QUICKBOOKS ONLINE FOR BEGINNERS

Step-by-Step Guide to Mastering QuickBooks Online for Small Business Owners and Entrepreneurs - Simplify, Streamline, and Take Control of Your Finances Hassle-Free

Liam Meyer

Table of Contents

Introduction

Now more than ever, private and public companies, Non-Governmental Organizations, corporations, and small businesses are paying more attention to their record-keeping, balancing, and accounting as a whole. The current era, often referred to as the Jet Age, witnesses instantaneous transactions, rapid money movement, and an accelerated pace in all activities.

There has never been a better time for any business to have a firm grip on their book-keeping. Championing this new trend in the online side of things is the QuickBooks software.

Developed and distributed by Intuit, QuickBooks is an accounting computer program. While initially less advanced than the dominant QuickBooks Desktop upon its 2004 release, QuickBooks Online (Q.B.O.) has undergone substantial development. Intuit consistently enhances the software by introducing new features and services tailored for small businesses.

Targeting primarily small and medium-sized businesses, QuickBooks offers both on-premises accounting applications and cloud-based solutions. These encompass handling business payments, bill management, and payroll functions.

Utilized by numerous small businesses and non-profit organizations, QuickBooks has introduced various program editions over time to cater to diverse business needs. QuickBooks has outpaced competitors in multiple industries, providing enticing deals for effective cash flow and expense tracking, especially in sectors like engineering and architecture. The introduction of QuickBooks for Nonprofits offers online accounting software with user-friendly features tailored for non-profit bookkeeping.

Although there is a QuickBooks non-profit version, QuickBooks Premier Nonprofit is favored due to its affordability and adaptability to non-profit organizations' requirements.

Before delving into QuickBooks, a fundamental question arises: "Will QuickBooks Online work for my organization?" The answer lies in understanding the two primary reasons for tracking company finances—to ensure smooth operations and generate reports for entities like the Internal Revenue Service, supervisory authorities, and other organizations overseeing checks and balances. QuickBooks simplifies these financial tasks, allowing you to track results and manage your business efficiently, even on the go, anytime and anywhere.

Introduction to QuickBooks Online Essentials

What is QuickBooks?

This is accounting software that has a combination of products that are useful for small and medium-sized business owners. They are vital accounting tools used for business payments, bill payments, and payroll. For some, QuickBooks, there are the cloud-based ones that can be very useful for businesses.

In 1983, the first version of QuickBooks was using the Quicken Software. This software did not function as a double-entry package. The software was invented using simple, easy-to-understand accounting techniques that can be understood by a business owner who has no accounting background.

By 2000, the software featured more complex audit processes, making the job much easier. In 2014, a newer version of the software called the QuickBooks online. To use this, the users have to pay a monthly subscription fee to be able to access the software.

There is a newer version of the QuickBooks Online known as the QuickBooks Online Plus. This QuickBooks Online Plus has two views that can be used. These views are called QuickBooks Accountant and QuickBooks Business.

In both views, you can easily perform various tasks. However, the type of view used may change how you access the task command. While the navigation bar of one might be on the left side, the other might have its navigation bar at the top.

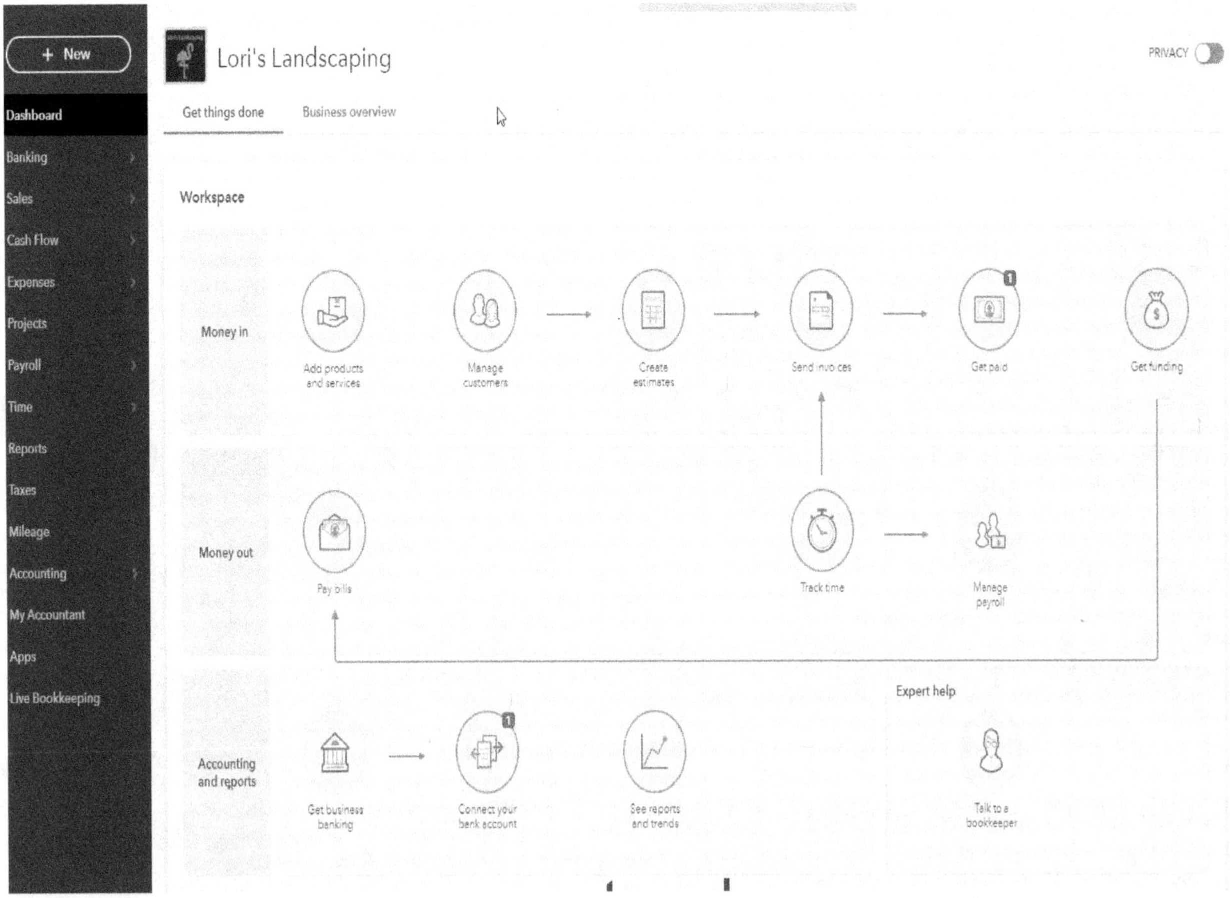

The accounting view gives you a full view of all business and accounting tasks in your QuickBooks. On the other hand, the business view streamlines the content in his view to day-to-day business tasks.

To switch between the two views, click on **Settings** at the top right side of your screen.

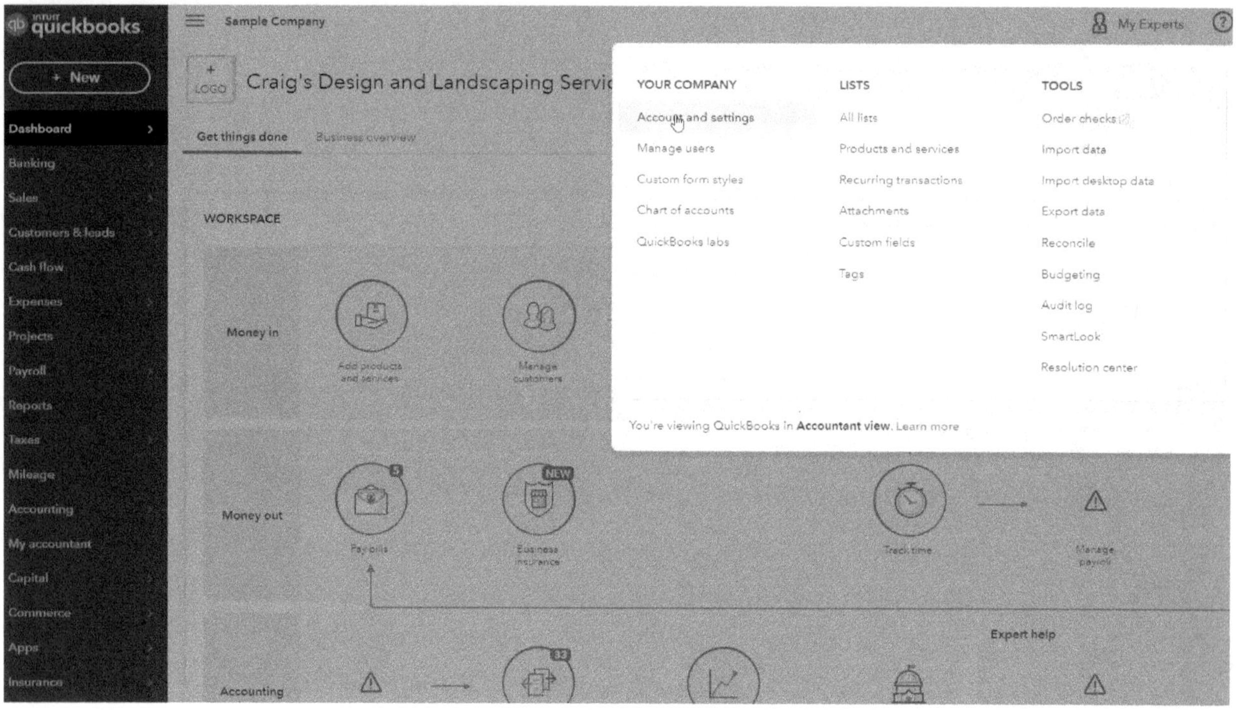

Here, click on the switch to business view or **accountant view.**

Comparing QuickBooks Accountant vs QuickBooks Business

Now, I am in the Business view of QuickBooks.

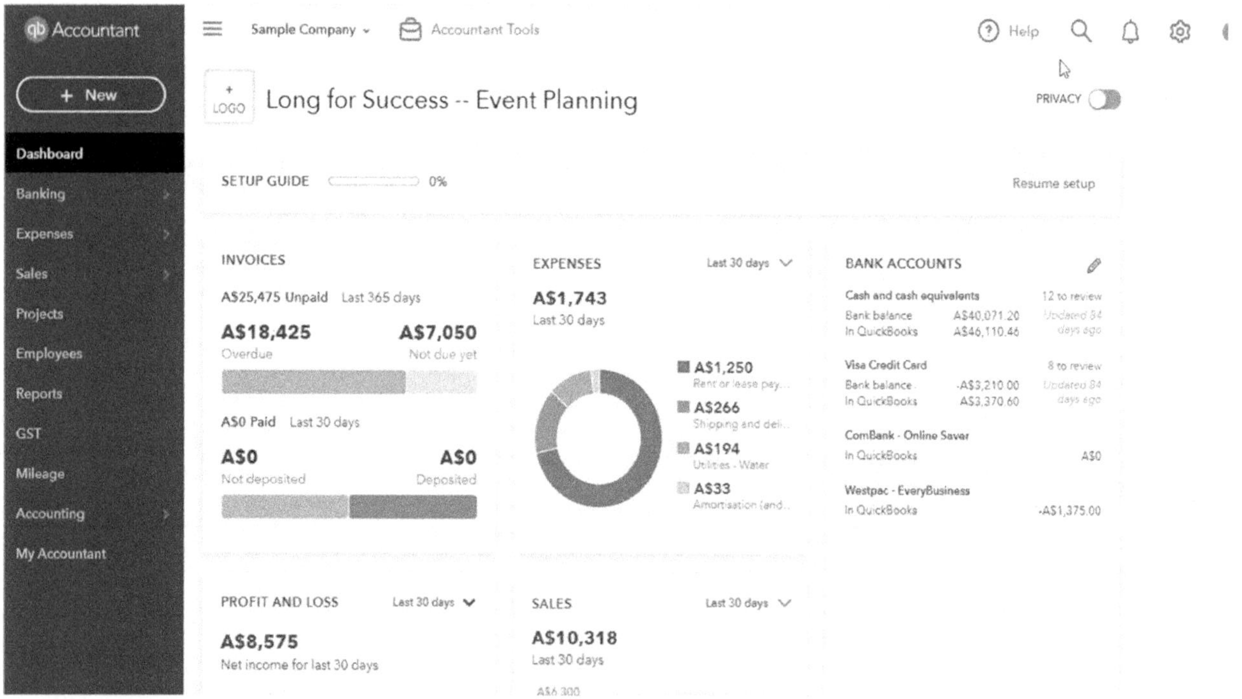

Here, the cash flow chart is going to show us past transaction data from your linked bank accounts. You can adjust the figures as suited to your business. In the Accountant's view, you cannot see the cash flow chart is not visible.

In the accounting view, the languages of tasks are much more technical and less understandable for a business owner with zero accounting background. Both views perform almost similar functions, the difference lies in the view.

Understanding Cloud Computing

In terms of scalability, data storage, server security, recovery of lost data and maintenance, cloud computing is a much better option for any business owner in comparison to the on-premises system. Cloud computing is more affordable and has a more advanced technological setup.

Cloud computing involves providing on-demand computing services via the internet, with a pay-as-you-go model. Rather than managing files on a local server, the same files can be economically maintained over the internet.

The deployment model and the service model are the two models commonly used in cloud computing. The deployment model is broken down into three categories: public clouds, private clouds, and hybrid clouds. Public clouds are cloud services that are owned by cloud service providers and are accessible to the general public via the internet. Someone else is in charge of managing the private cloud, which is controlled by a single corporation. The hybrid cloud is an integration of the characteristics of both the public cloud and the private cloud.

On the other hand, the service model is divided into IAAS, PAAS, and SAAS. Cloud computing is mostly by I.T. administrators. They are used for hosting and managing your cloud computing services.

The Multi-Currency Nature of QuickBooks Online

1. Open the **QuickBooks Online** website.

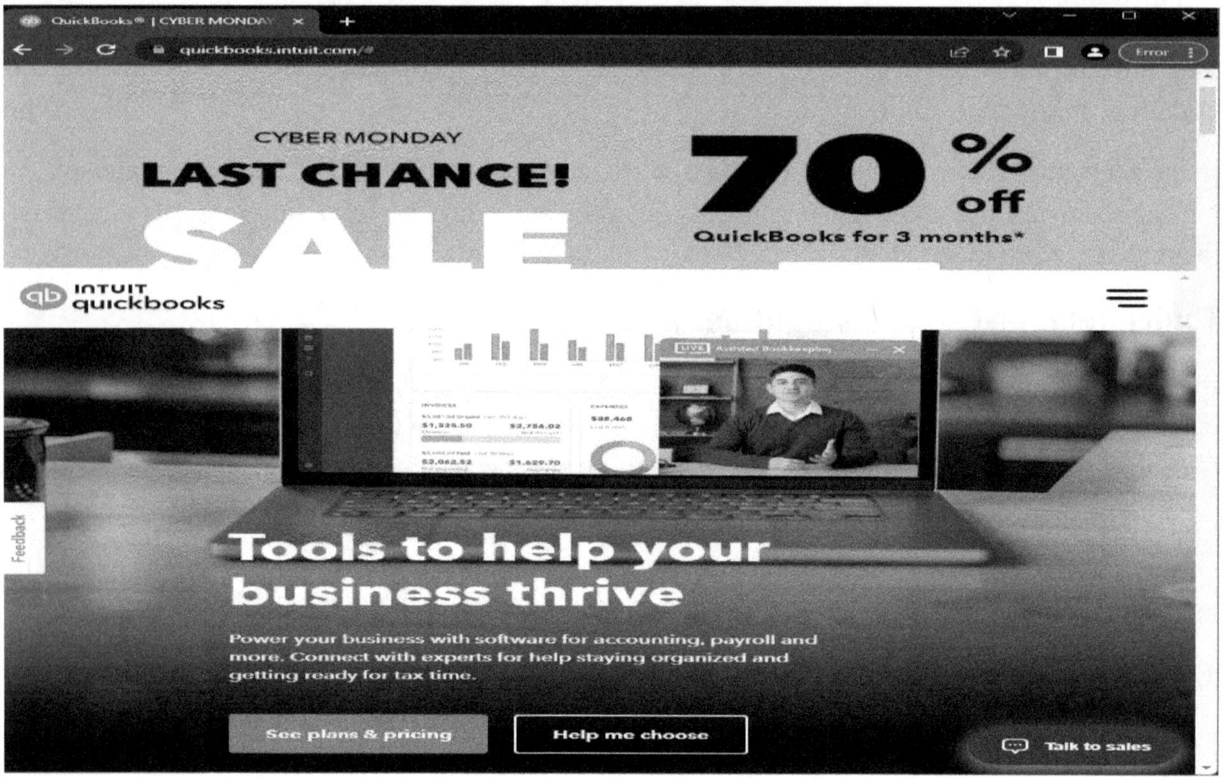

2. On the left side, click on the **sign-in** option from the drop-down.

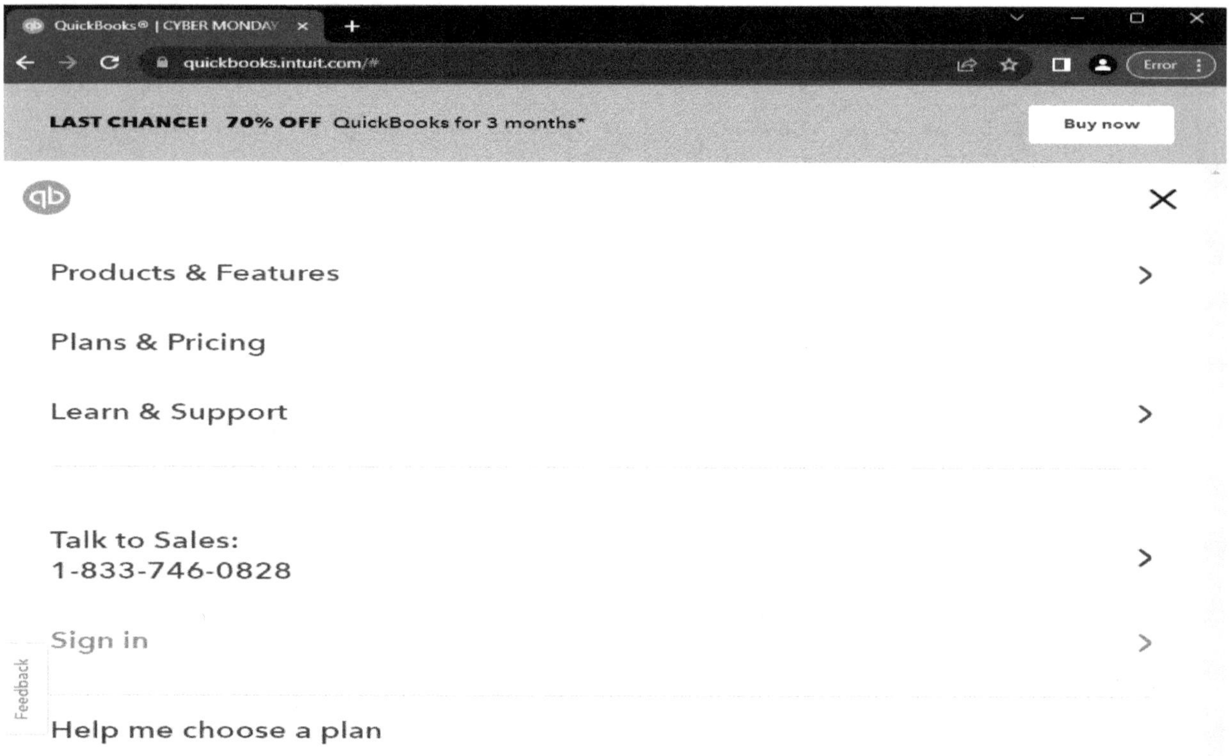

3. Select **QuickBooks Online** from the drop-down.

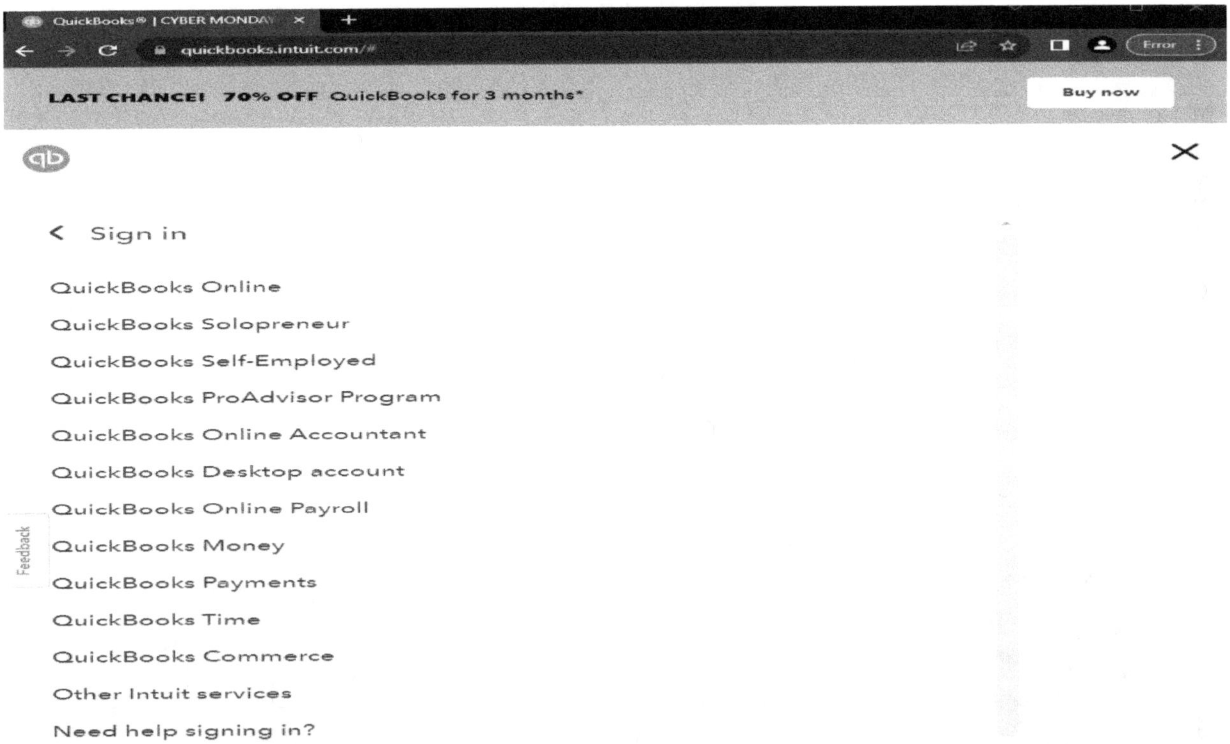

4. Input your email address.

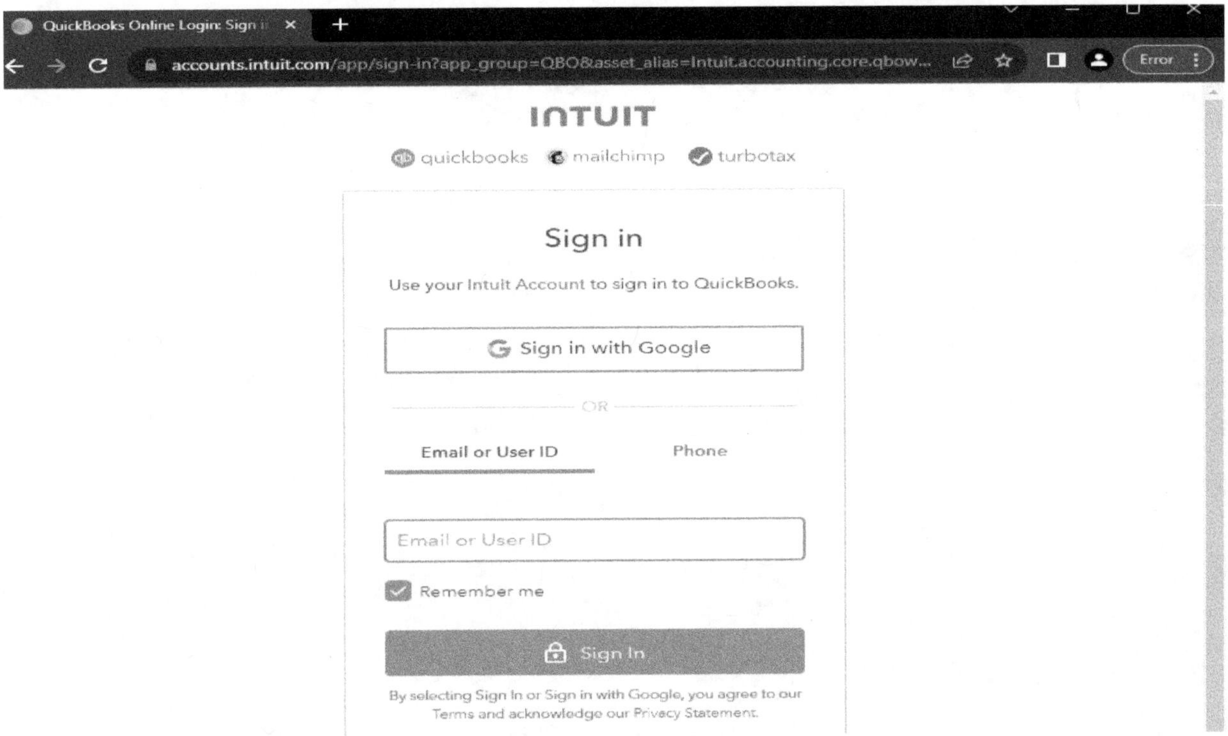

5. Next, to turn on the multiple currencies option, click on the **Settings icon** at the top right side of your screen. Click on **Account and Settings.**

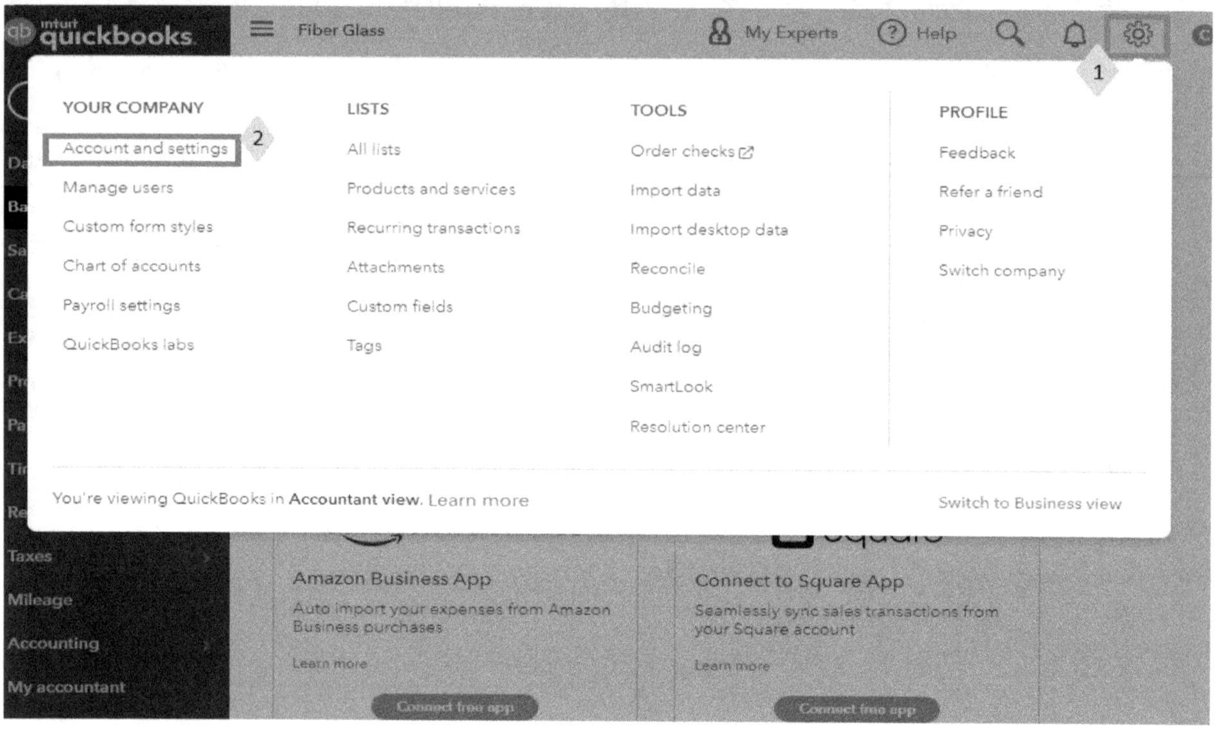

6. Click on Advanced settings.

7. Scroll down and choose the **currency option.**

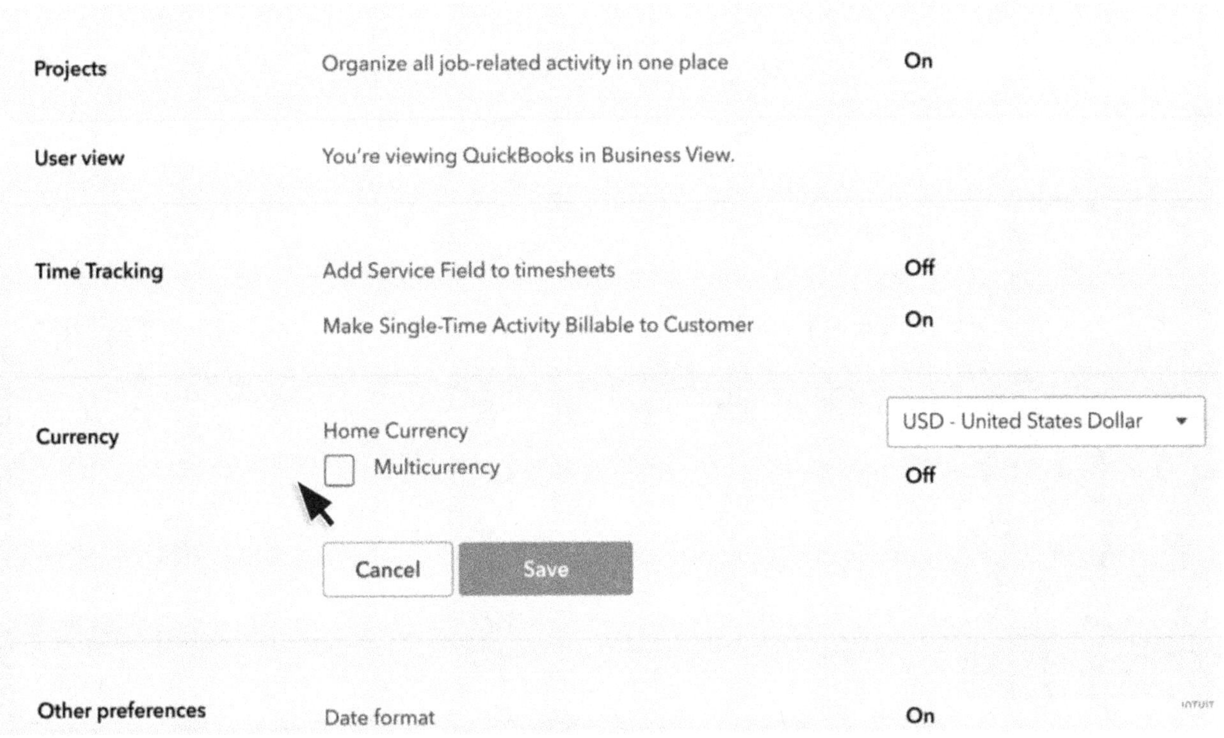

8. Click on the **pencil-like icon** to switch on the multi-currency option.

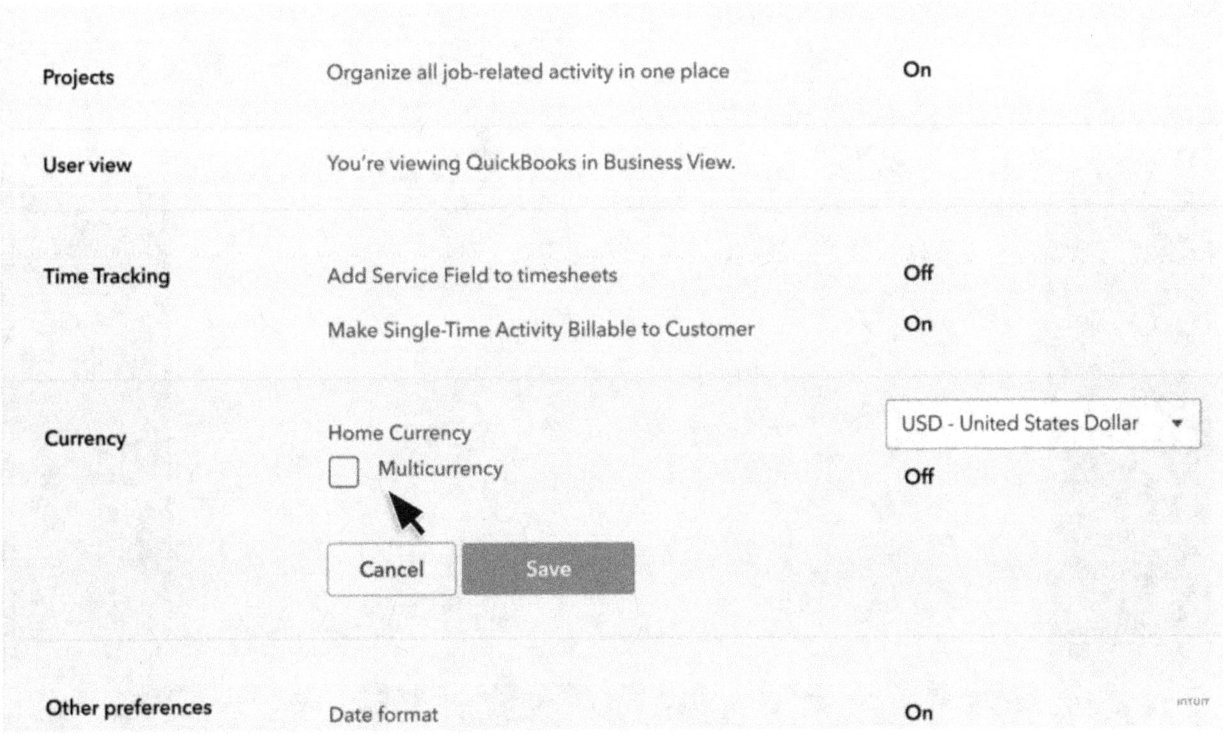

9. To test-run one of the currency options, click on the **accounting option** on the left side of your screen.

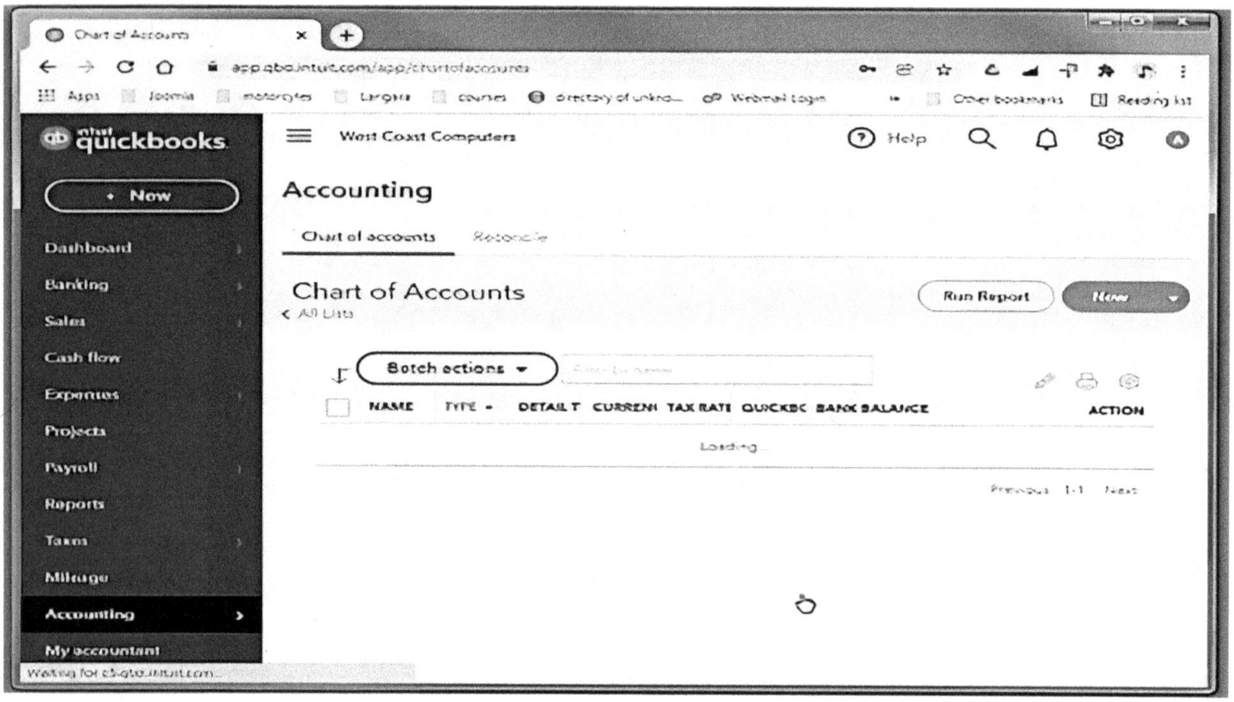

10. Under the **charts of accounts,** fill in the account details options. Here I will be using the dollar currency.

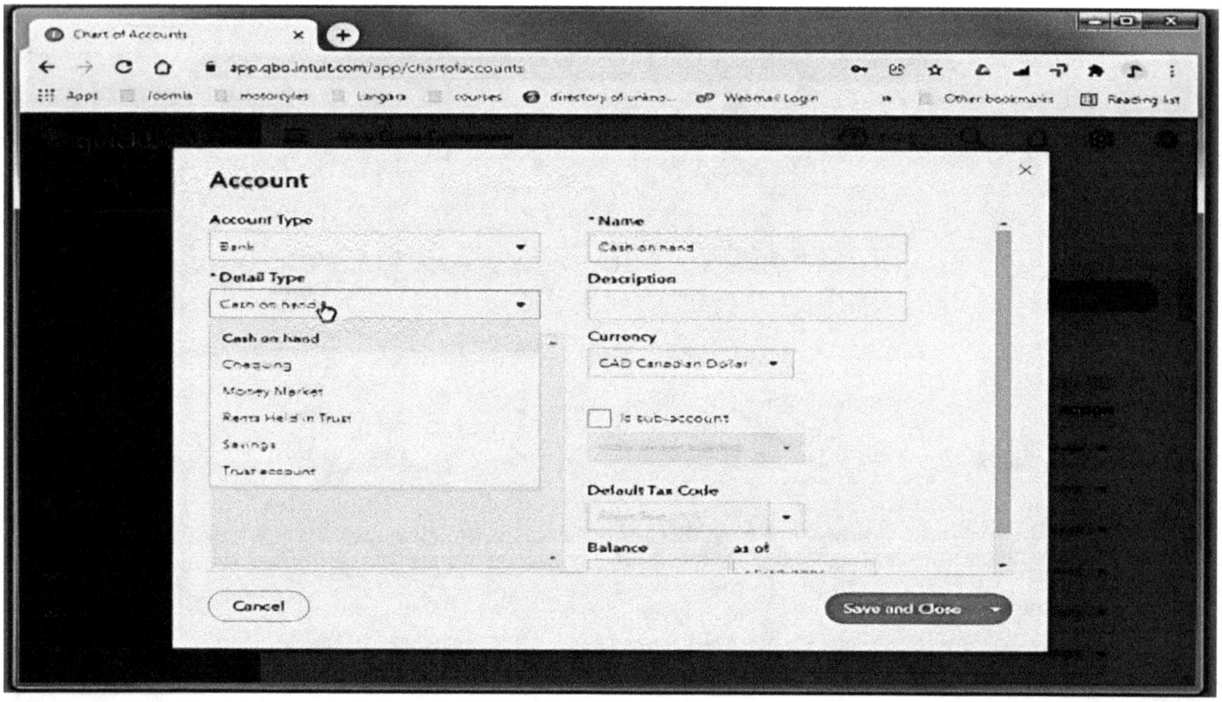

11. To make a transfer from your savings account to the currency account, click on **new** on the left side of your screen.

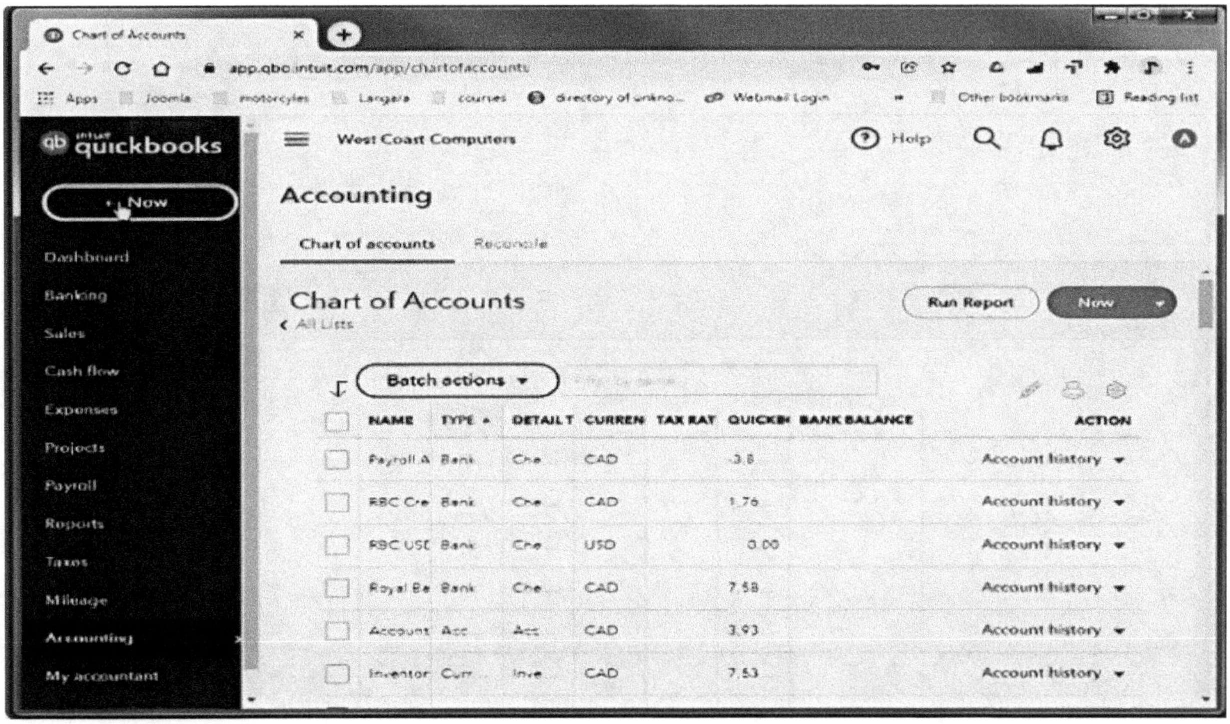

12. Select journal entry.

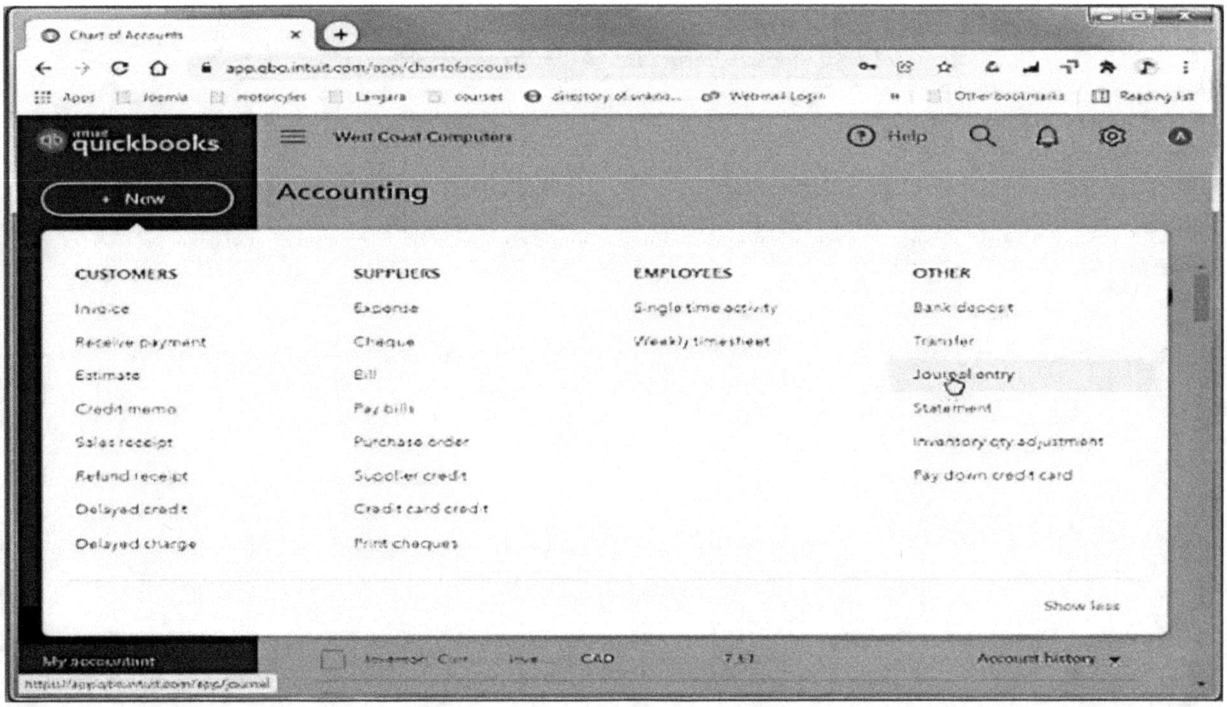

13. Click on the **currency tab.** From the drop-down, select your preferred currency and input the amount you intend to transfer.

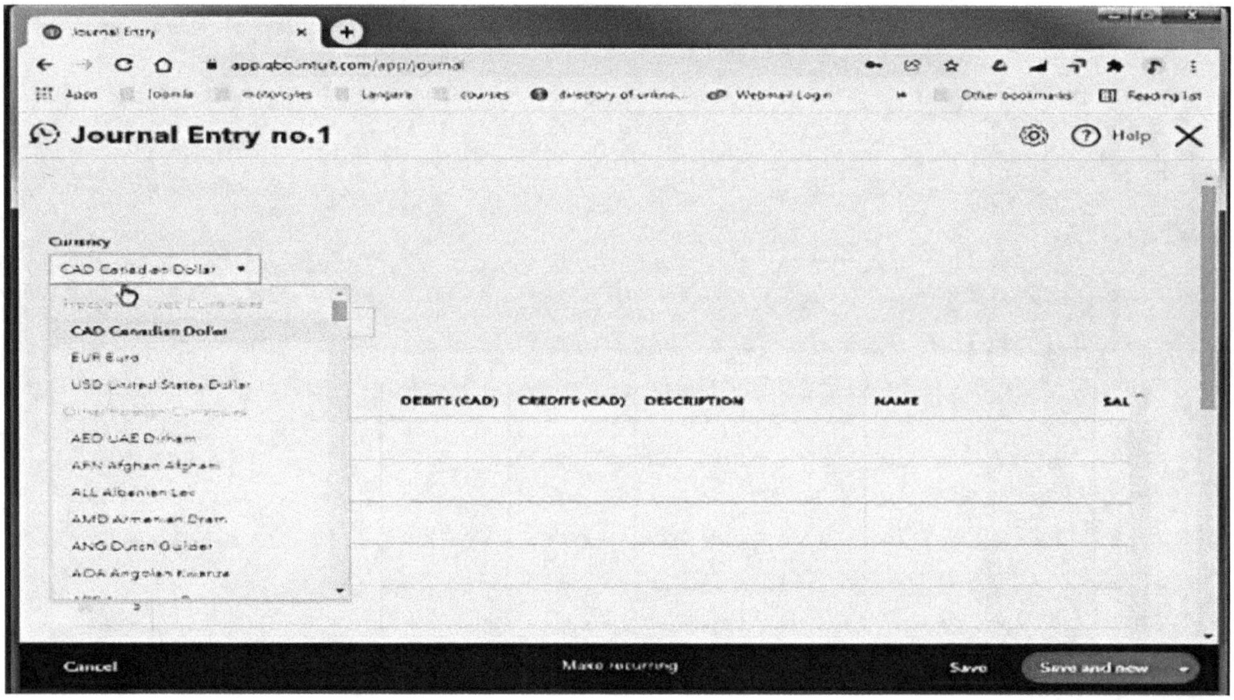

14. In the journal, you will debit the account that has been created and credit your savings account.

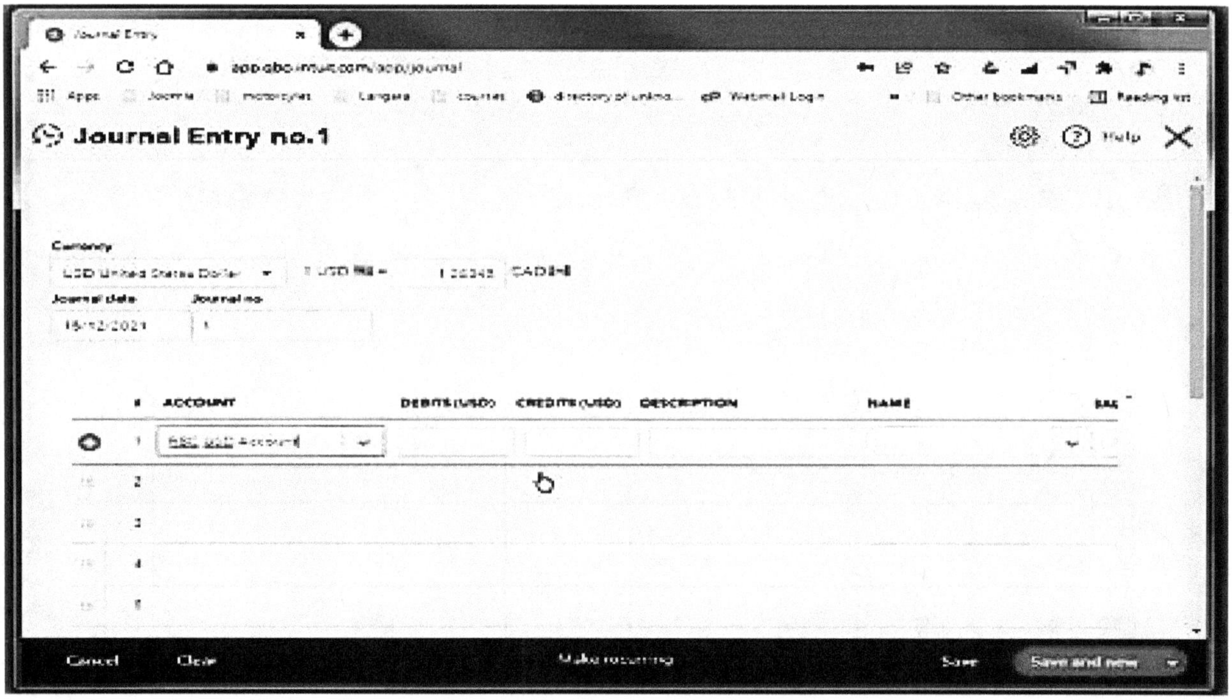

So, QuickBooks Online is not limited to a single currency. For multiple currencies, simply switch on the feature from your **Settings tab.**

How to Run the Payroll Option

The payroll is a schedule for easy payment for your employees simultaneously. It makes multiple payments easier to run without stress. To run the payroll option;

1. Click on **new.**

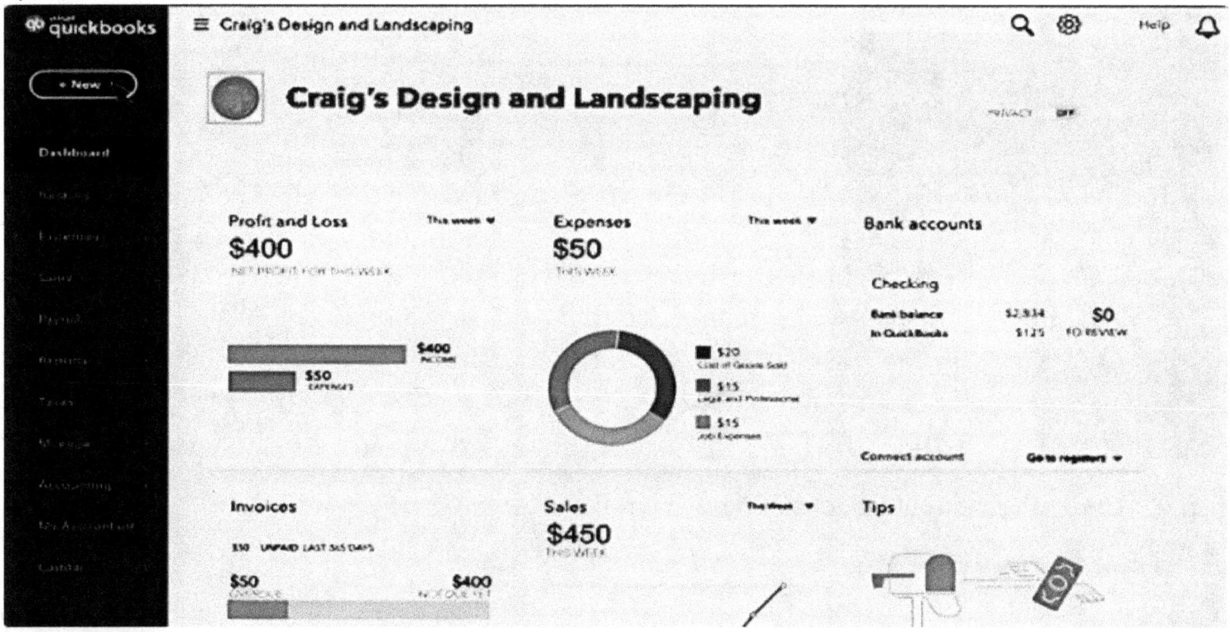

2. Select the payroll option.

3. Click on Payroll, and select overview.

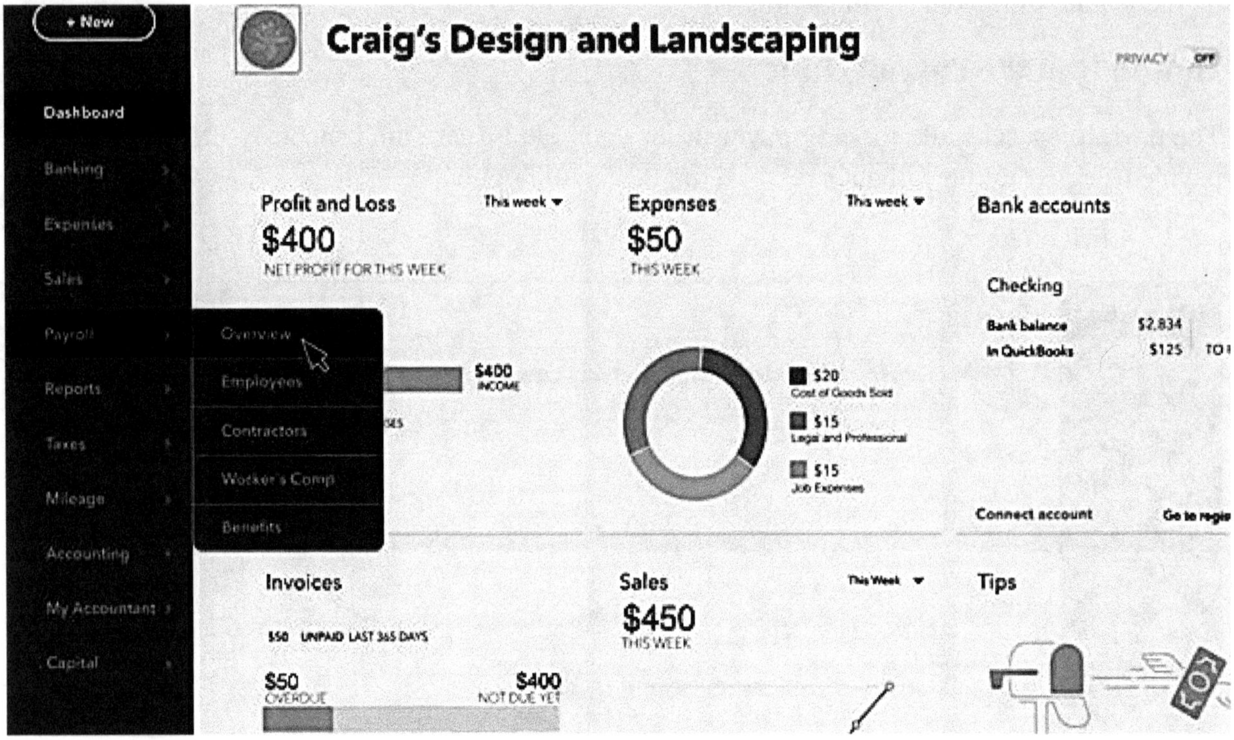

4. Under the shortcut tab, click on run payroll.

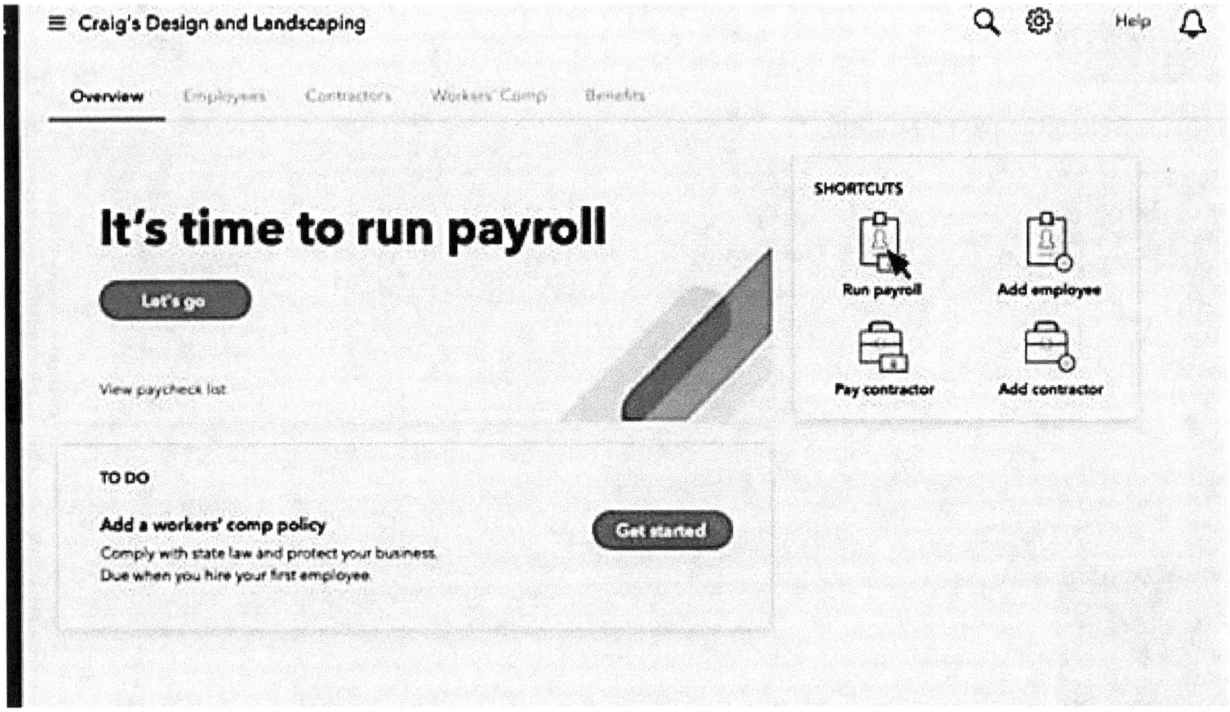

5. Under the **bank account** option, choose the type of account you intend to make the payroll payments from.

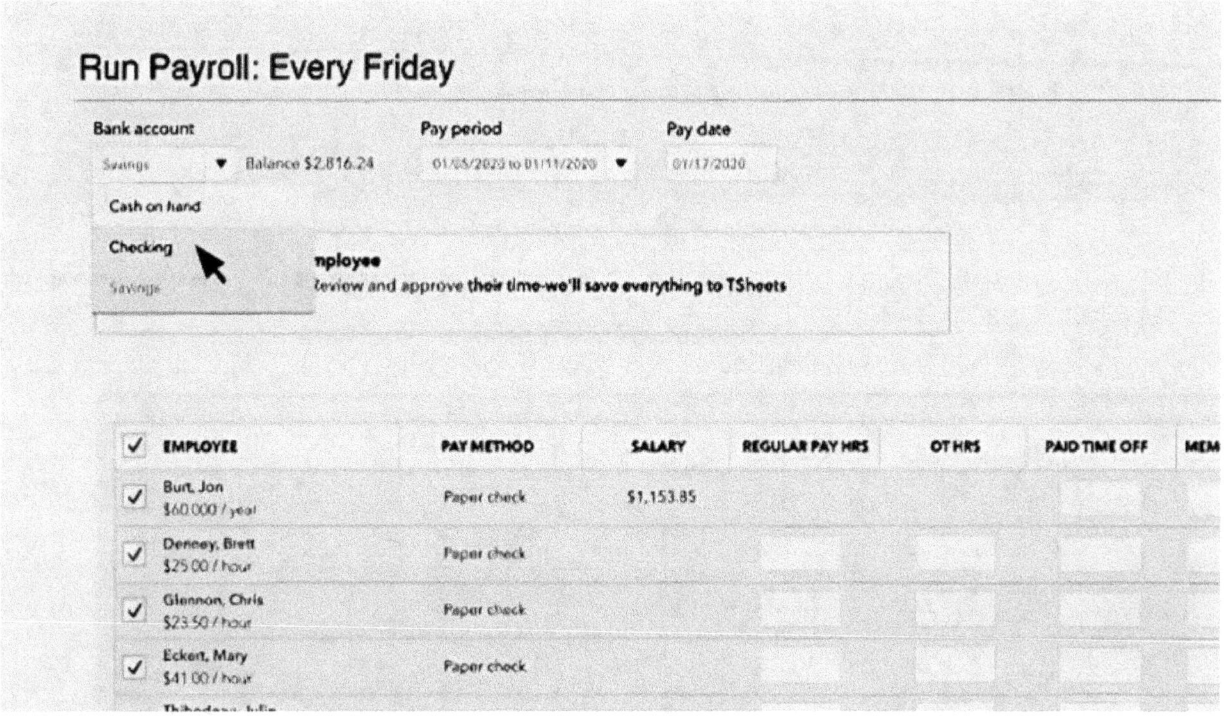

6. Confirm that the **pay period** and **pay dates** are correct.

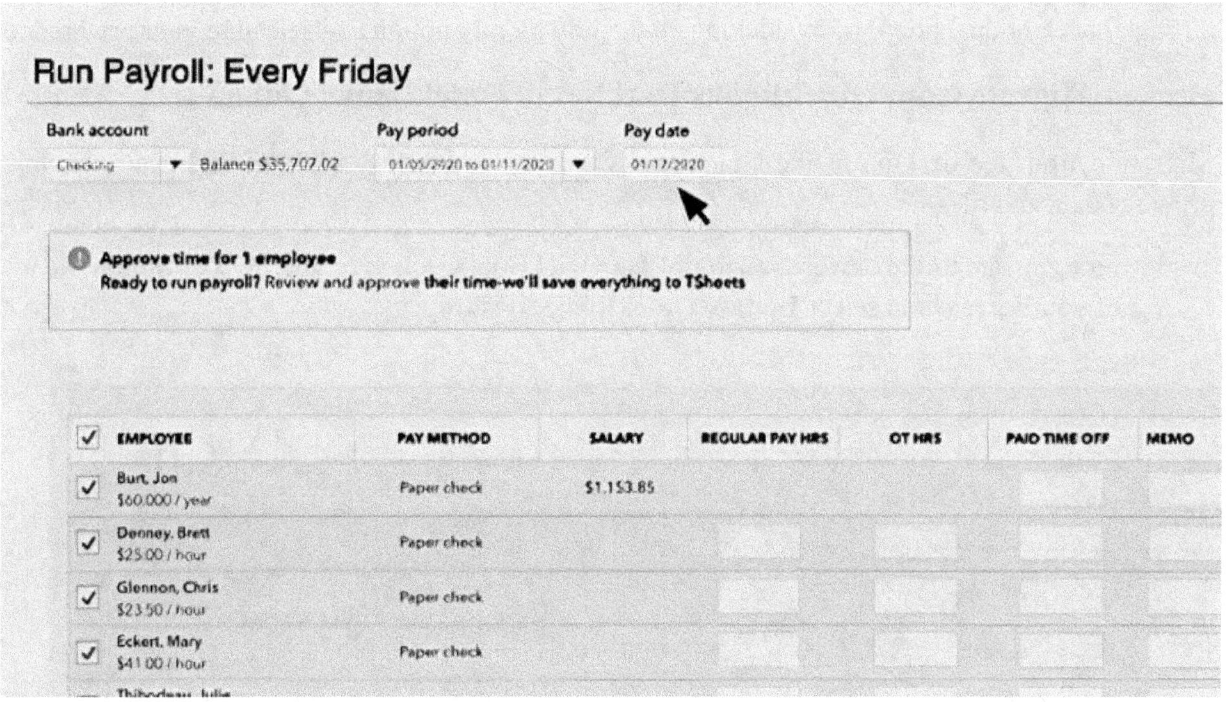

7. All the employees on this payroll will be displayed.

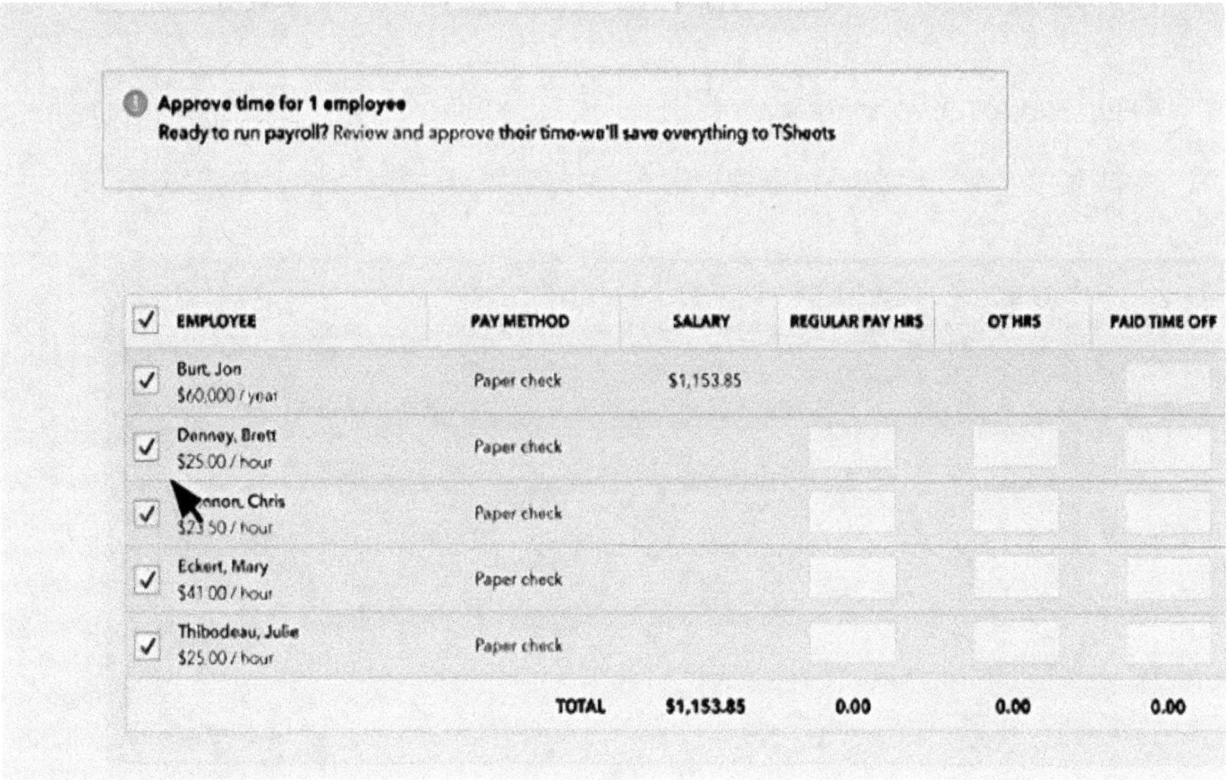

You can deselect an employee's name to remove him from the payroll. Also, you can decide to pay through check or direct deposit by clicking on the **how to pay** option and selecting your preference.

How to Migrate from QuickBooks Desktop to QuickBooks Online

Migrating from the desktop to the QuickBooks online can be done without losing any of your previous data and files.

1. First, update to the newest version of the QuickBooks. Click on the **help option** at the top of your screen, and select **Update QuickBooks Desktop.**

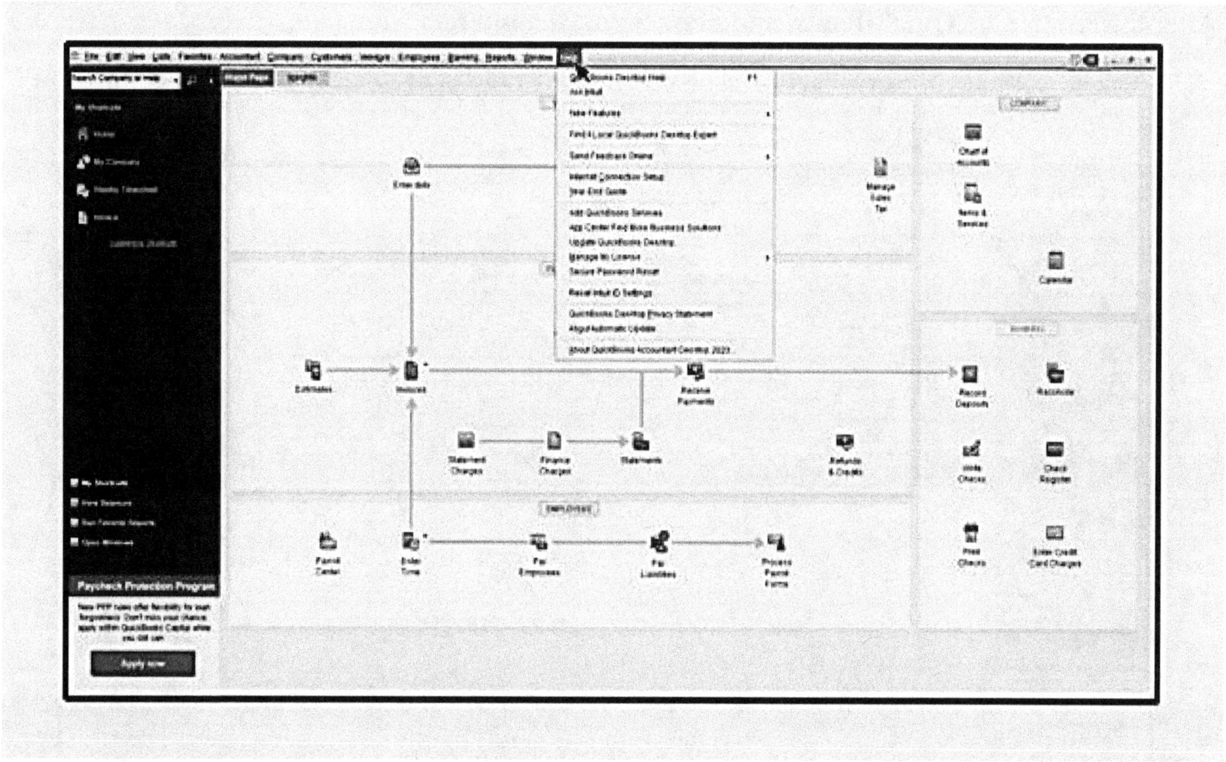

2. Click on Update Now.

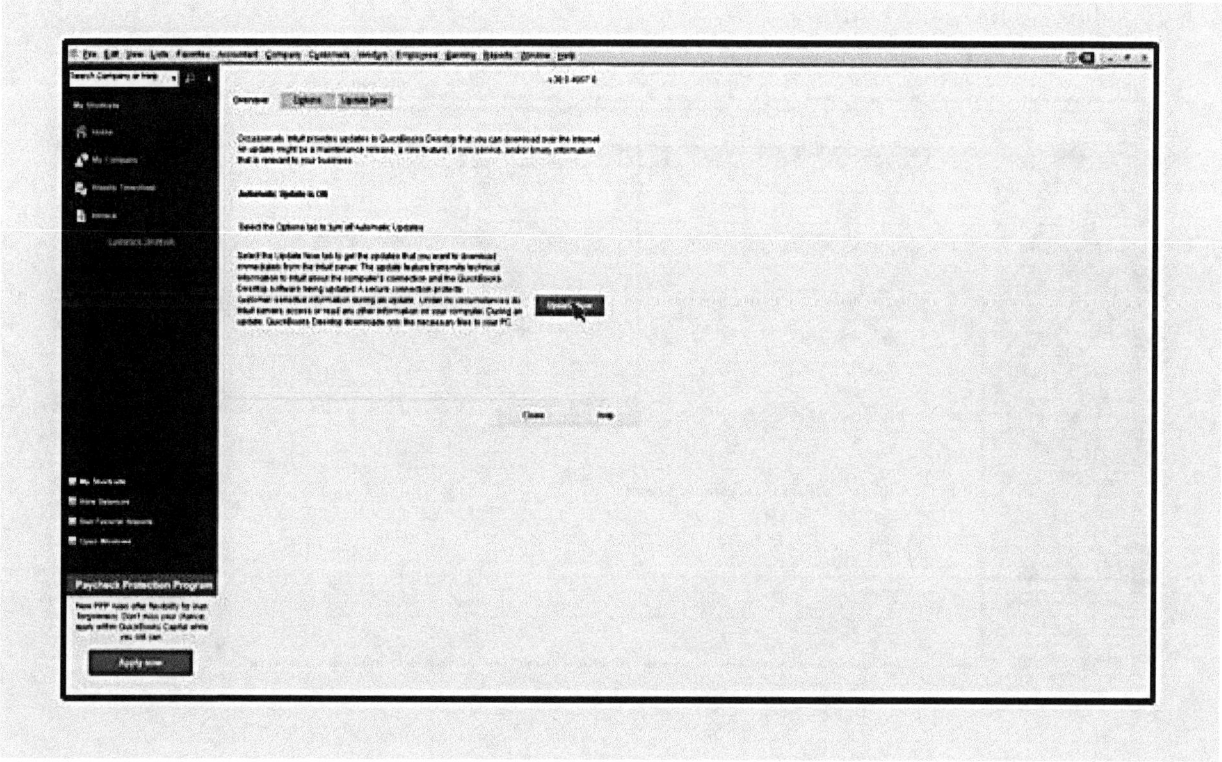

After this, restart the **QuickBooks, and restart your computer.**

1. Next, select Company, choose the Export your Company File to QuickBooks Online.

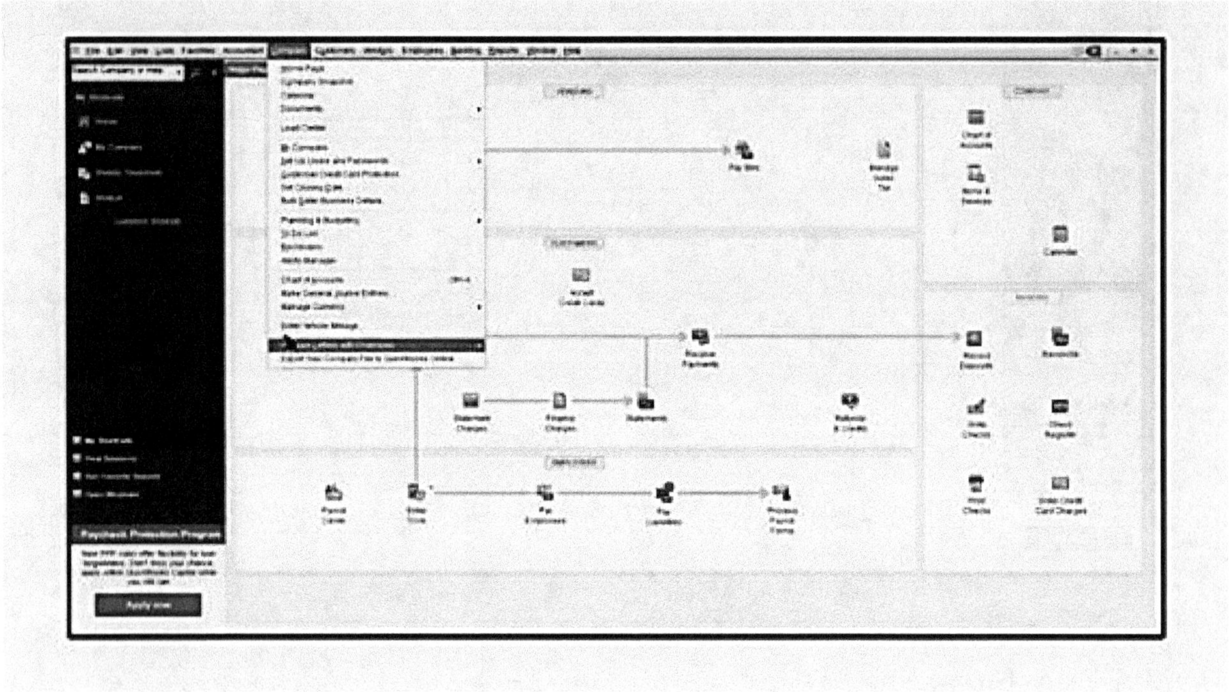

2. Click on Ready to move.

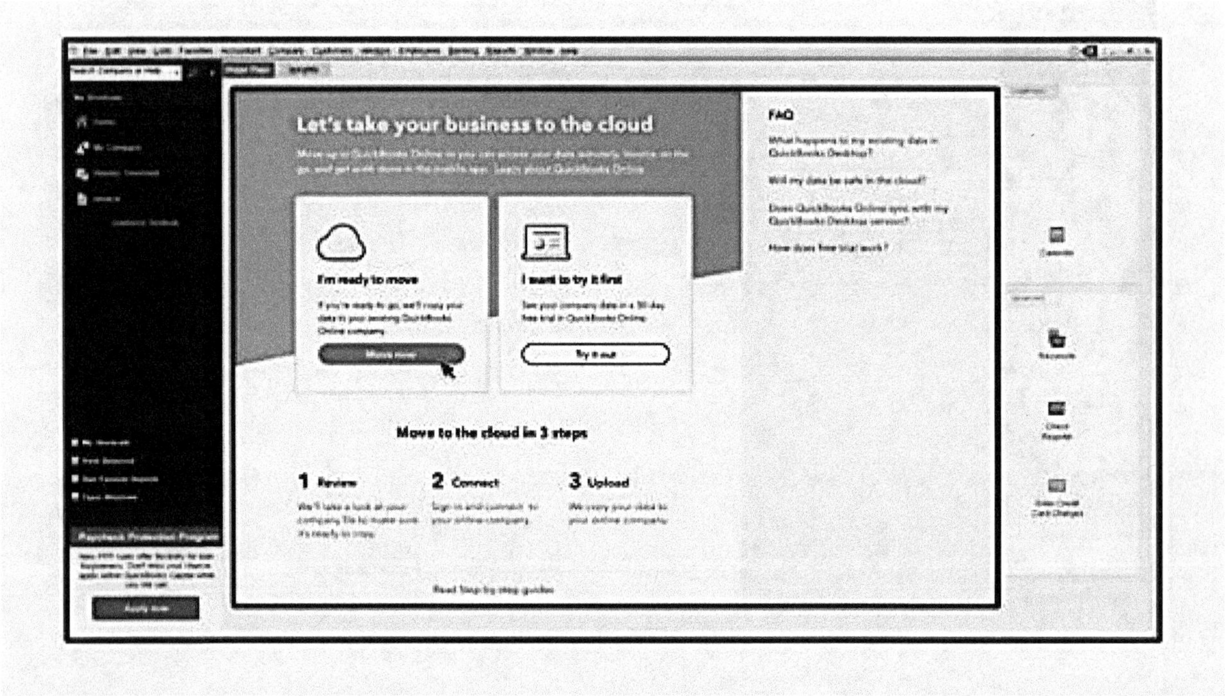

3. If you want to try the **free trial** option for 30 days, click on **Try free.**

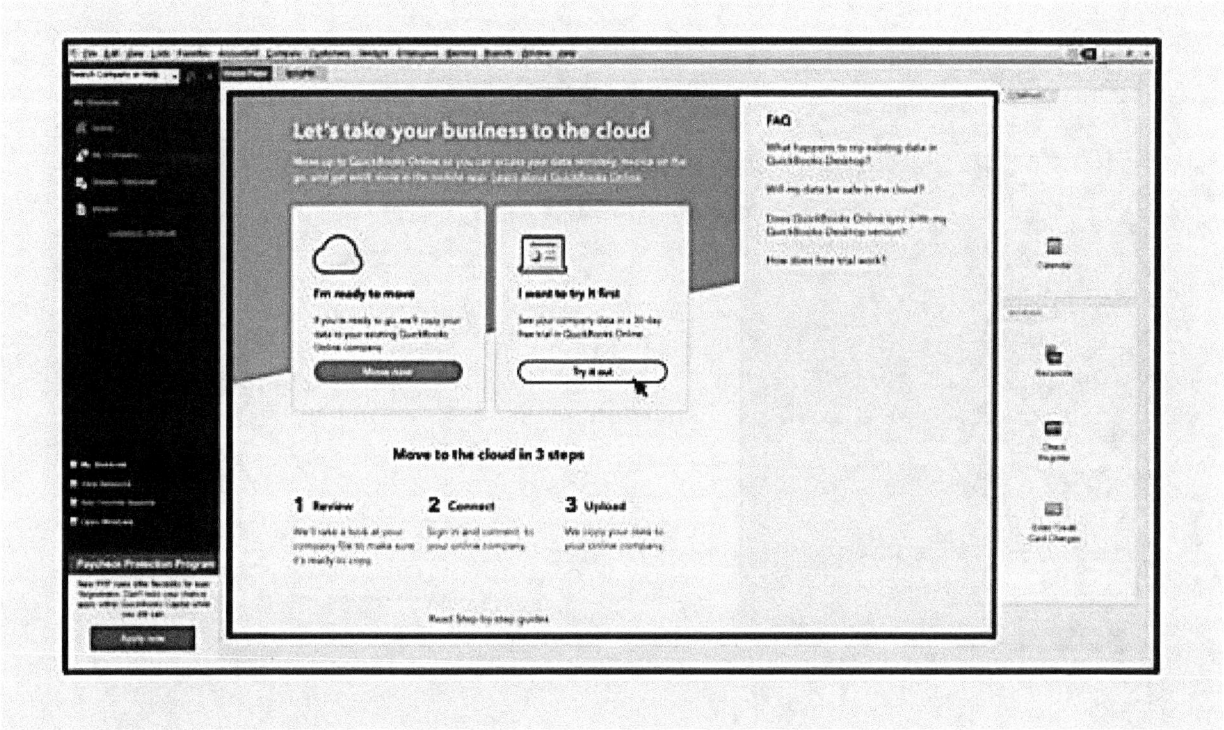

4. Click on **continue.**

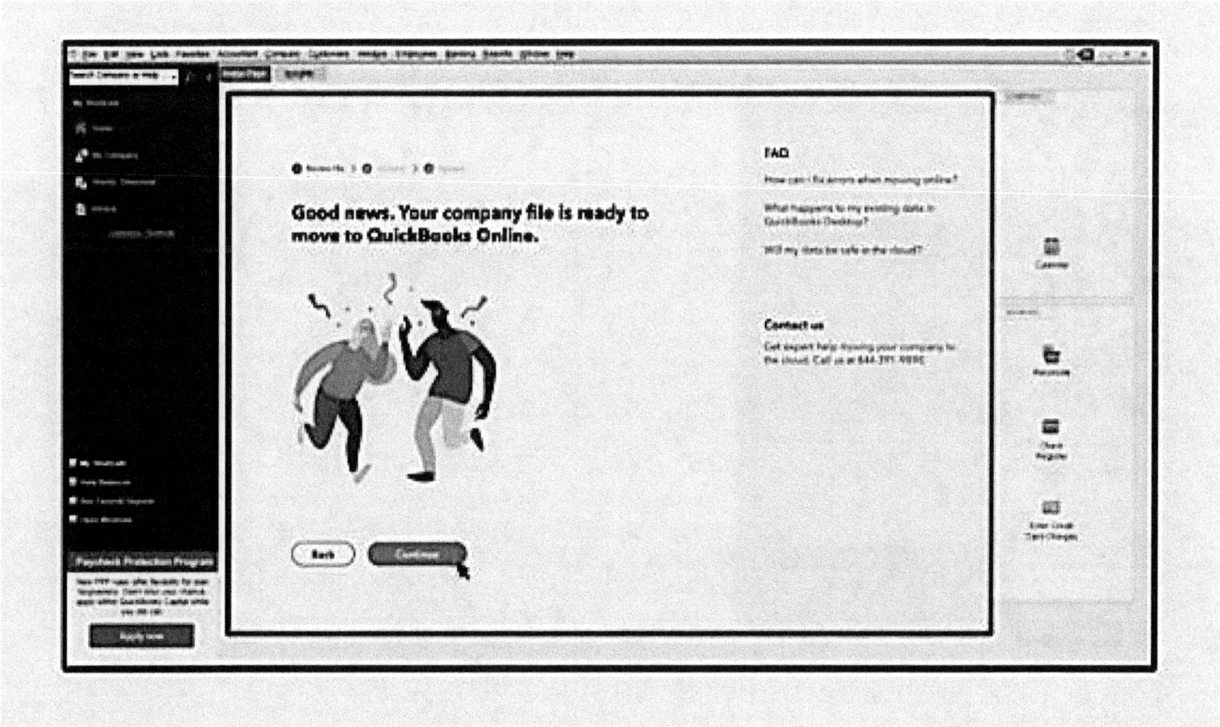

5. You can sign in to an existing QuickBooks account or create a new one.

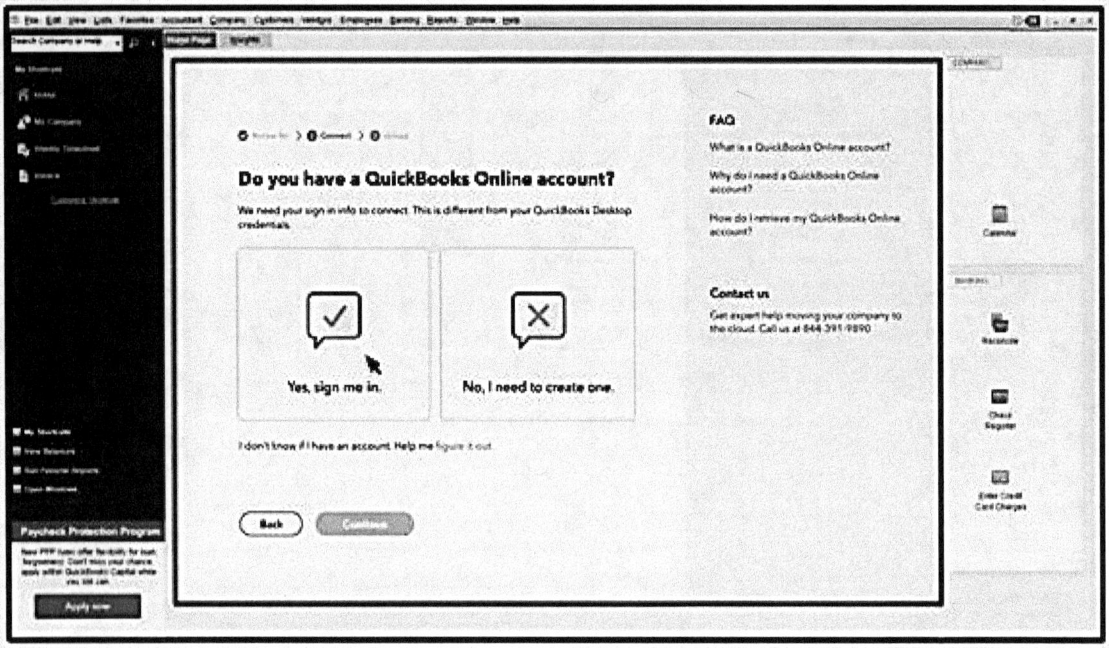

6. Input your **email** and **password** to create a new account.

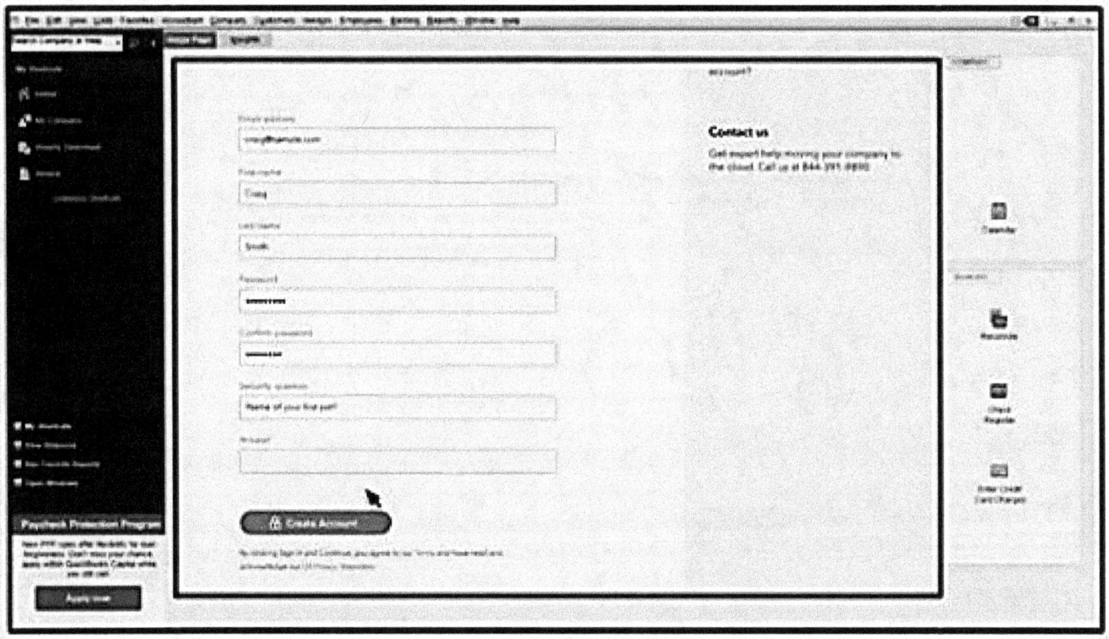

7. All your other details will already be preset. Simply click on **continue** and choose the **upload** option.

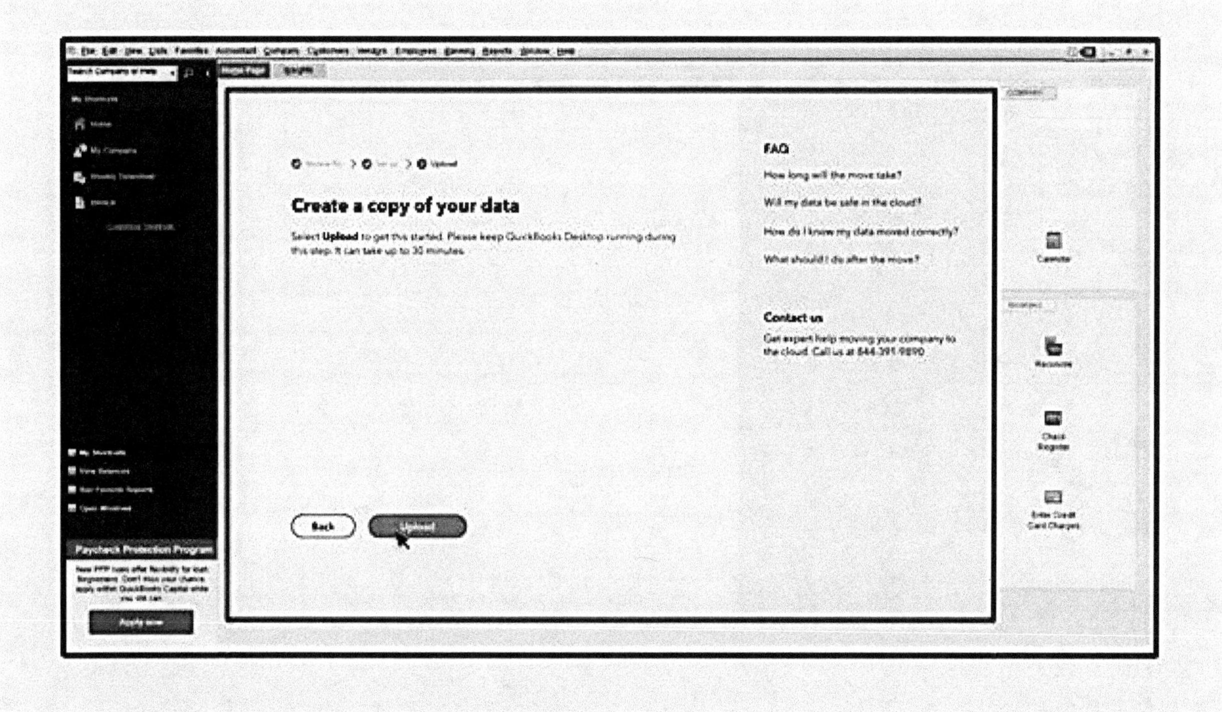

8. Once this is completed, you will receive an email for further access instructions.

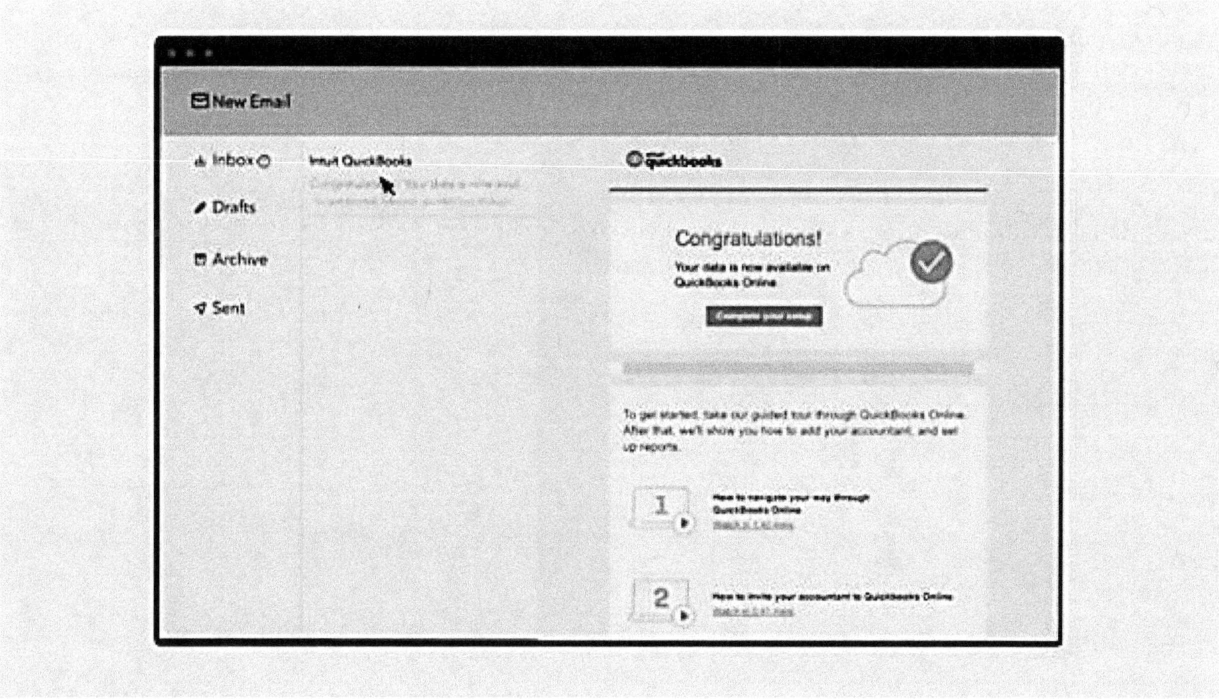

9. Your new account with all files from the QuickBooks Desktop will be displayed. You can cross-check the upload with your previous data to ensure that all information is duly uploaded.

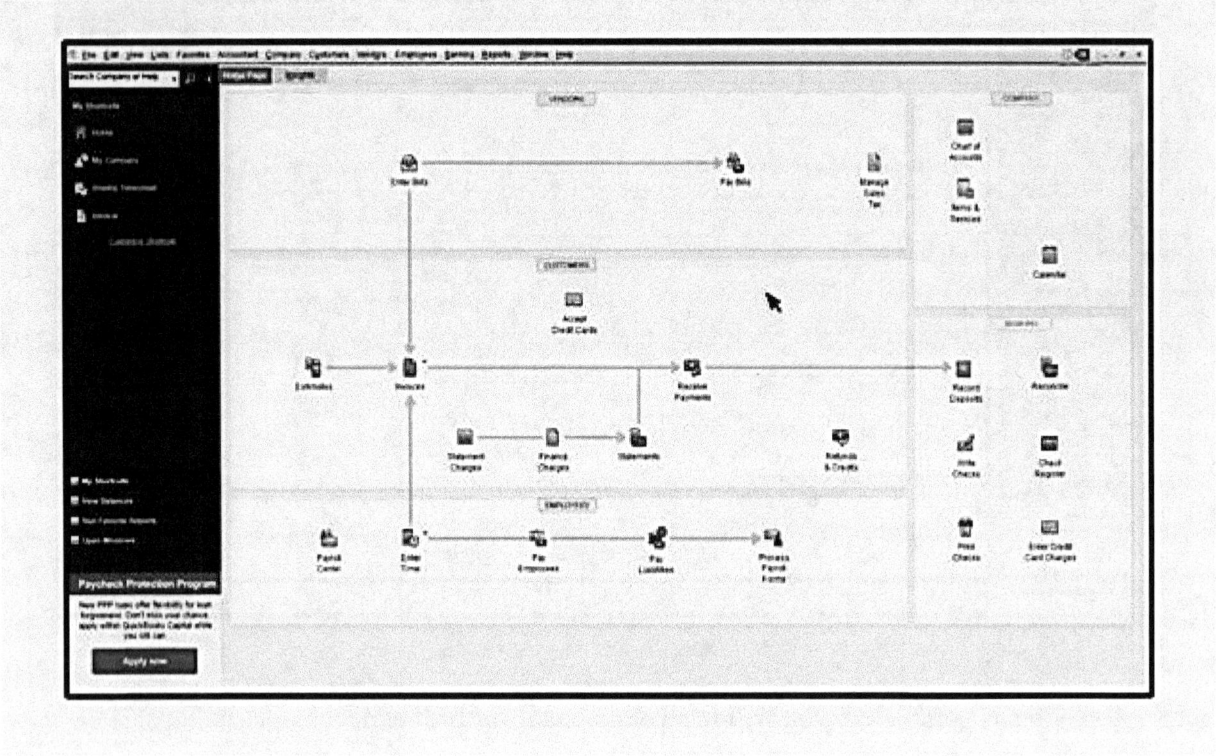

Configuration and Features of QuickBooks Online

Signing Up for QuickBooks Online

1. To create and sign-up for a QuickBooks Online, visit https://quickbooks.intuit.com/online/.

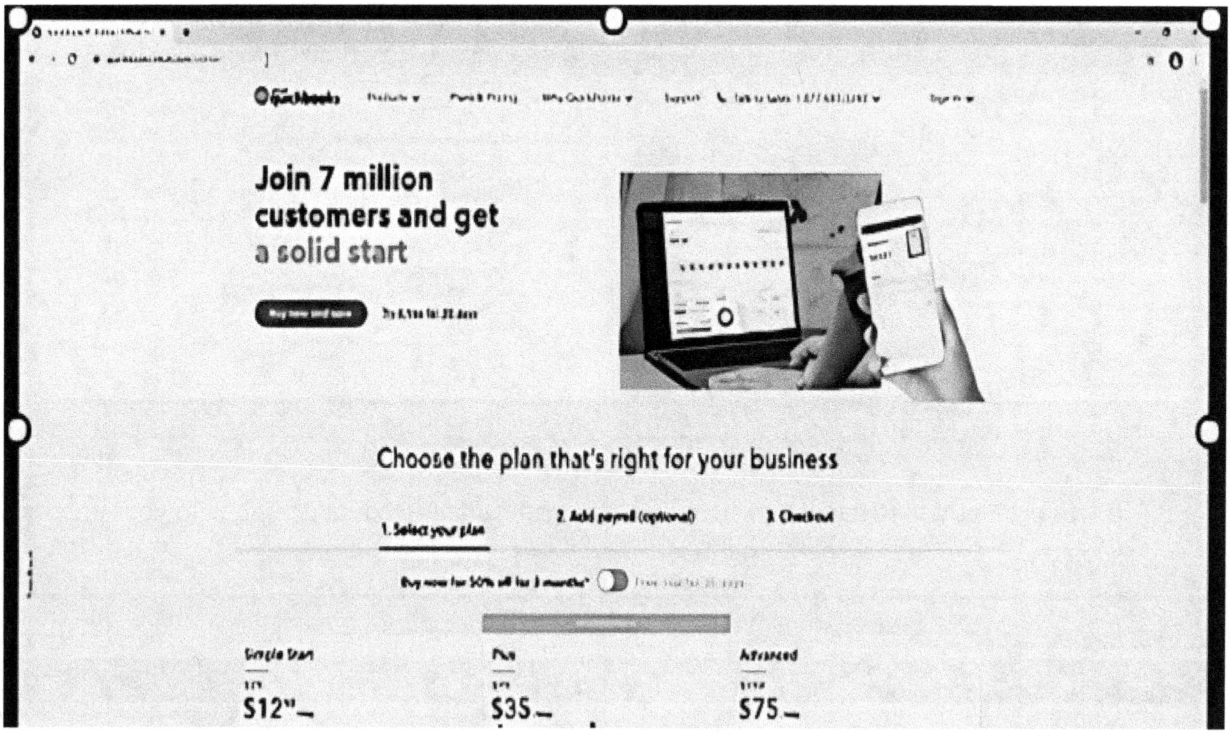

2. Next, choose a 30-day free trial or buy a subscription. Select your preferred subscription plan.

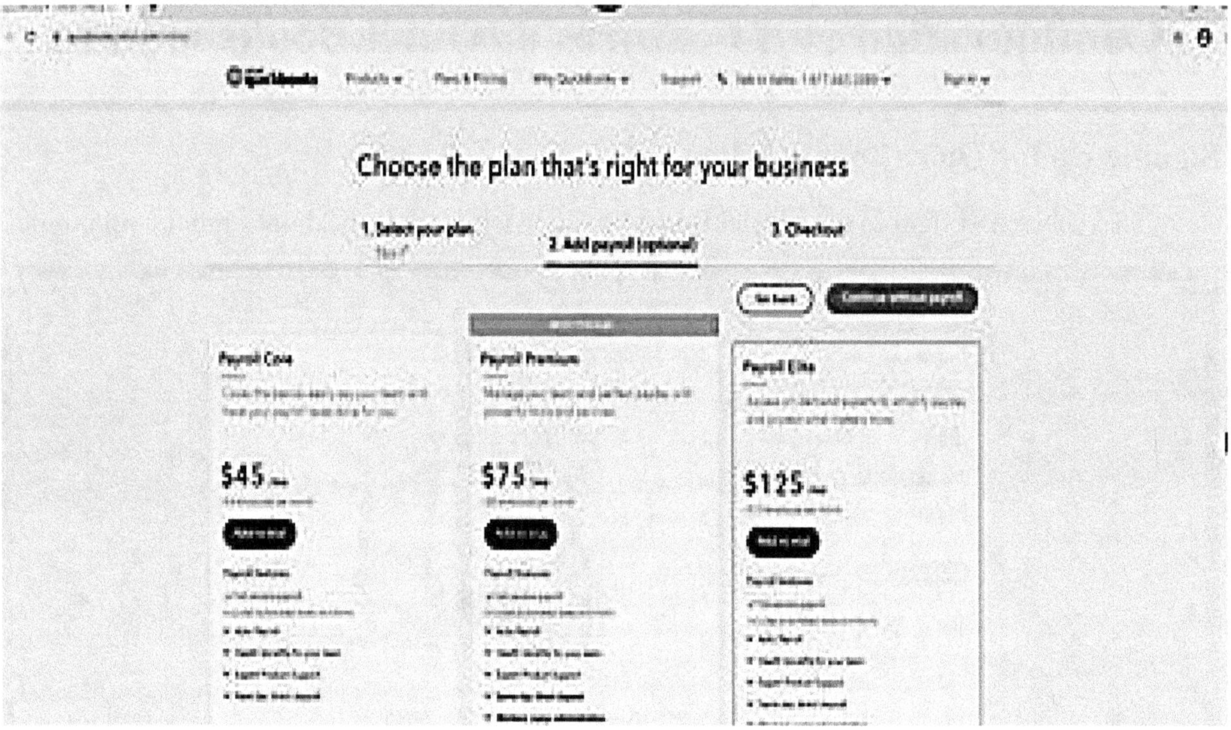

3. It will prompt you to the page where you can create a new account or sign in to your previous account.

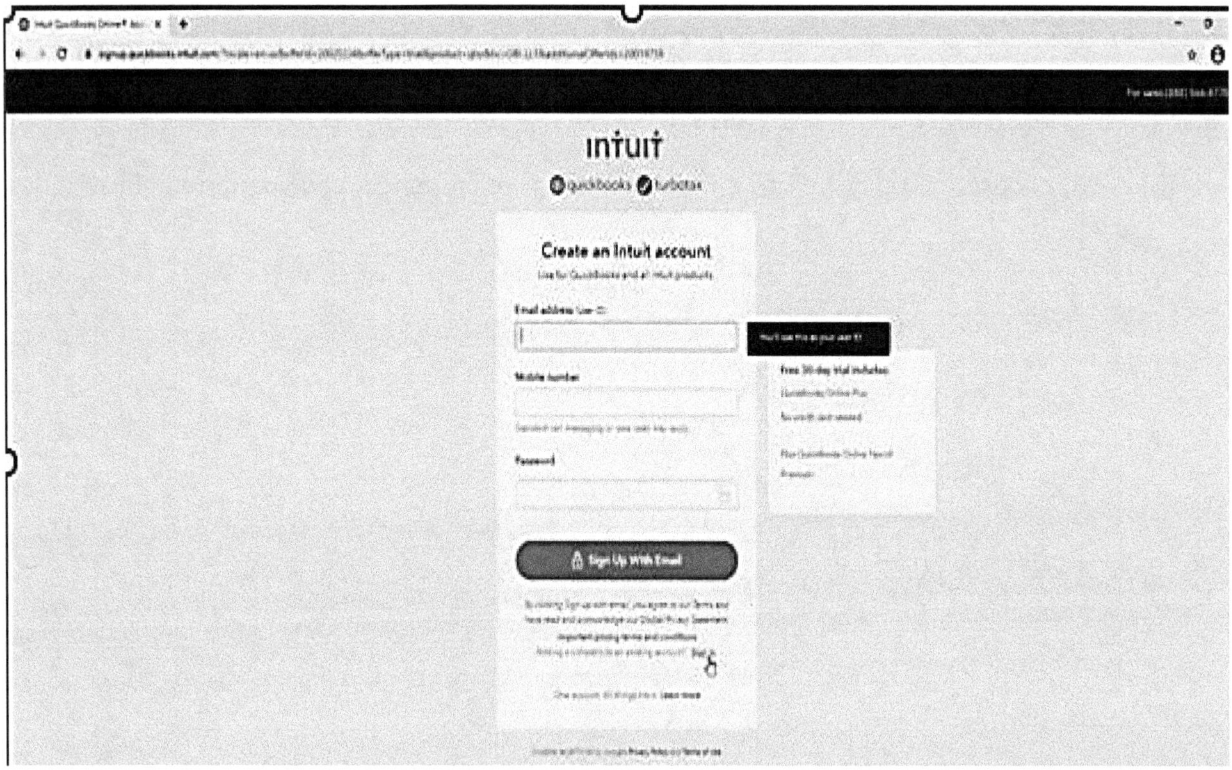

4. After creating the new account, proceed to set it up, and see your profile instantly.

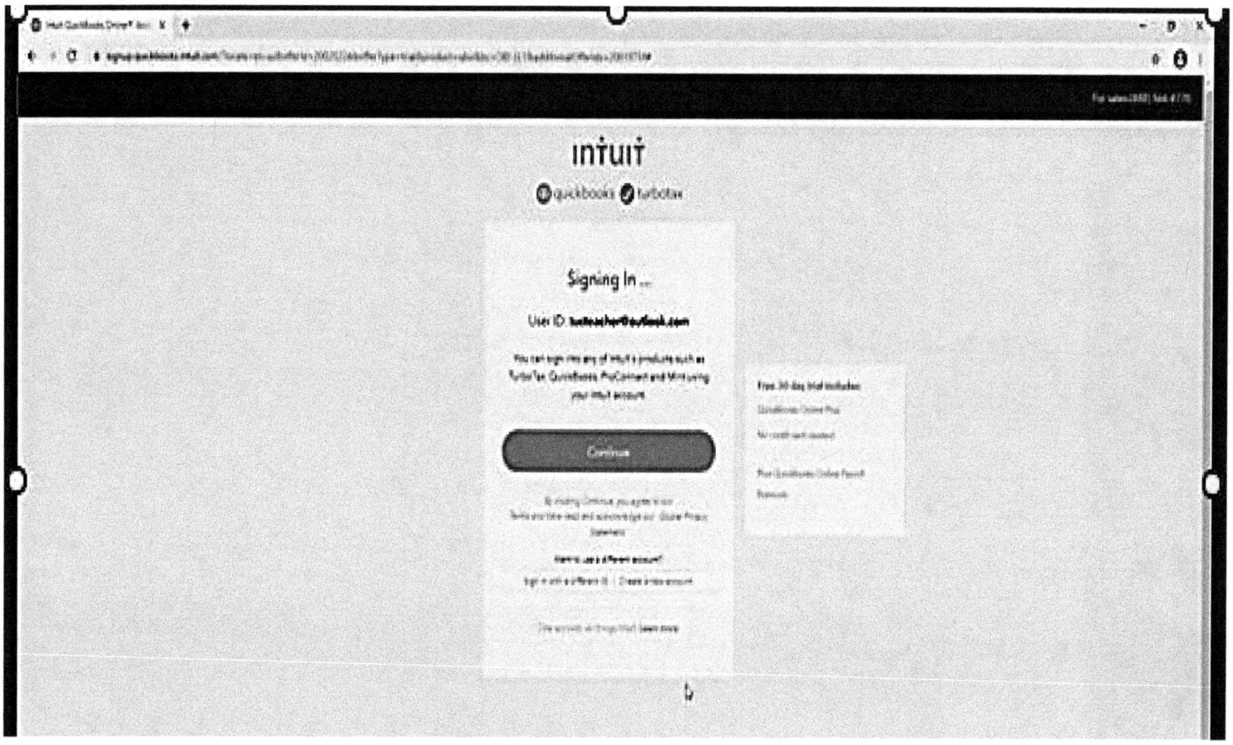

5. Type in your business name and other details.

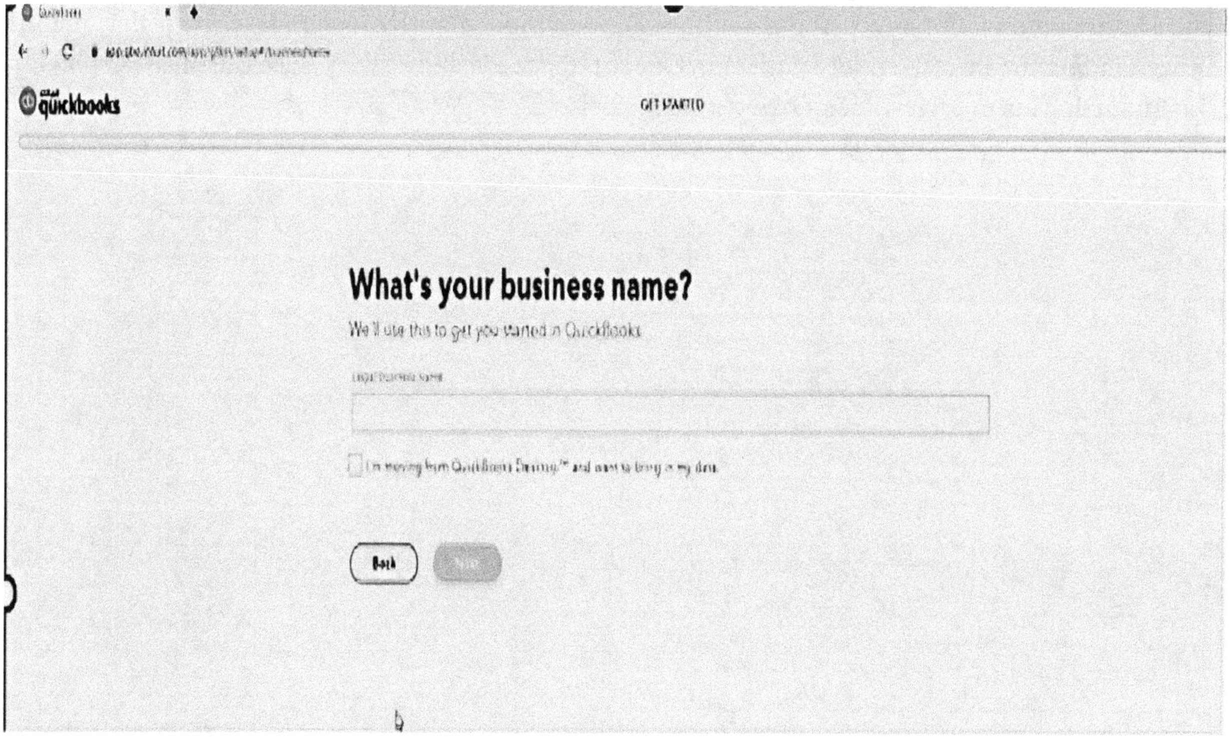

6. Your QuickBooks Online is ready for use.

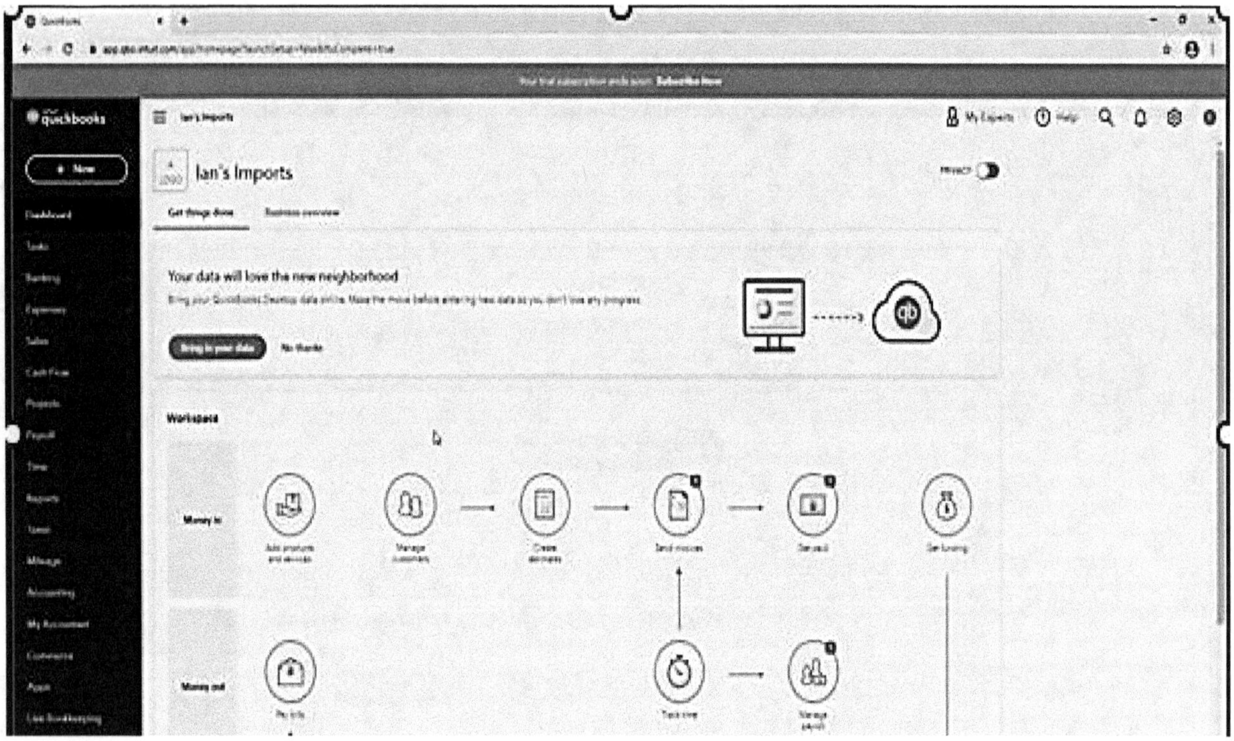

Understanding the Dashboards

The Dashboards of the QuickBooks Online have multiple screens in its Dashboard that require understanding to be effectively utilized. One of those dashboards is the **Business Overview Dashboard.** This overview looks like the image below:

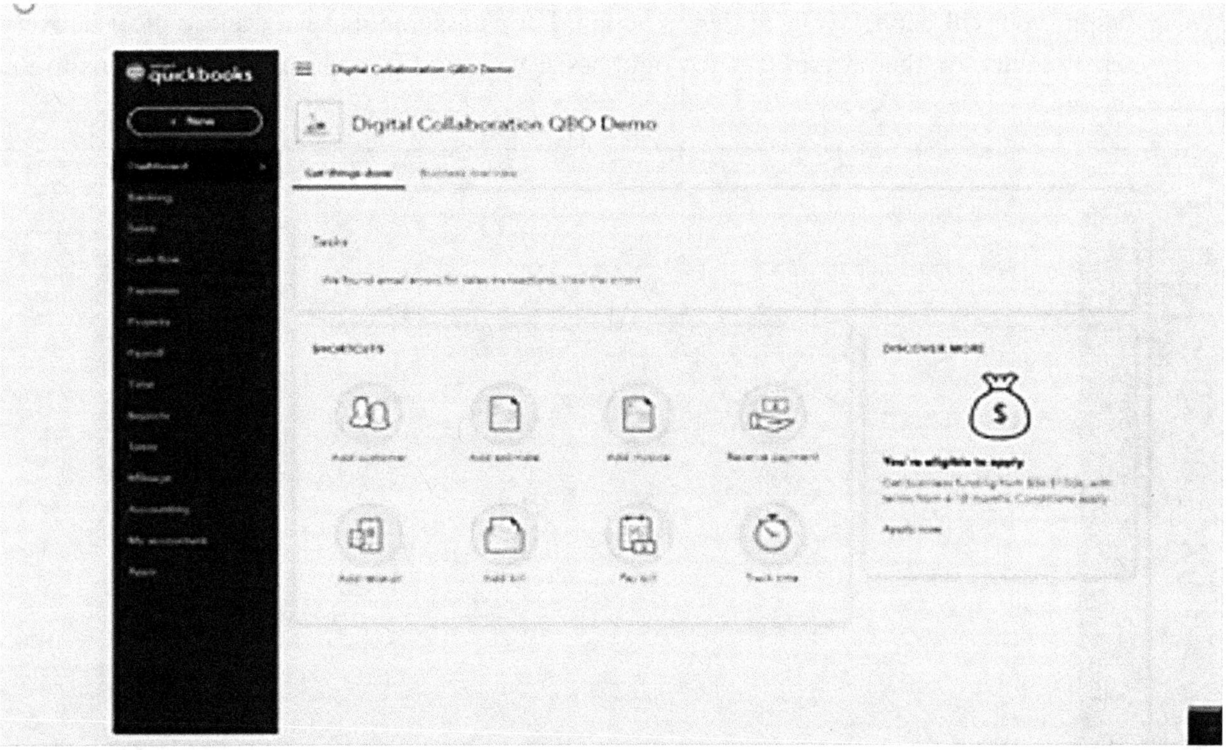

1. So, on the left side of your **QuickBooks Online,** click on **Dashboard** and choose the **Get things done** option.

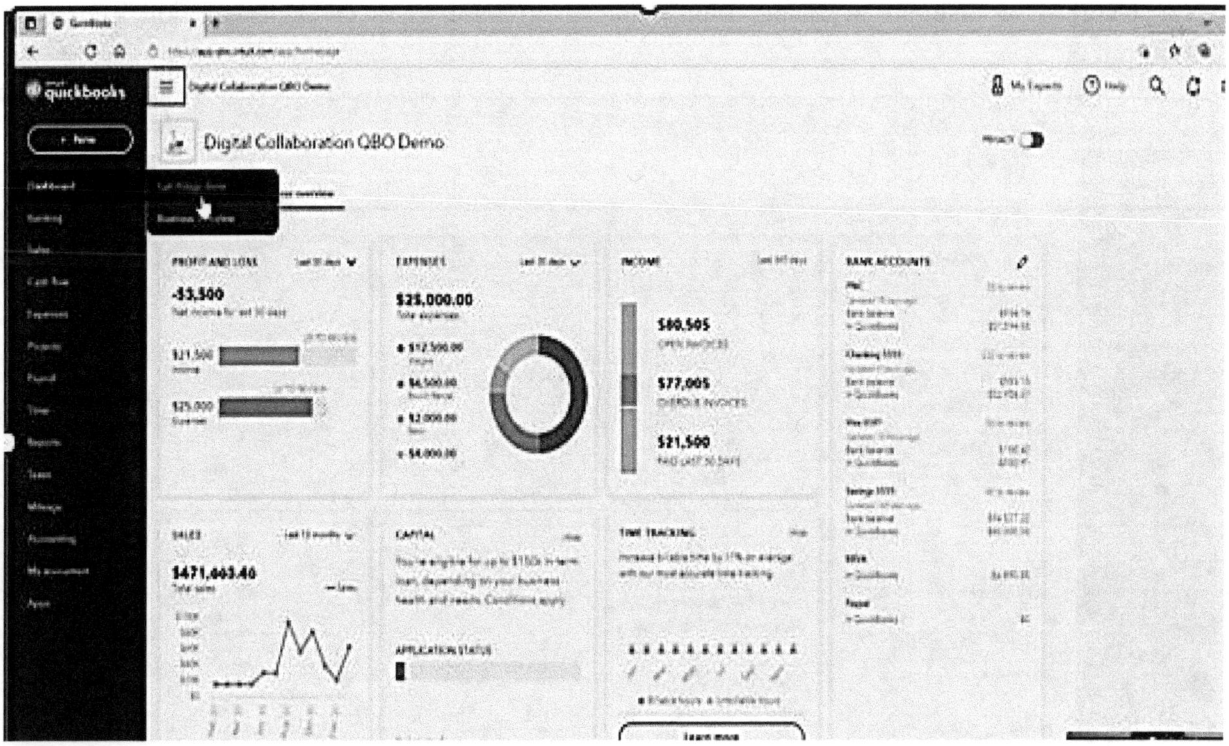

2. Next, you will choose your preferred action. Let us assume that we want to clear delivery errors, click on the prompt and it would assist you to affix appropriate corrections to the errors.

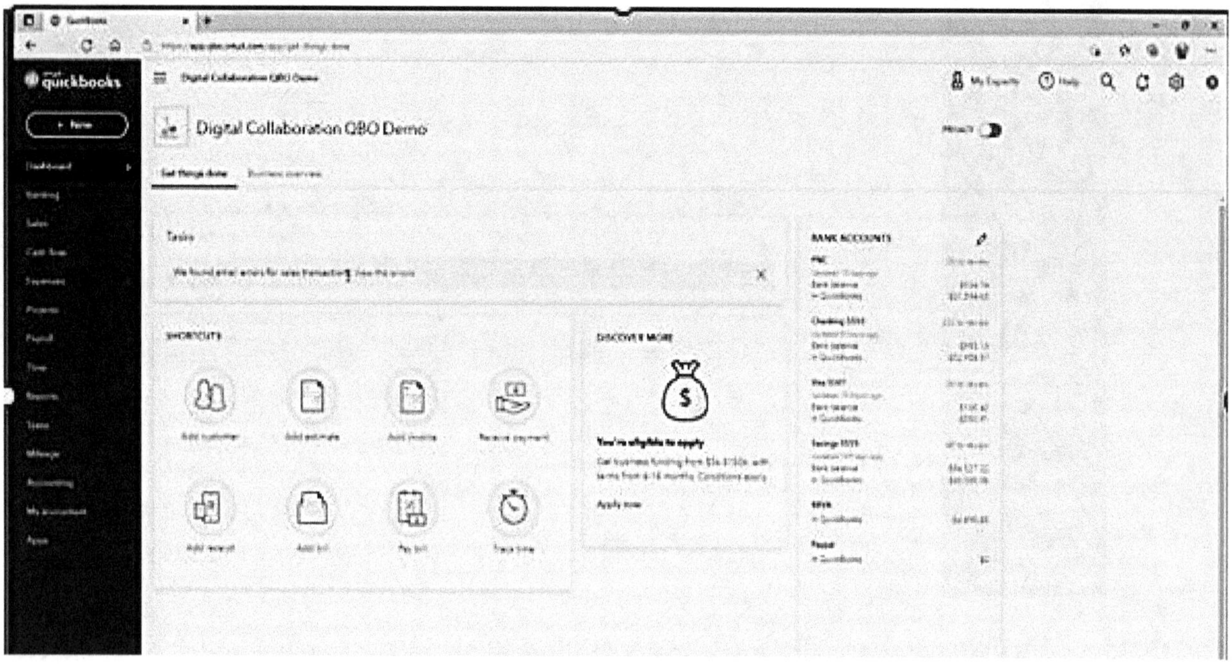

The Dashboard is mainly a shortcut to manage other functions on your **QuickBooks Online.** To view a variety of different widgets, simply click on the **Business Overview** option from your **Dashboard.**

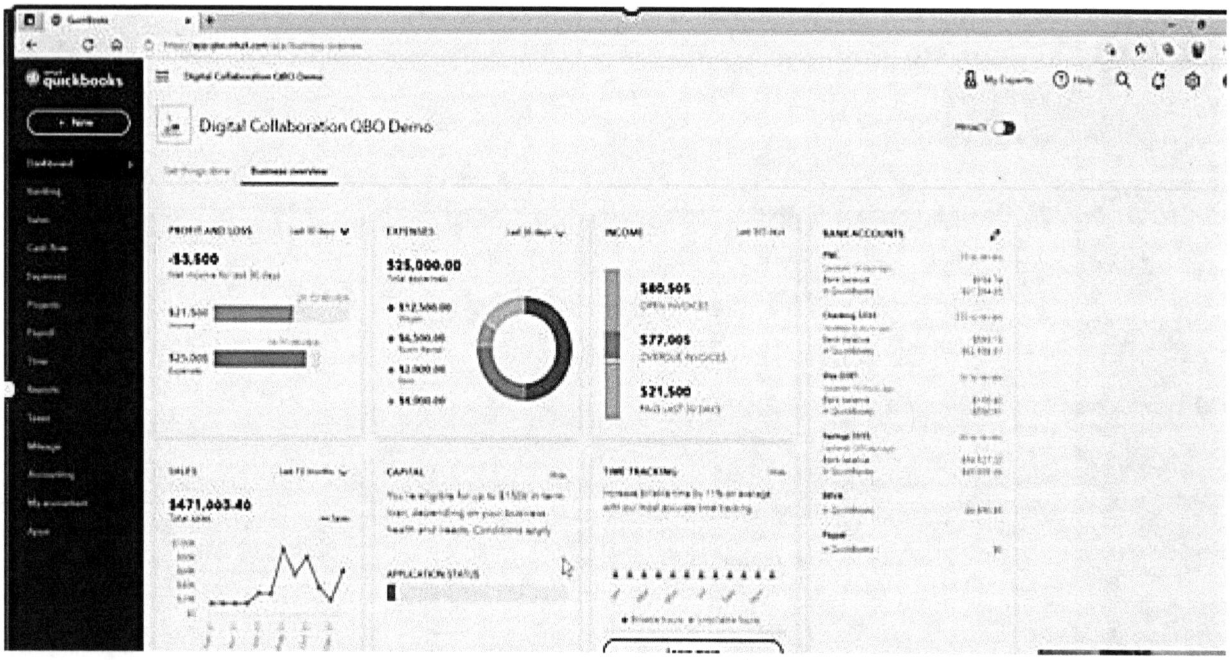

3. From your dashboard, you can choose the privacy option and choose to turn it off or on at will.

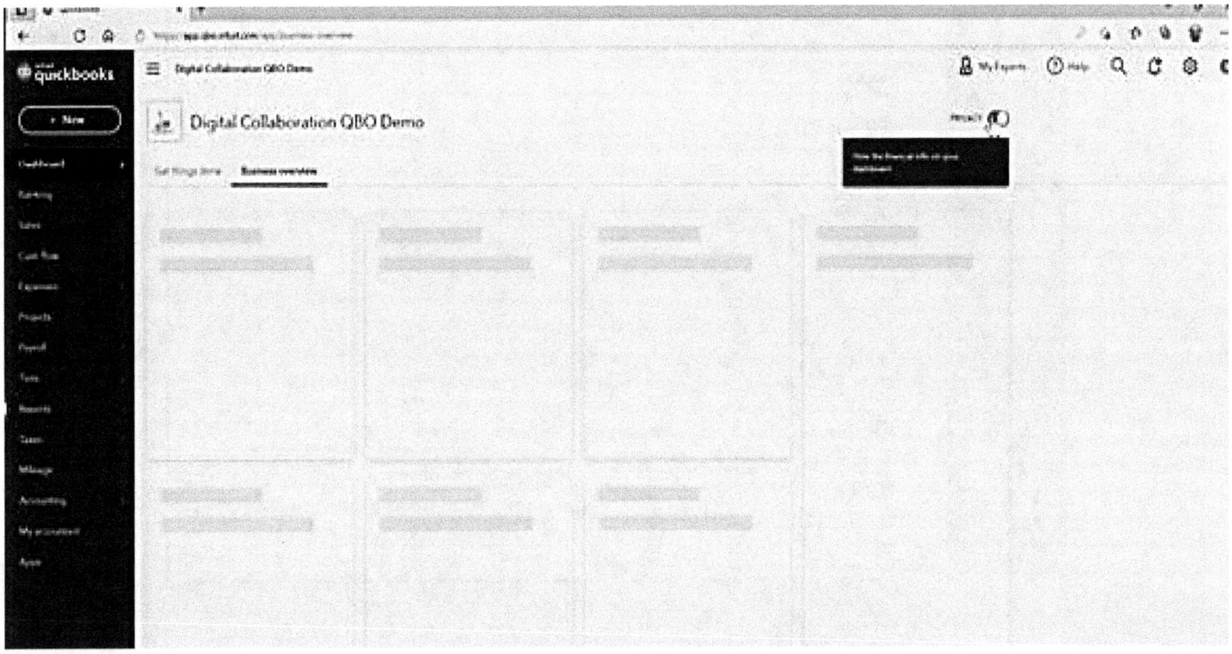

Charts of Account

Your charts of accounts are enabled to automatically connect to most credit and bank card accounts. However, when you want to connect them to online banking features, you might need to manually add some accounts to the charts. Some of these are loans, assets, and some banks and credit card accounts that are not supported in the QuickBooks online.

These can be manually added to your charts. To do this;

1. From your Dashboard, click on the Charts of an account option.

2. Click on **new.**

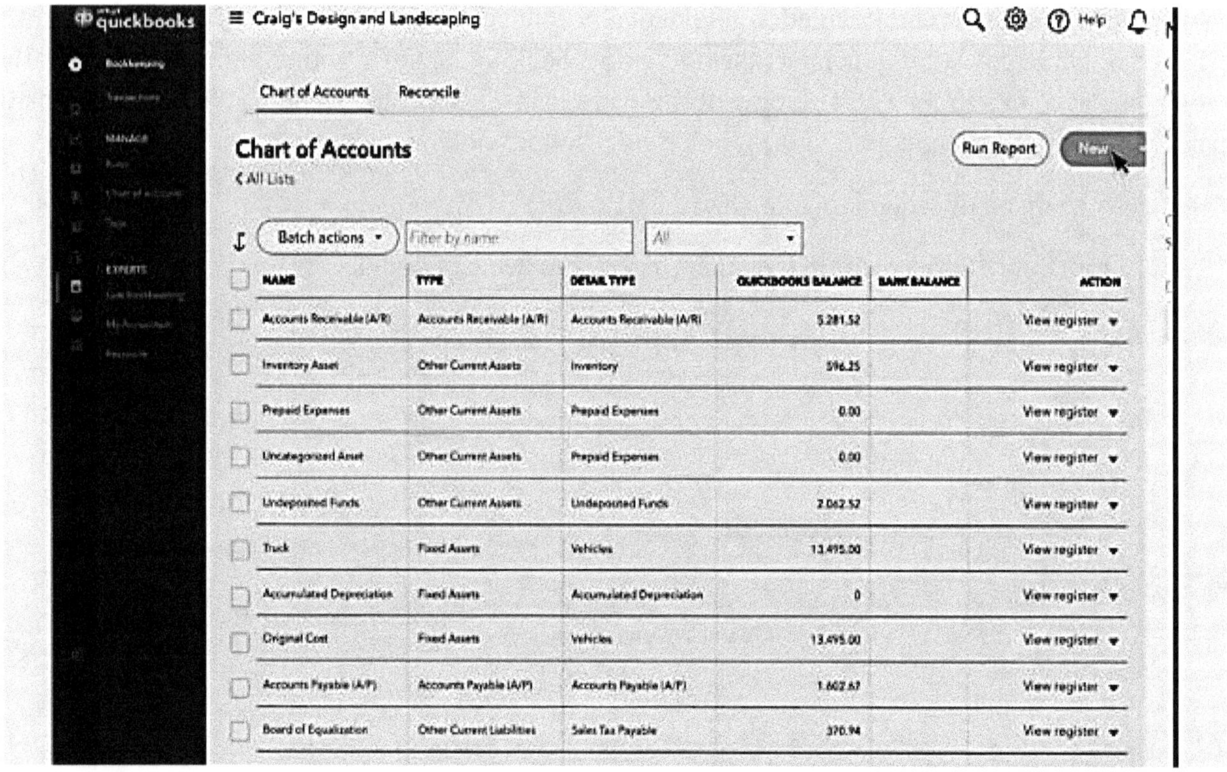

3. Click on the **select category** option.

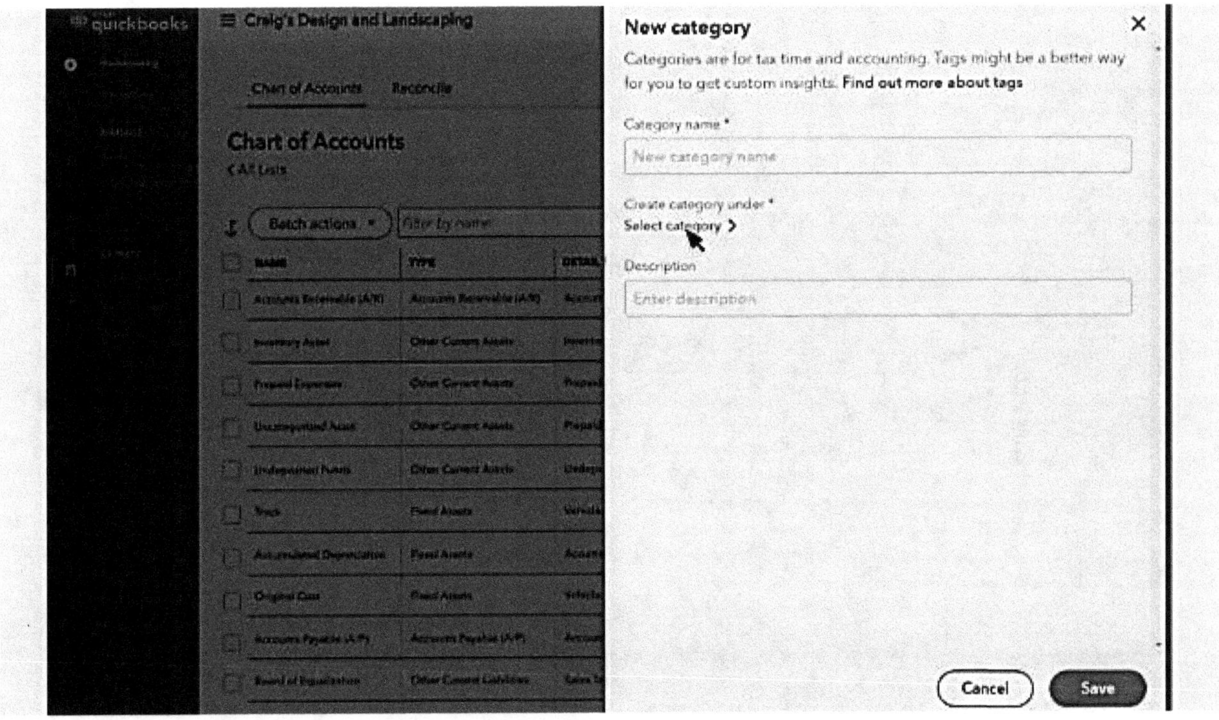

4. Choose the type of account you want to create. For this example, we will be using a business account so we will choose the **bank and credit cards** option.

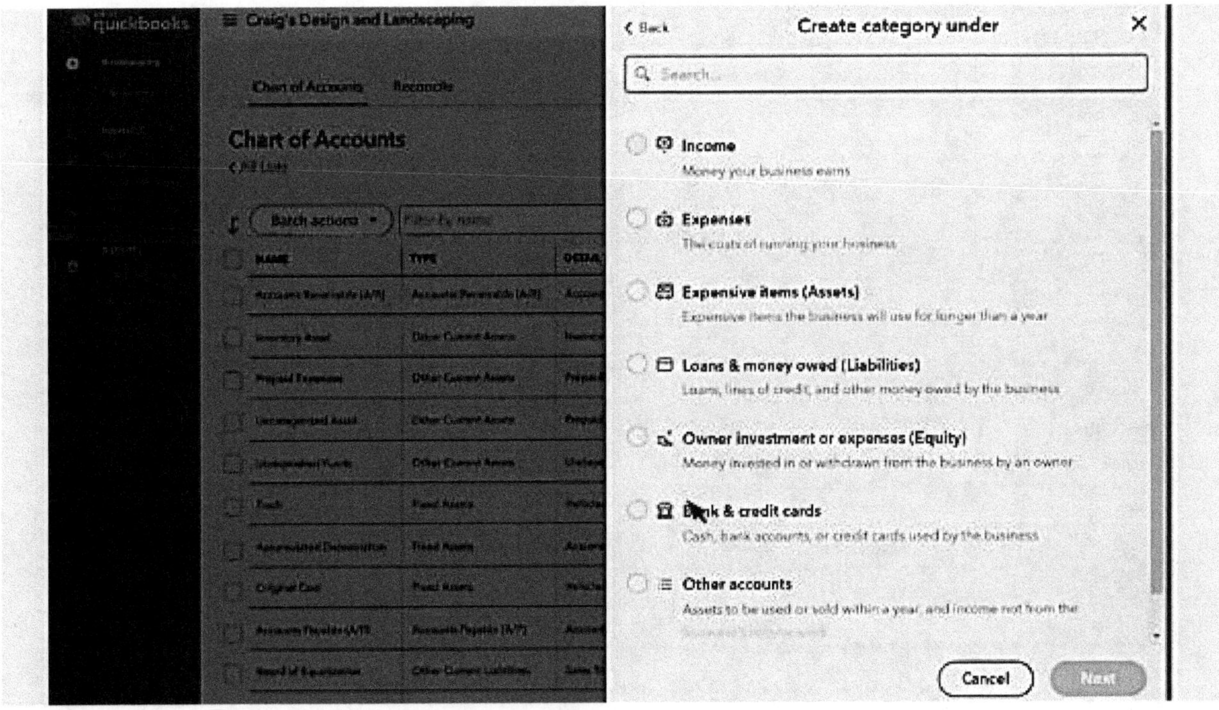

5. Select the **checking account** option.

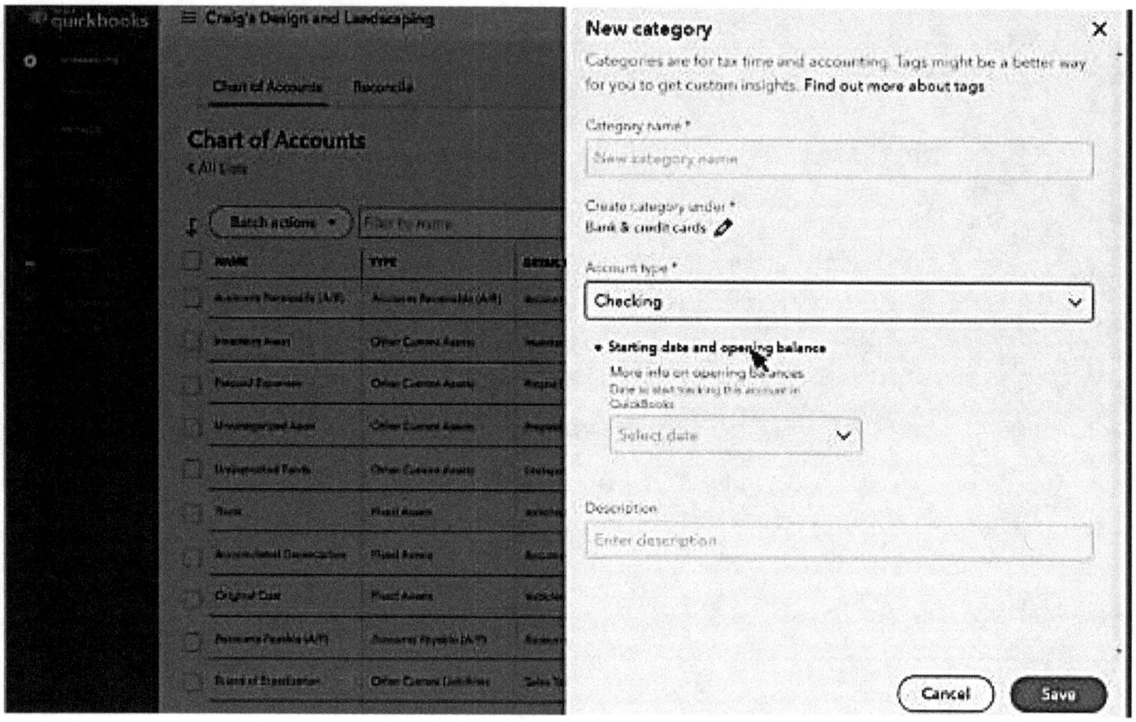

6. Select your category name and pick a day to start tracking all your business transactions in QuickBooks.

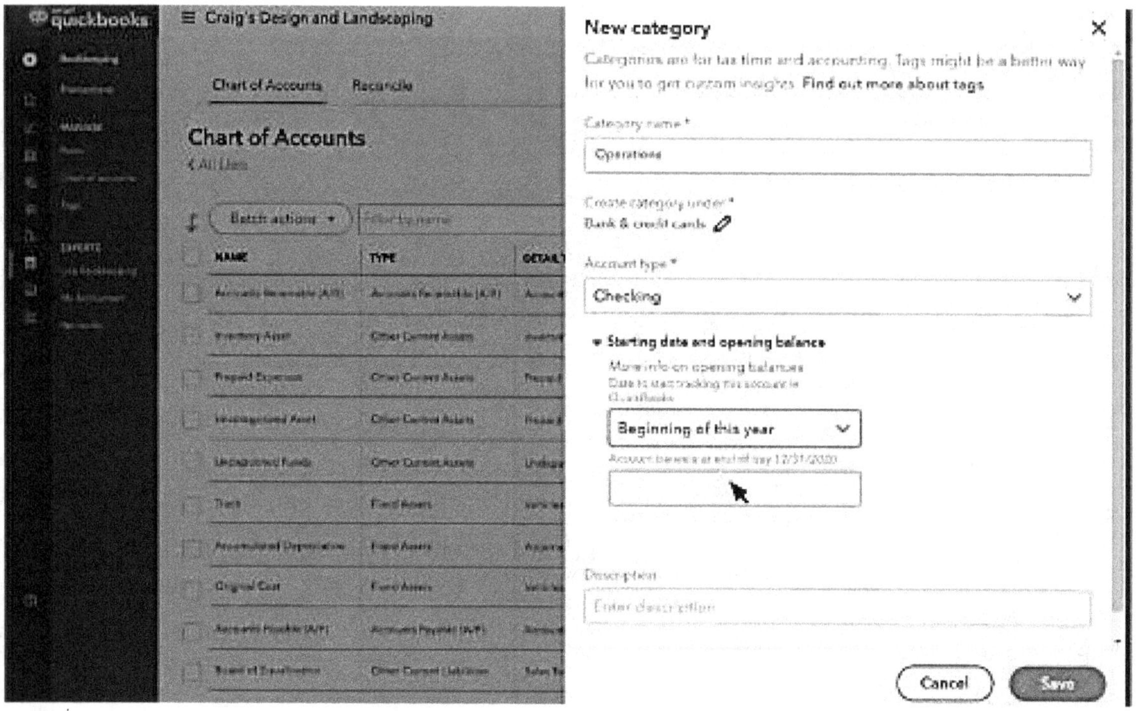

7. When you are done with this, enter the exact amount you wish to reflect in your real account.

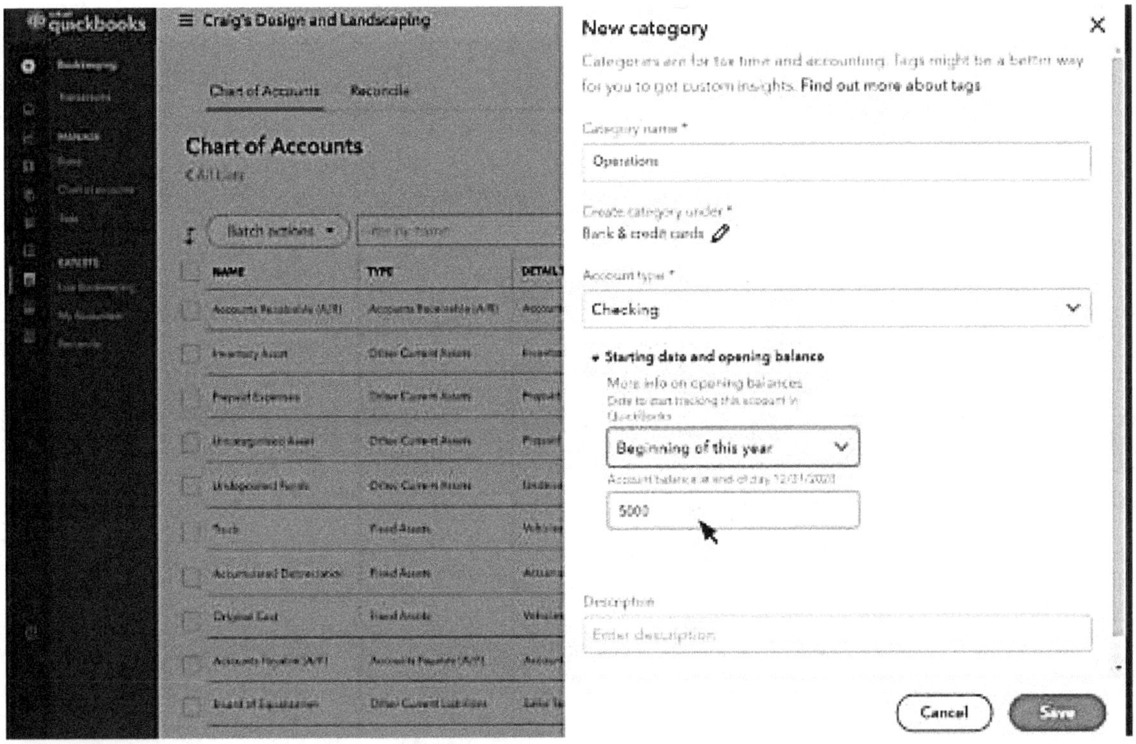

8. When the task is completed, hit the save button to avoid missing information.

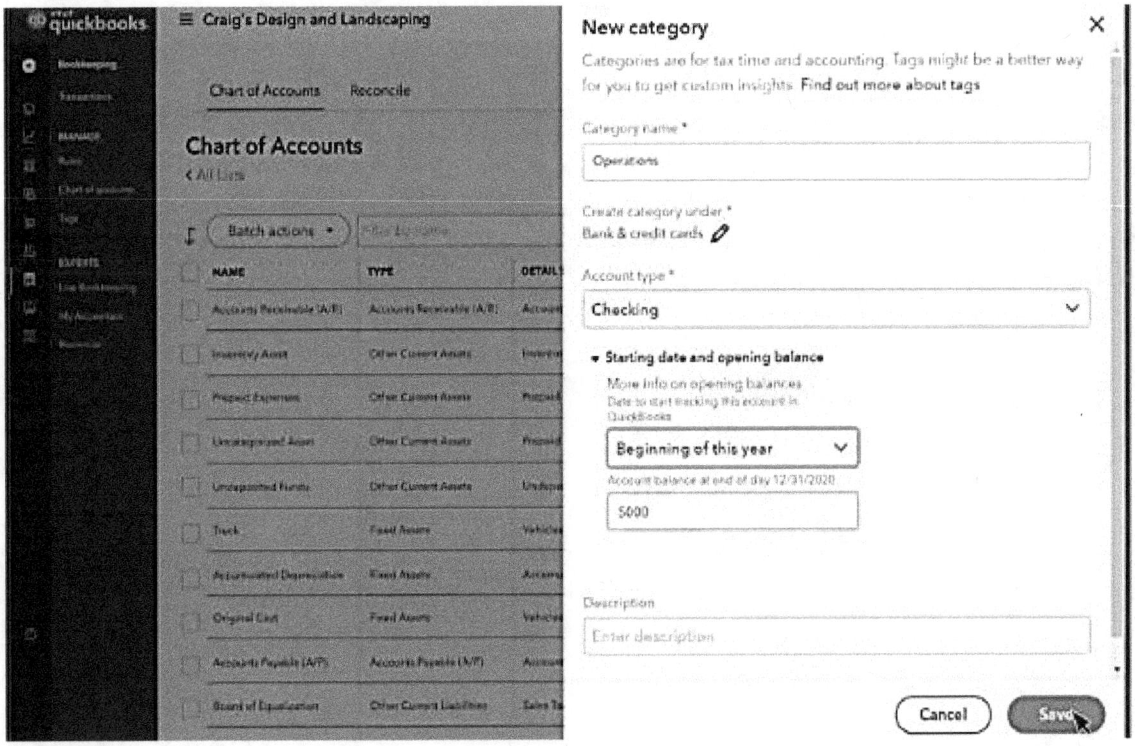

Now you are set to record new payments and deposits conveniently in your QuickBooks Online. If you intend to add more data to the account before the set date, seek the expertise of an accountant for better assistance.

How to Set Up Company Settings

In your QuickBooks online, to set up the company settings, you would need to enter basic information, like your contact and tax information to make communication with your customers and vendors easier.

Also, you can add your logo, your business address and phone number to the set-up. To do this;

1. Click on **Settings.**

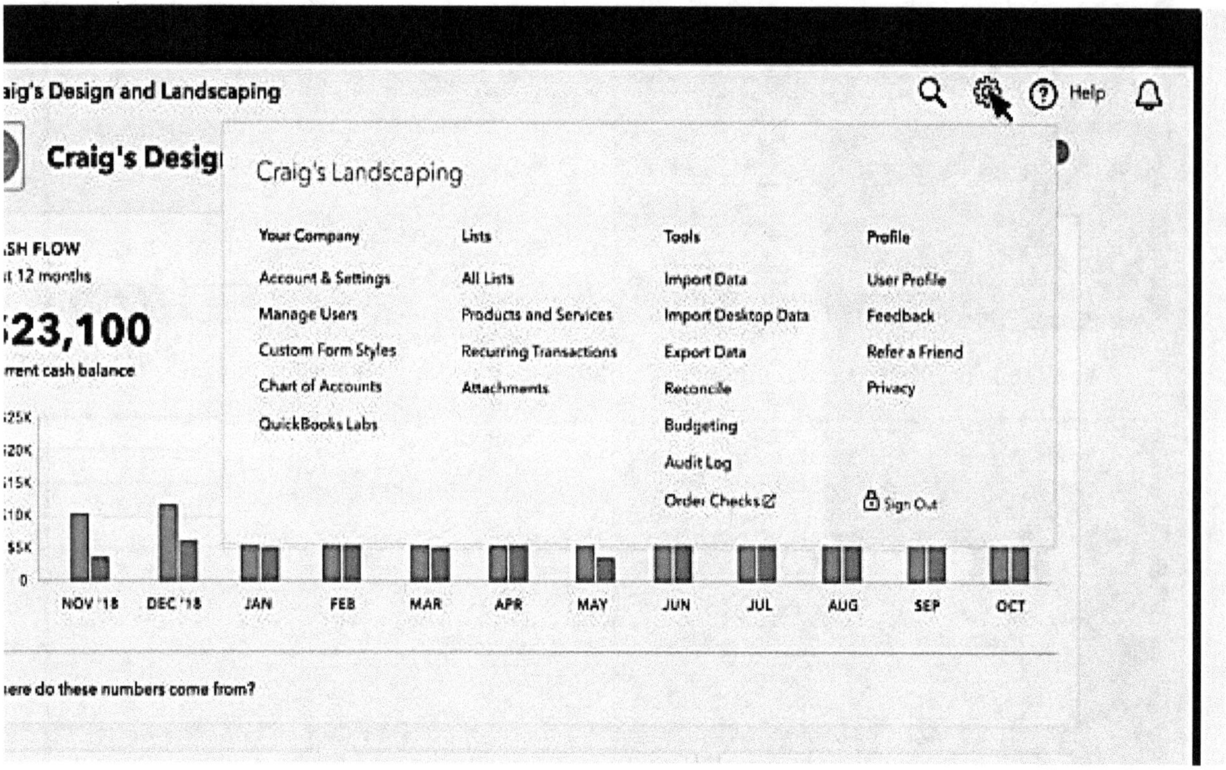

2. Select account & settings.

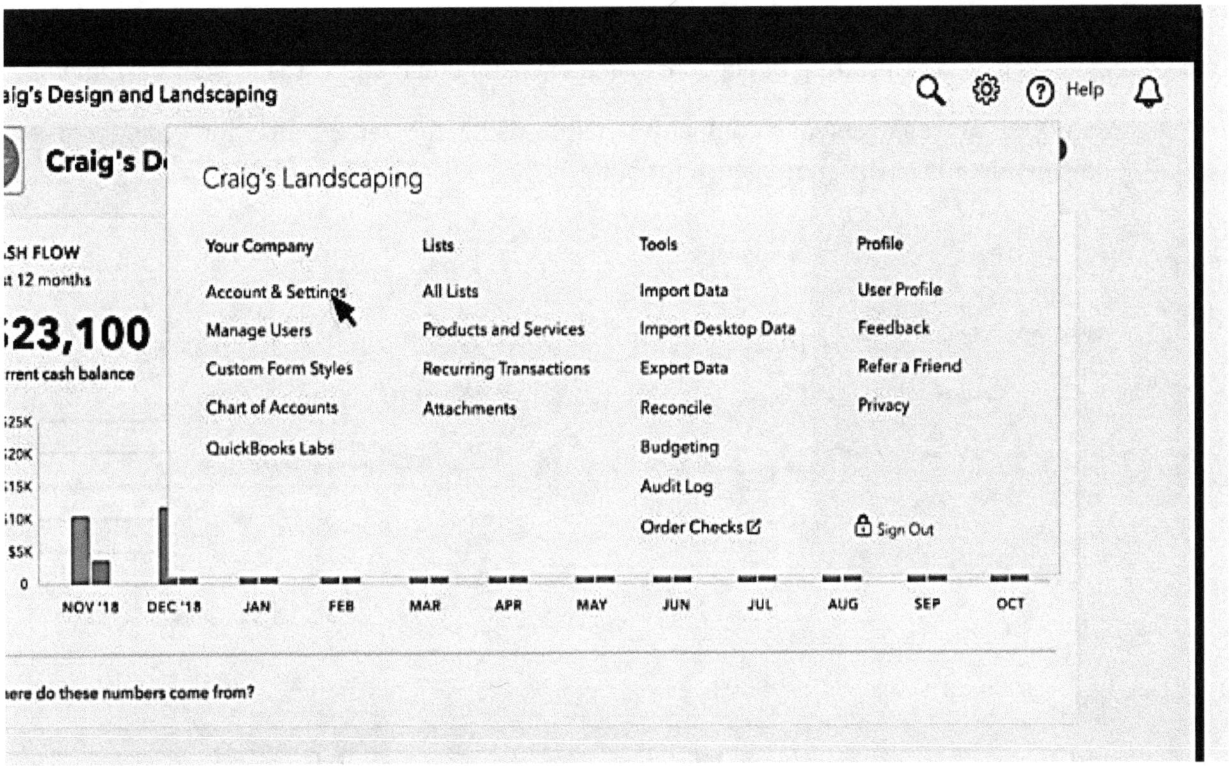

3. Here, you can view your company's logo.

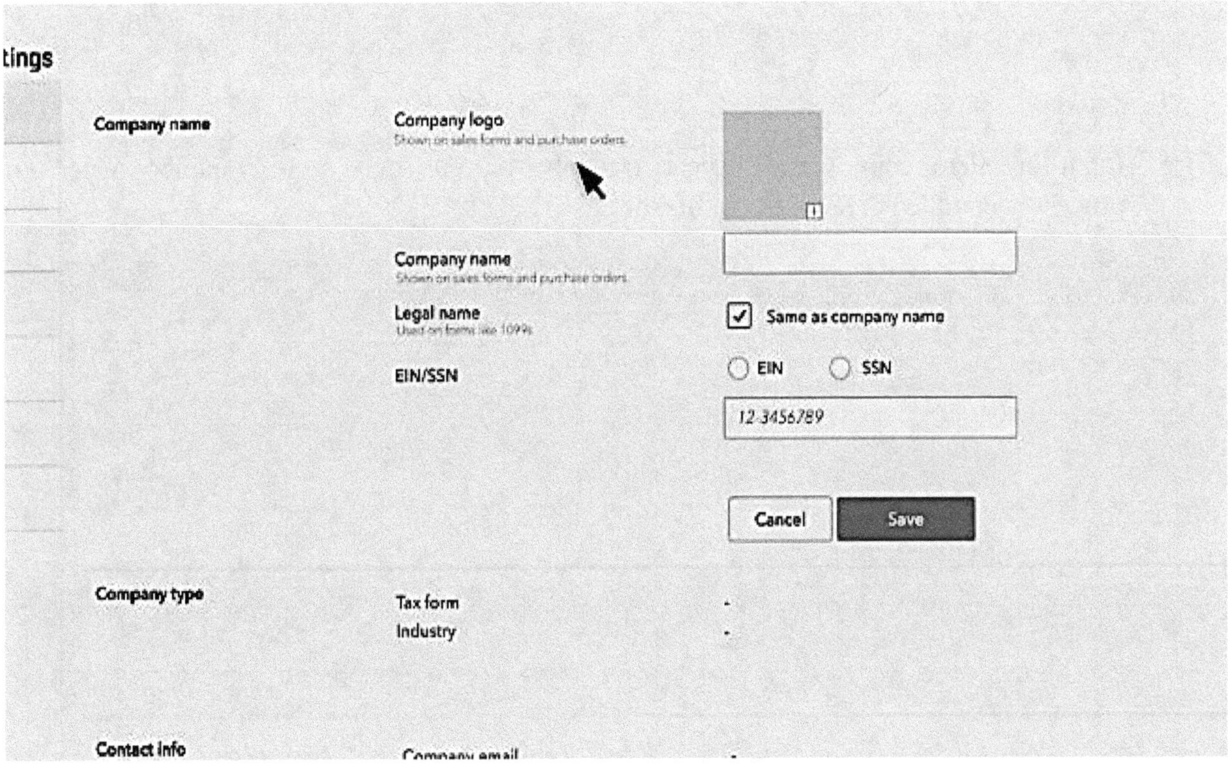

To set up the logo, click on the logo icon to upload it to your invoices and other vital categories of the QuickBooks like your printing of account statements and email addresses to your customers.

4. Also, you can change your company's name, using the same name for your legal and company details or different names for both.

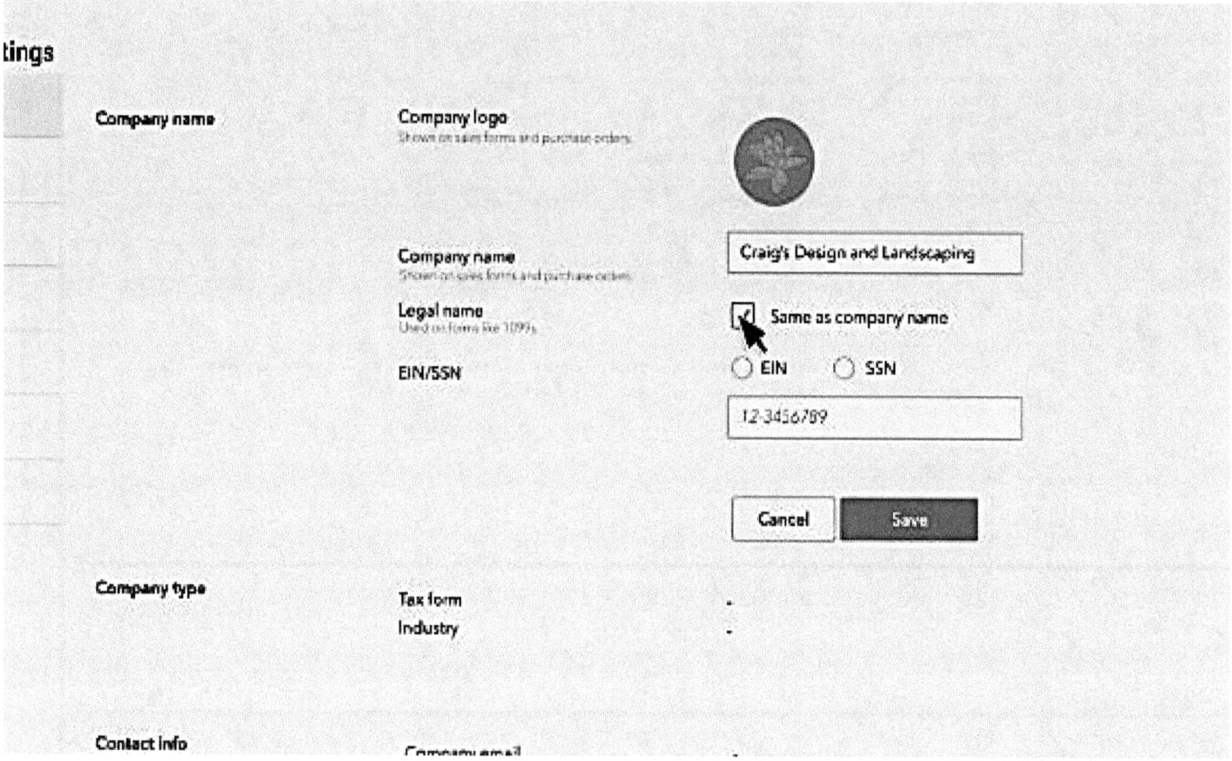

5. Input for federal employer identification number or your social security number. Once this process is completed, hit the **save button.**

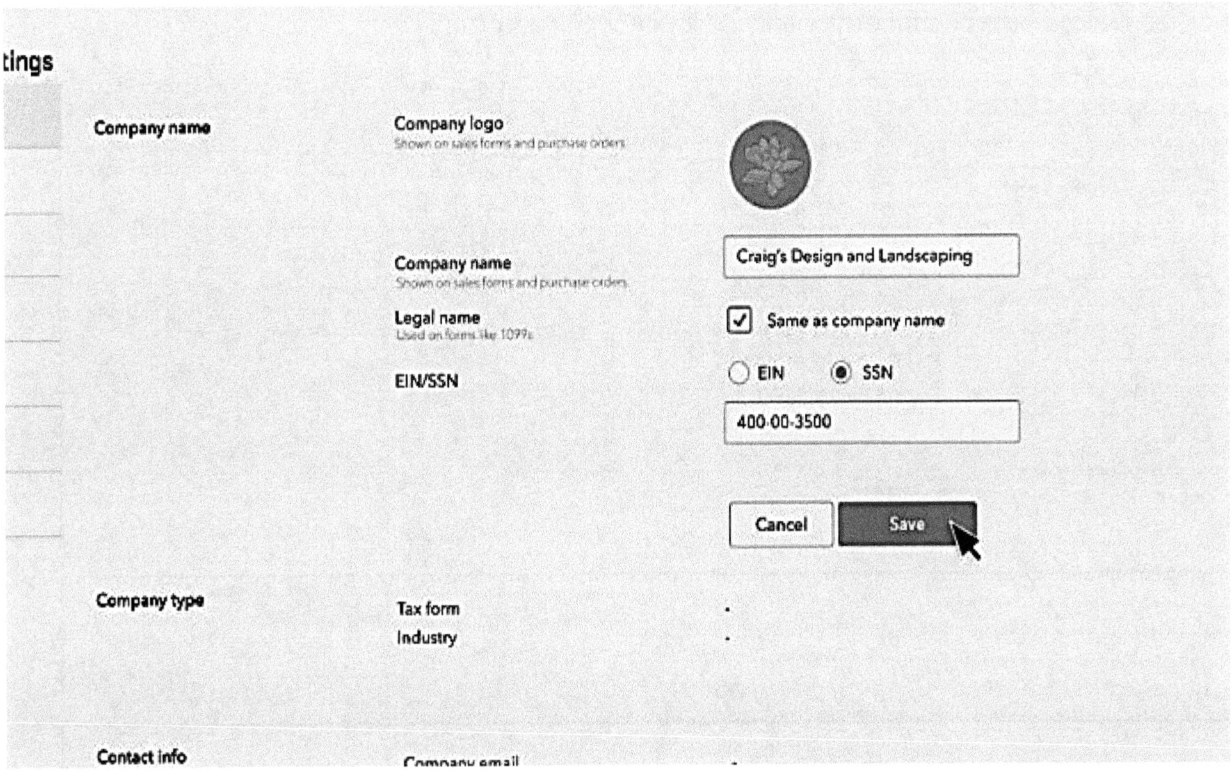

6. Under the tax form category, indicate the company's type.

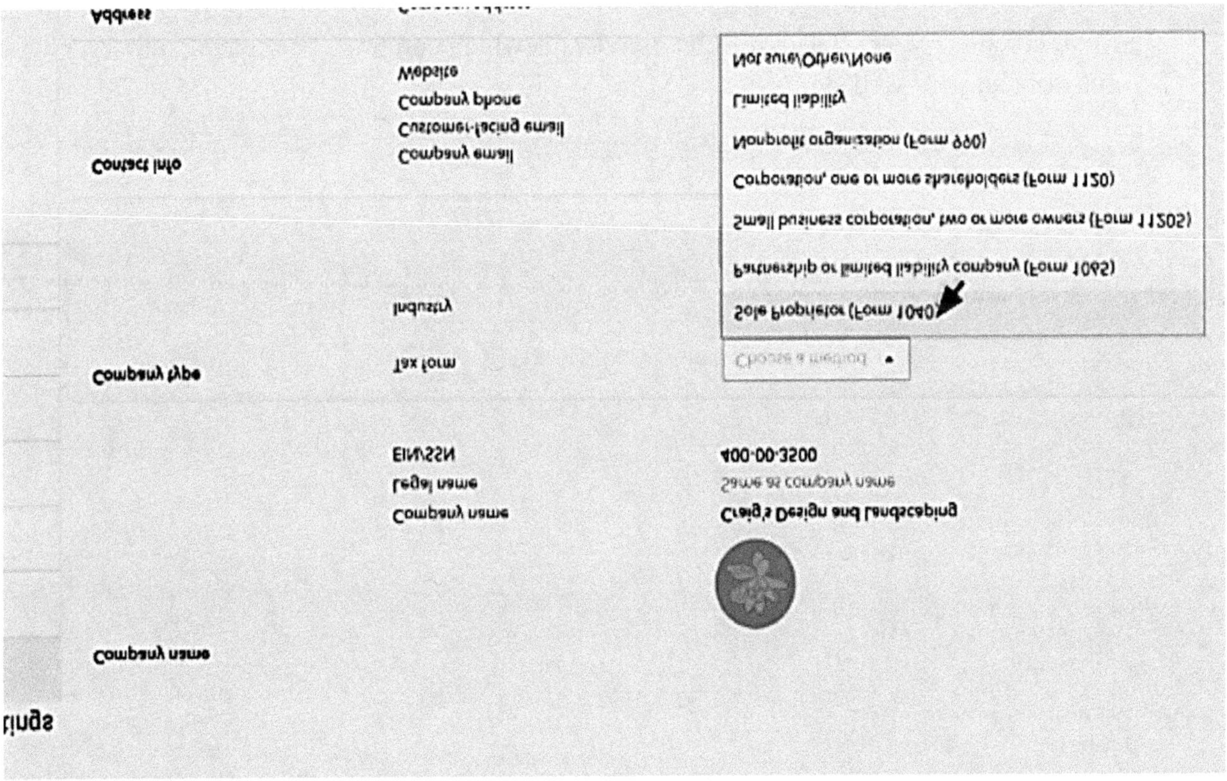

7. Select the type of industry and click on the **Save button.**

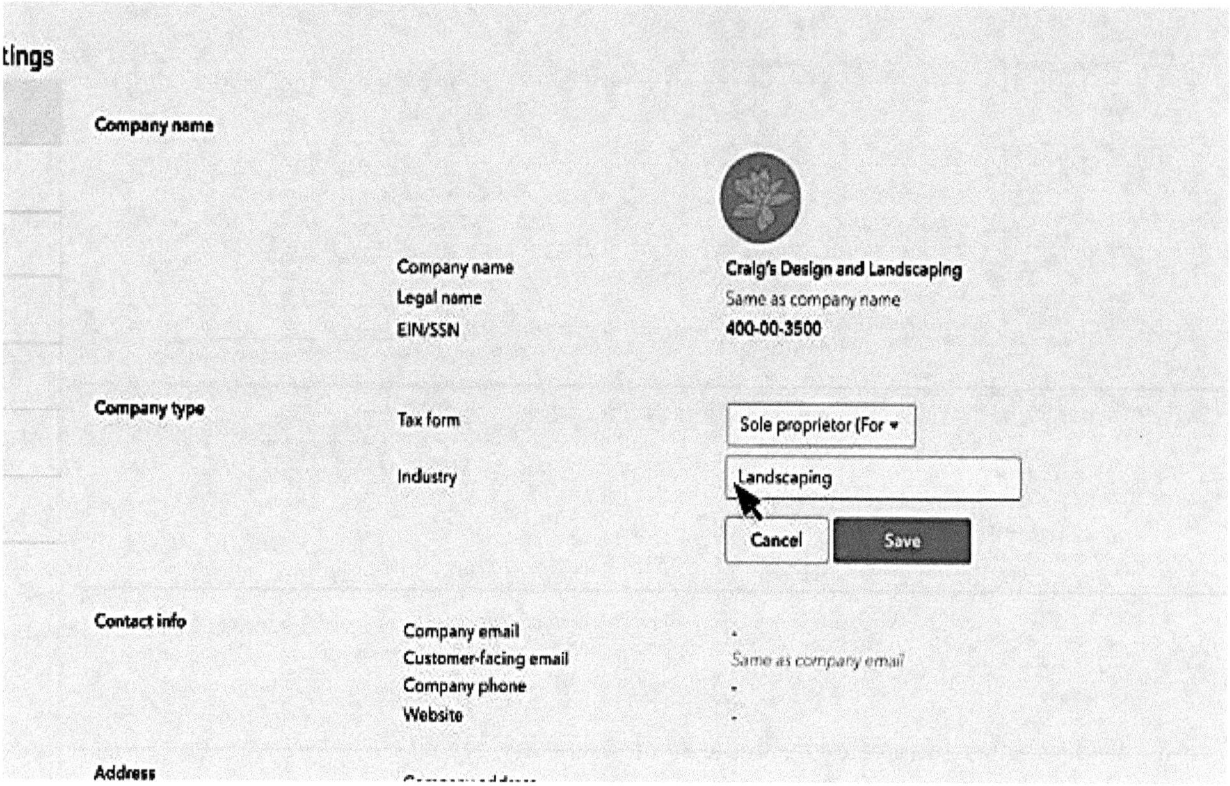

8. Next, complete your contact information details which comprise your email address, phone number and your website.

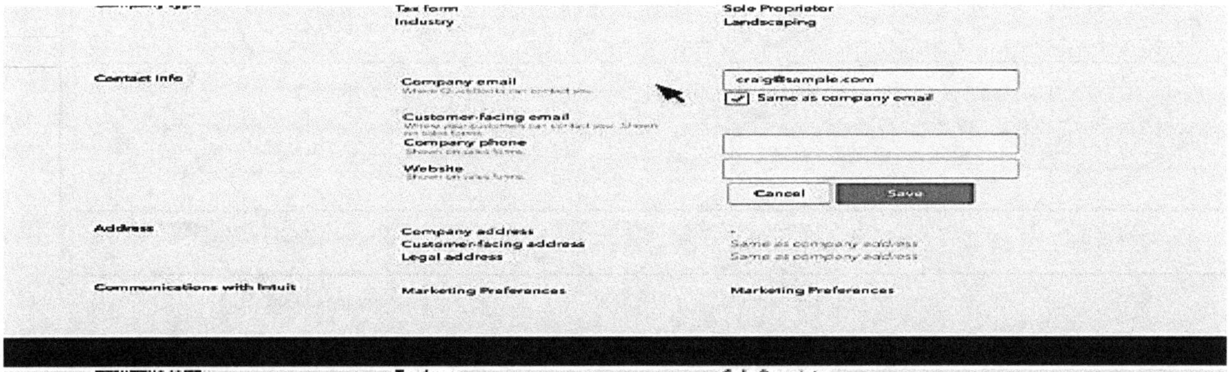

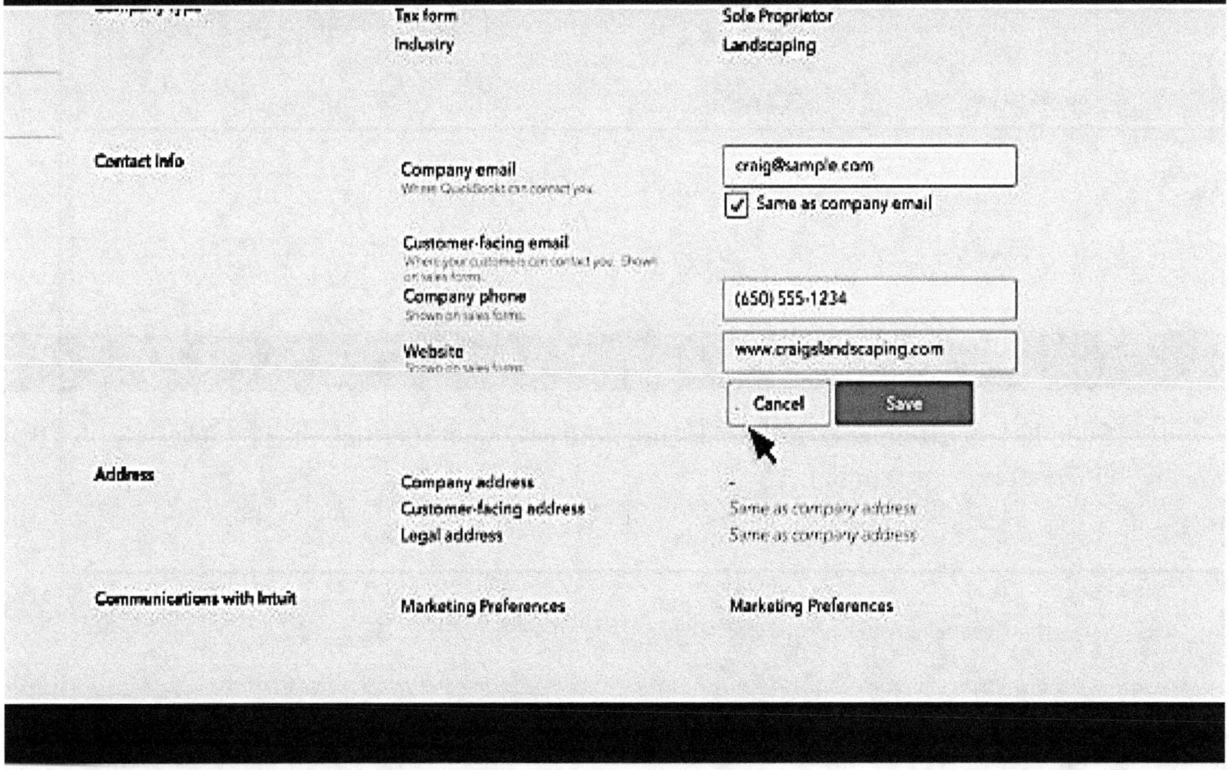

9. Input your house or company address as well.

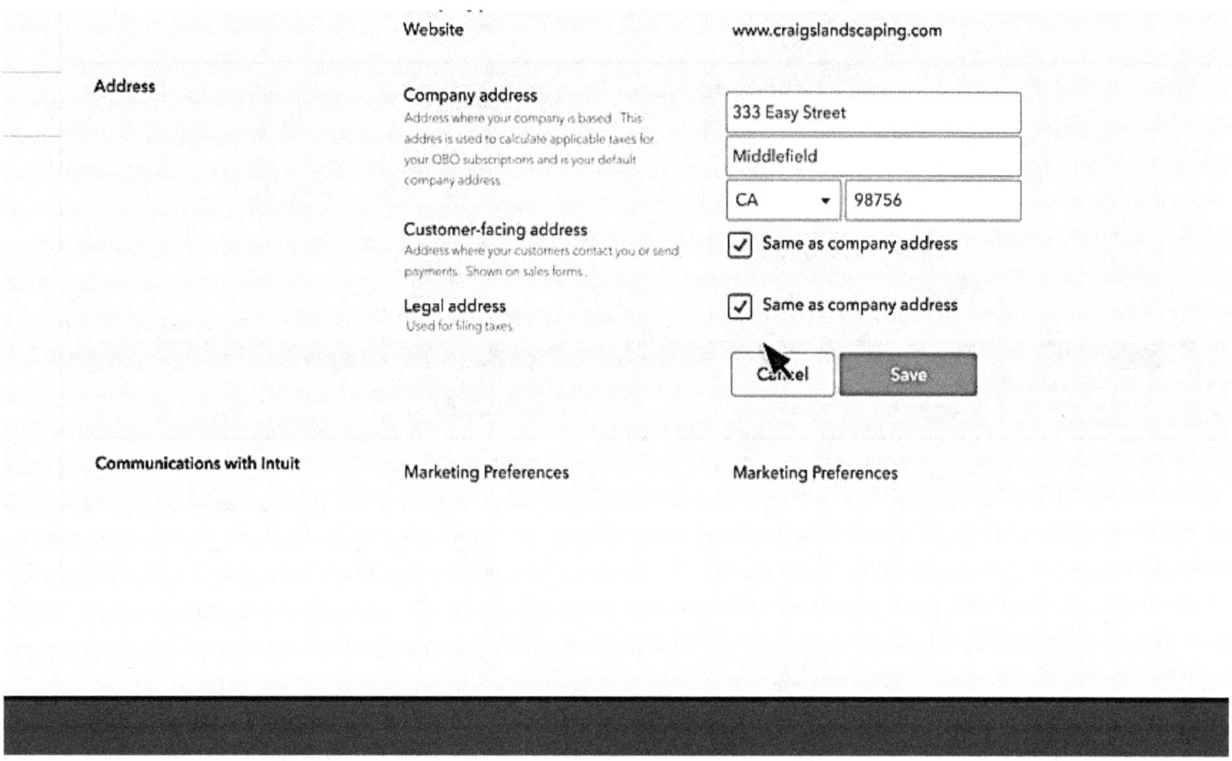

10. If you have a different **customer-facing address,** input it or tick the box that indicates that both addresses are similar.

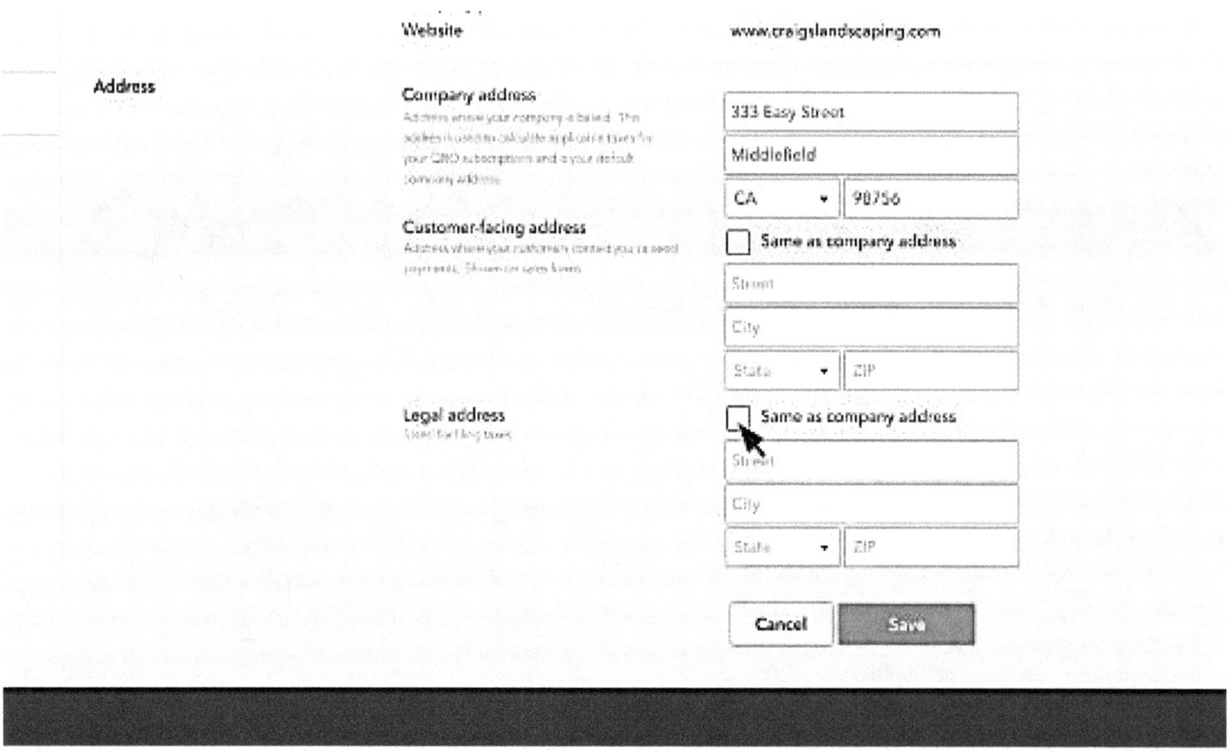

11. When the set-up is completed, click on **done.**

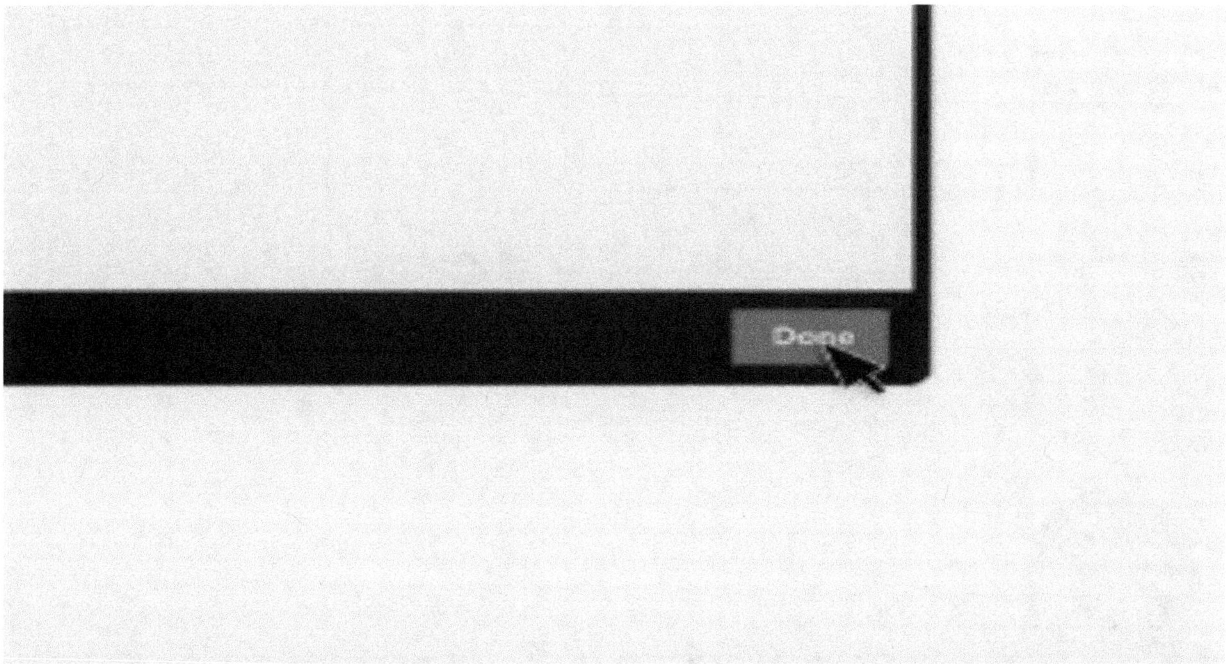

Now your company is ready to function on the QuickBooks online.

Customizing Sales Forms in QuickBooks Online

1. Quickly, click on the Settings icon and choose the account and settings option.

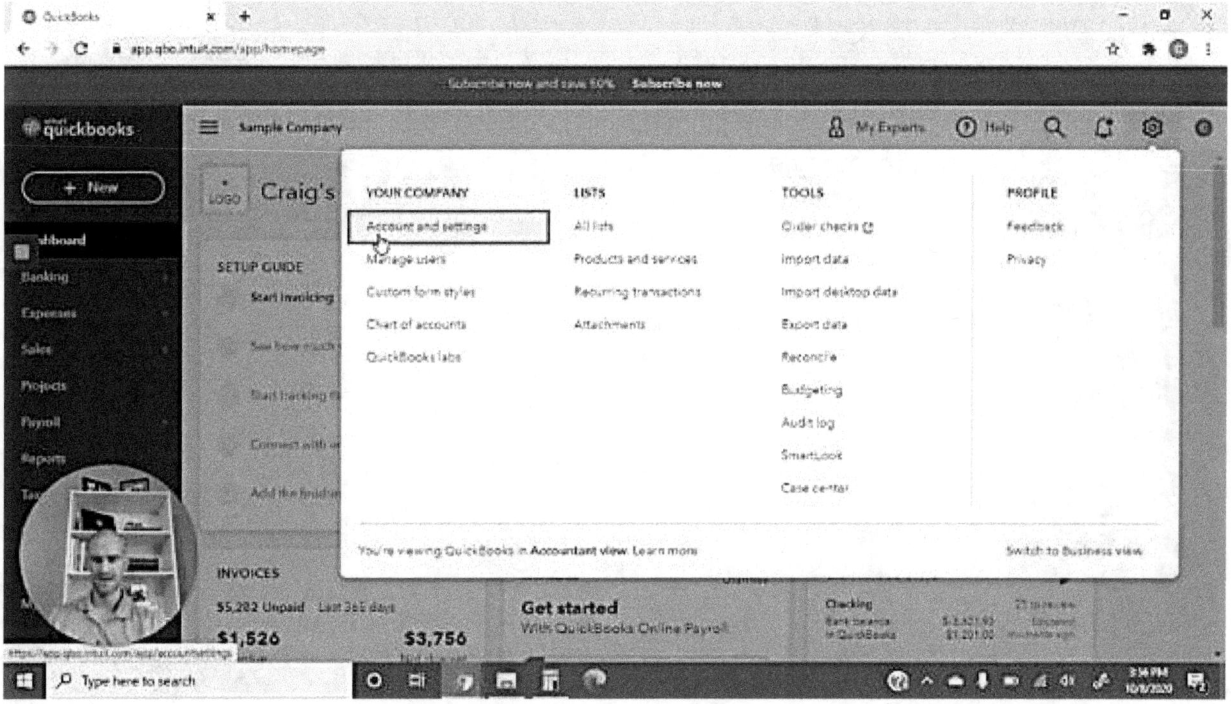

2. Next, click on **sales.**

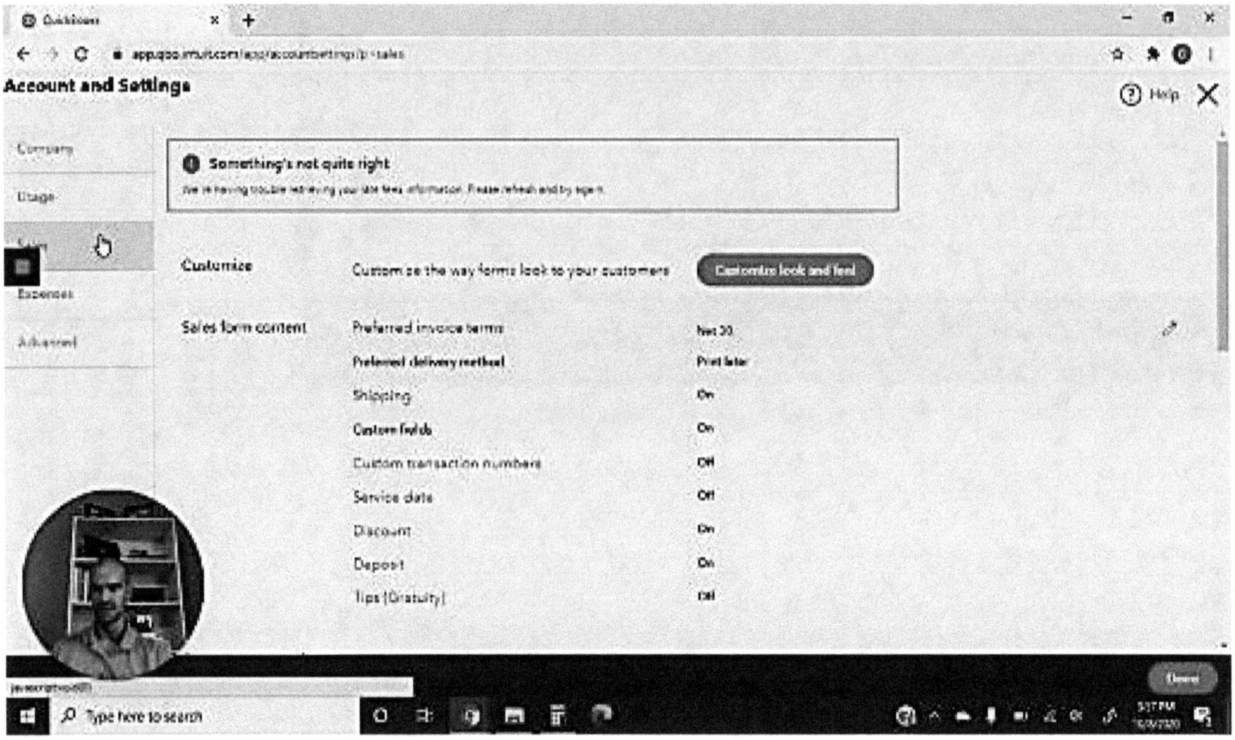

3. Select the option to **customize form style** and click on **edit.**

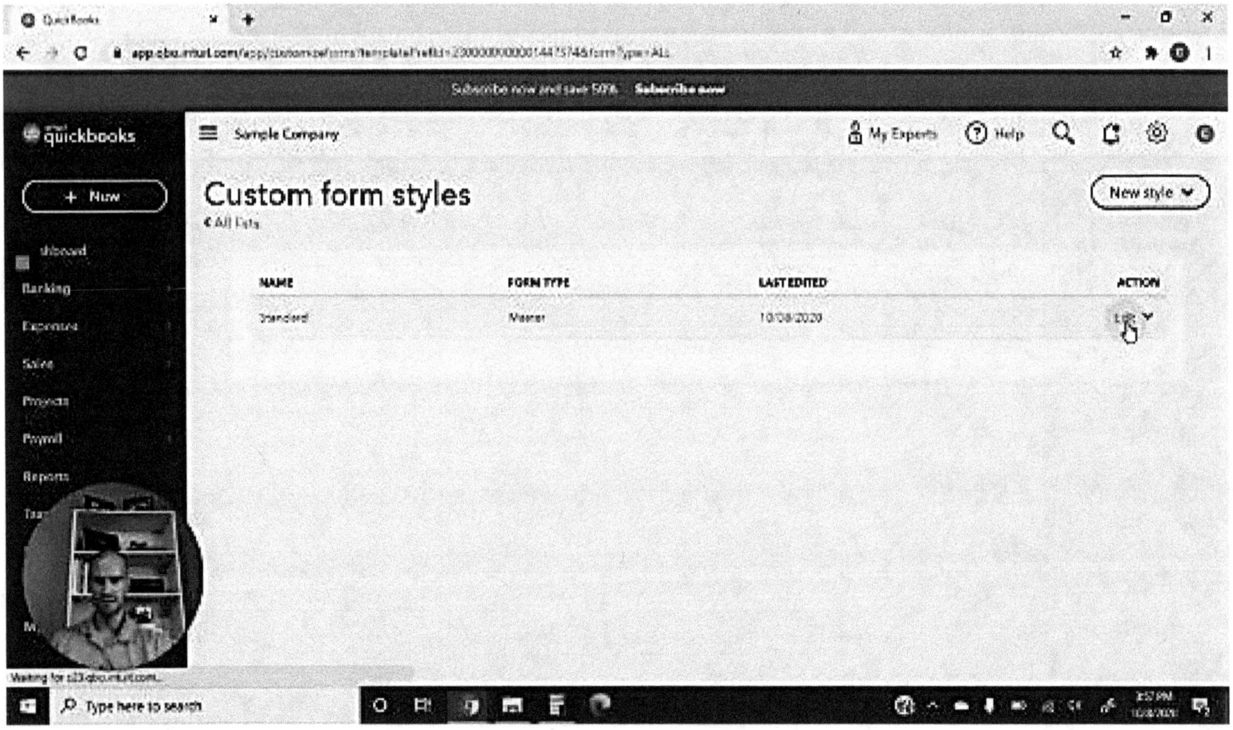

4. There are a variety of design template options to choose from.

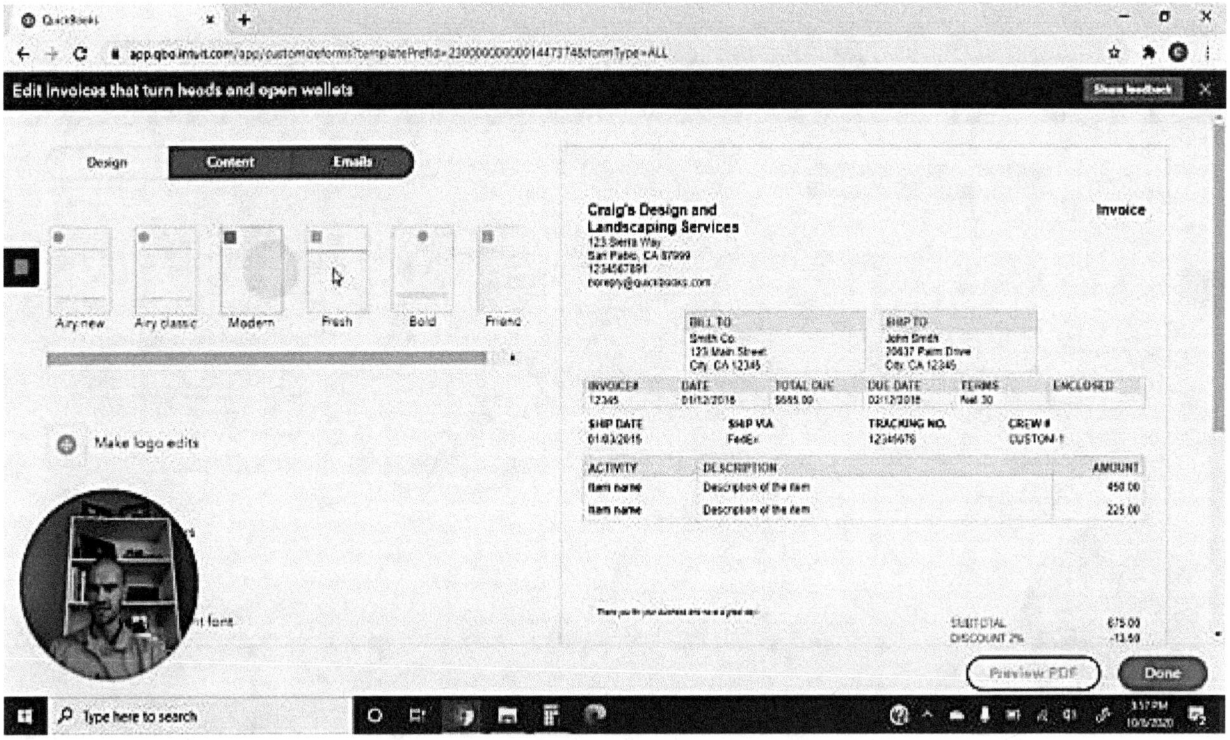

5. Also, you can select colors for your design.

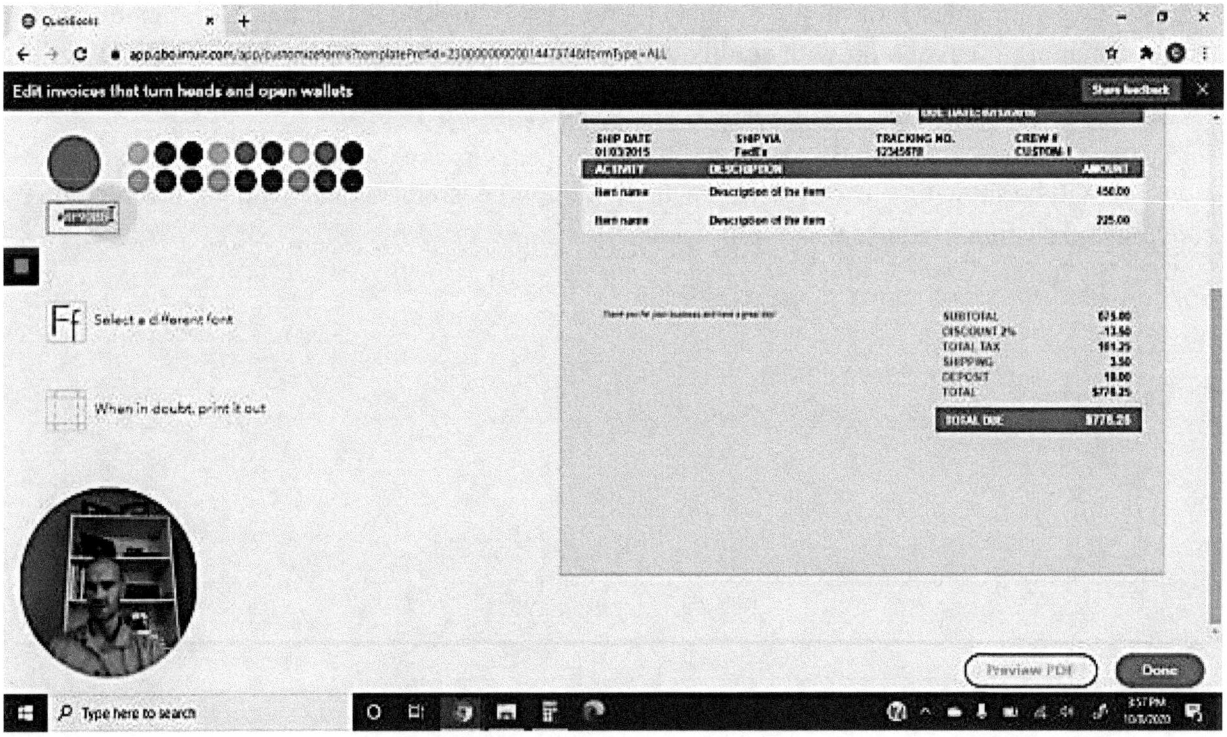

6. Play around with font styles to select your most preferred option.

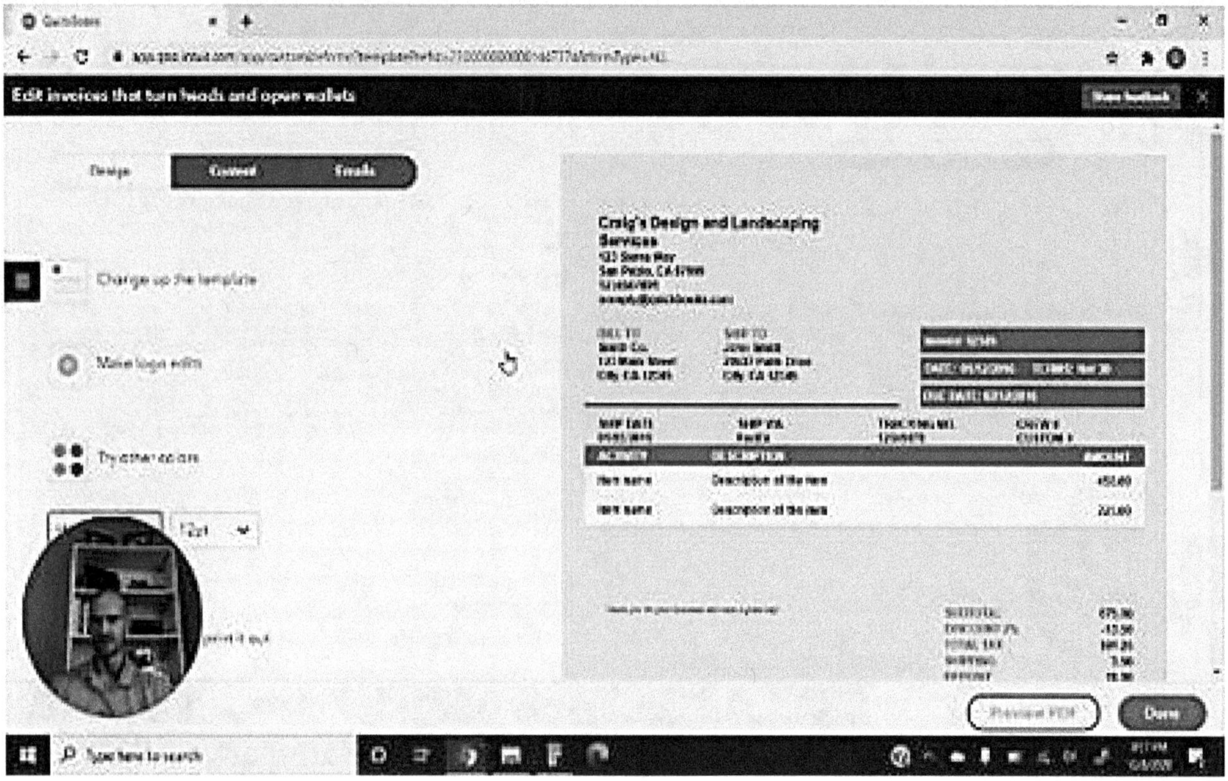

Customizing your sales form is not a cumbersome task. QuickBooks Online has streamlined the process, making it easy to do with readily available templates. Simply maximize them to get the best results.

Importing Customers' and Vendors' names into your QuickBooks Online
Here, we will be showing you the easiest method to import customers' and vendors' information by copying and pasting from excel.

So, now I have a list of names in an excel sheet.

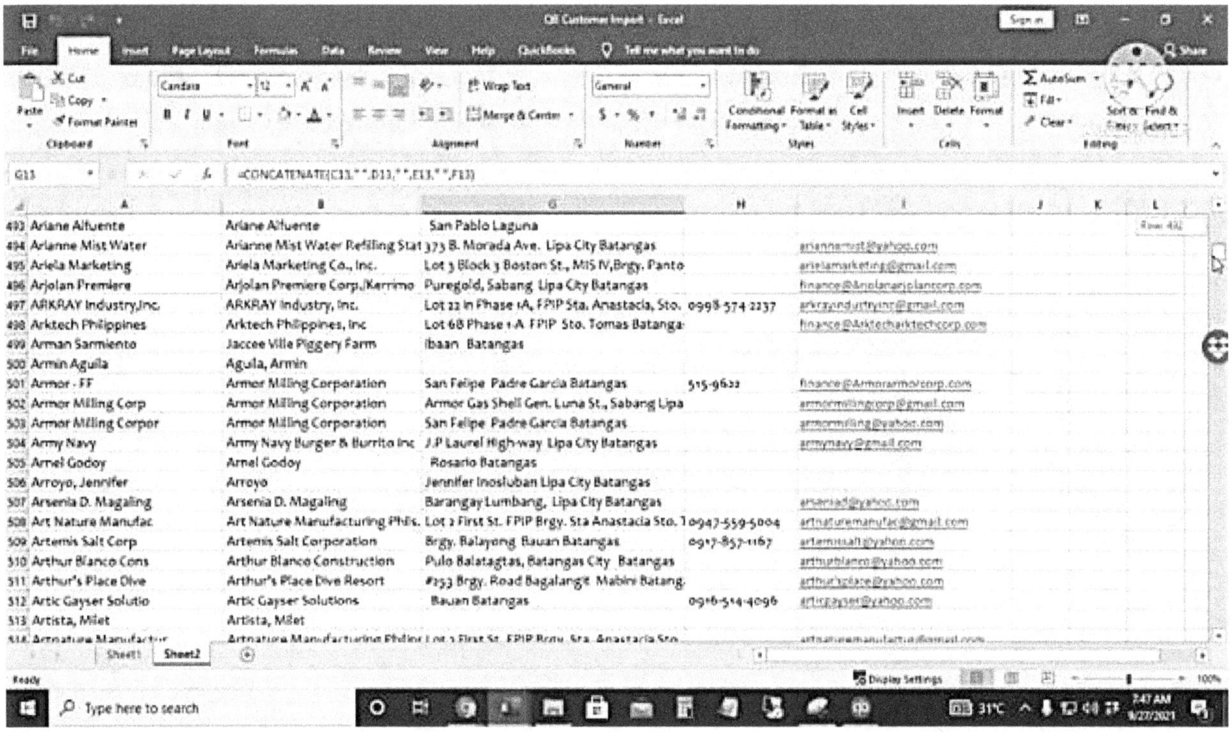

If you are to put the names in your QuickBooks Online one at a time, this will waste a lot of ample time.

1. In your QuickBooks Online, click on the customer section.

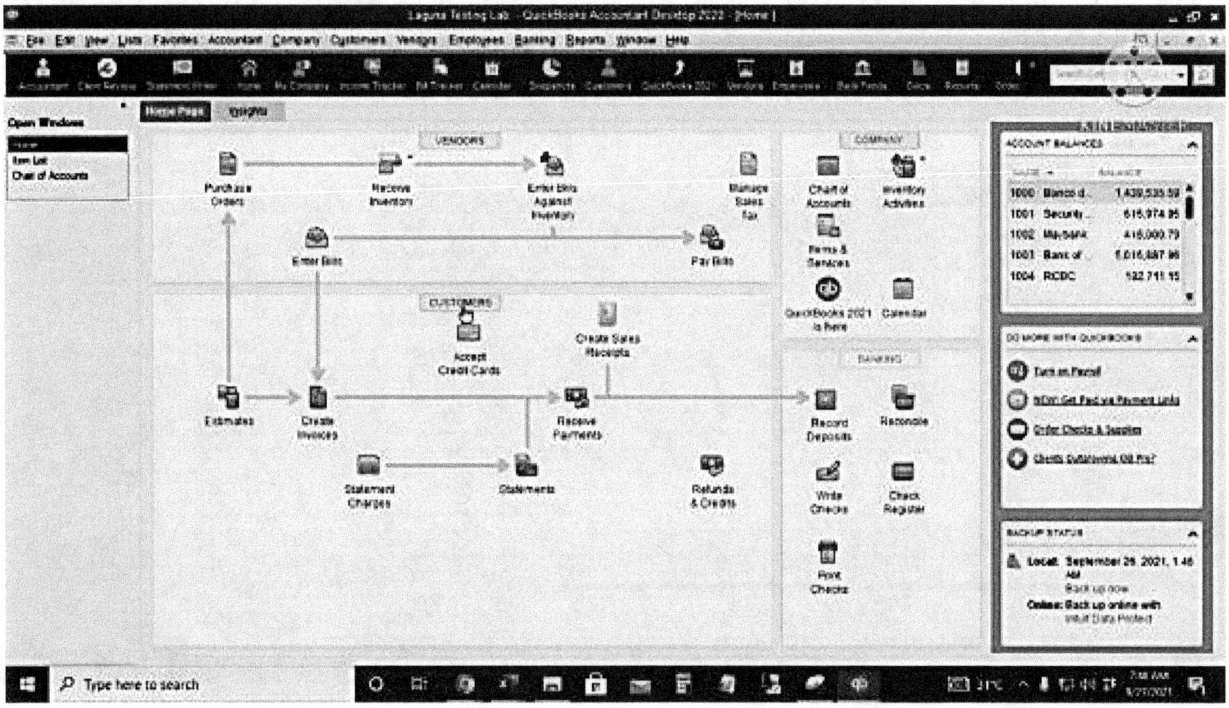

2. Right-click on the excel tab, and choose **add edit multiple customers.**

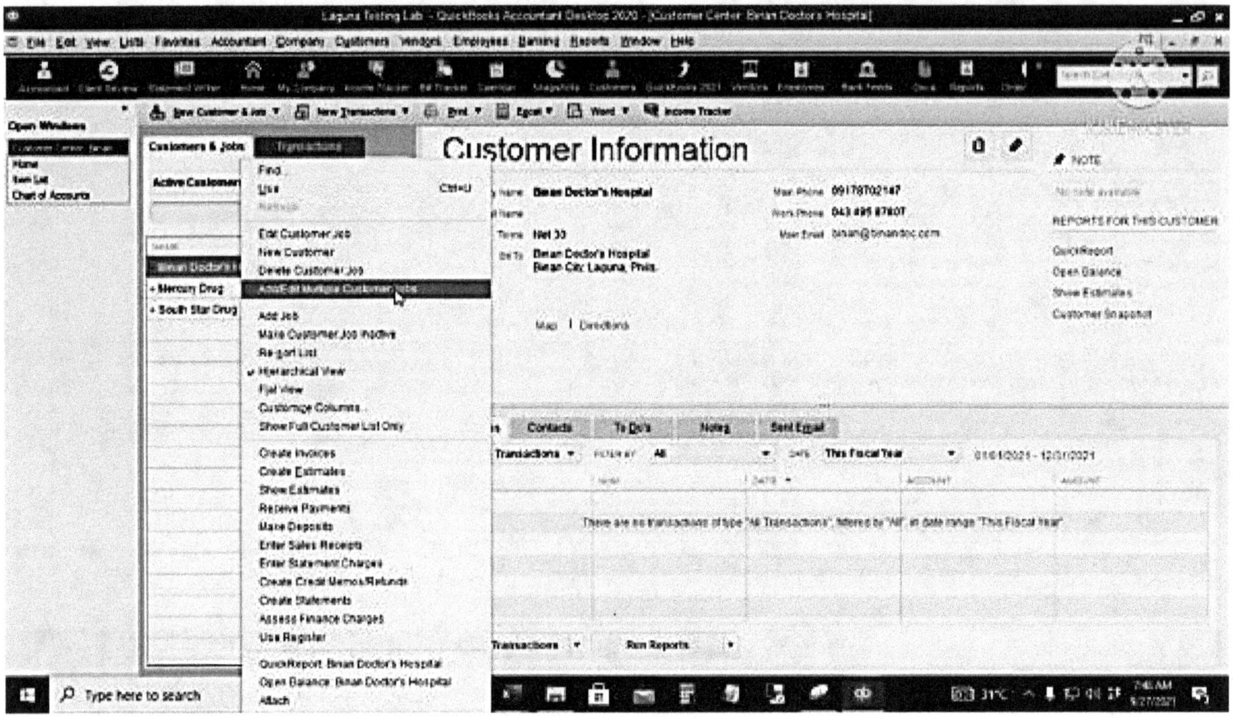

3. Click on the **drop-down arrow** and select **vendors** or **customers,** depending on the category you wish to update.

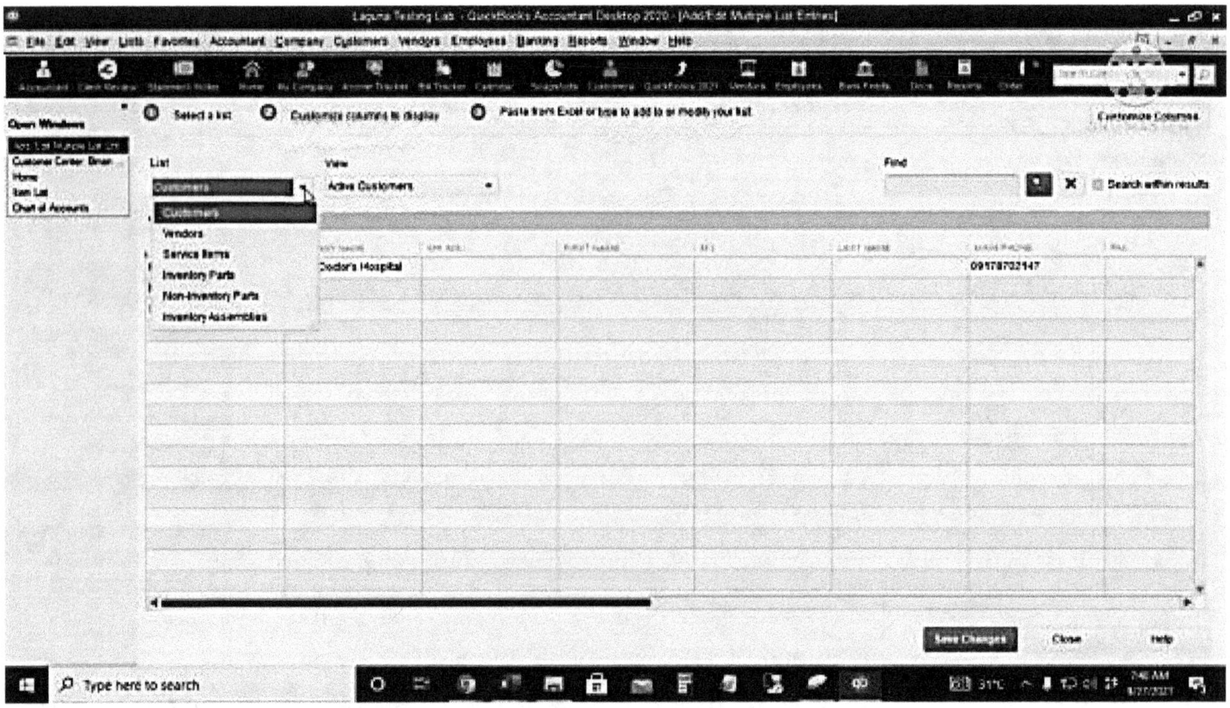

4. Go back to the excel sheet, highlight the customer's name or any other information you are working with and click on **the shortcut keys CTRL+C.**

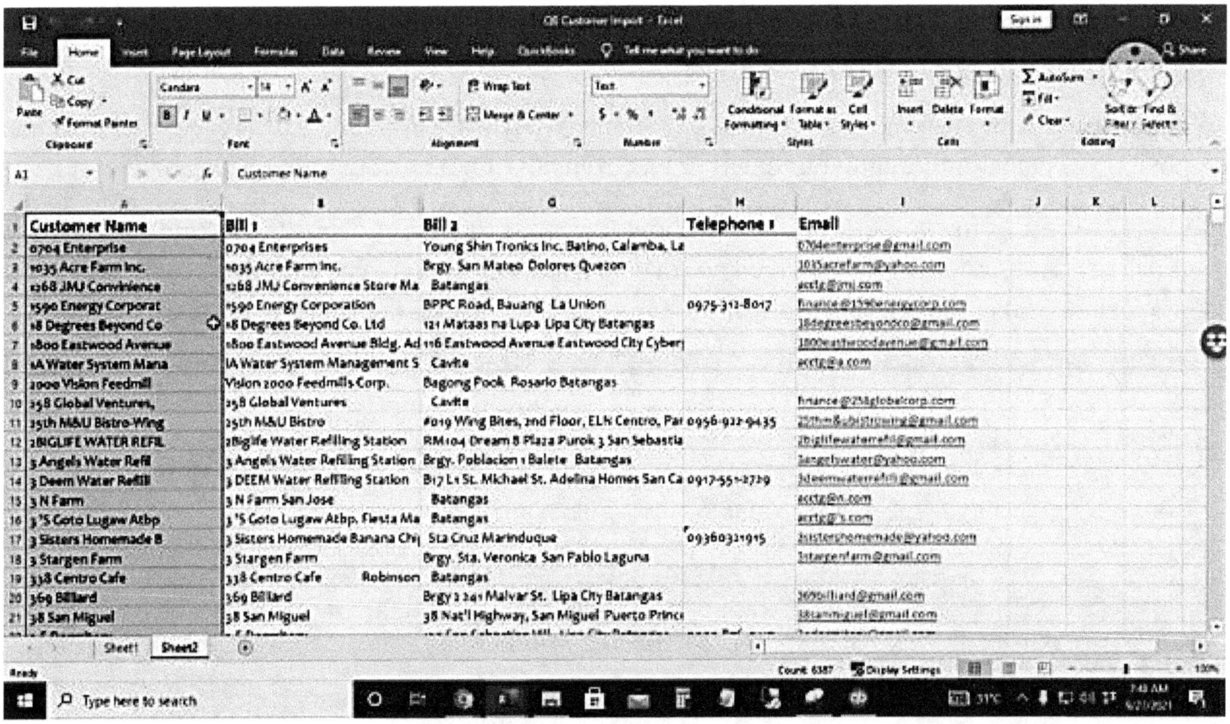

5. Use the **CTRL+P** to put the data in **QuickBooks Online.**

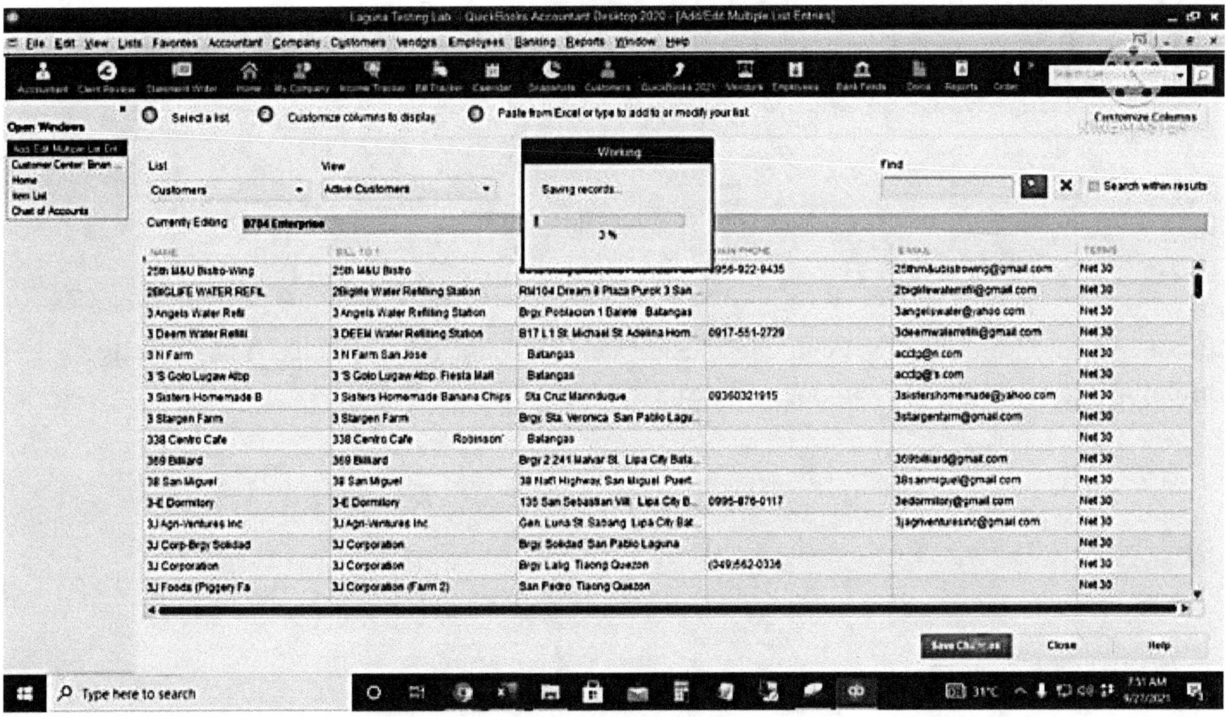

With this done, you are good to go.

Dealing with Records in the QuickBooks Online

Record-keeping is the core of QuickBooks Online. At this point, we will walk you through how to record diverse deposits in QuickBooks.

When dealing with customers, some will pay immediately after issuing a sales receipt, while some deposits will come in through your email or electronically for a customer that pays an invoice.

So, now we are going to put you through how to record incoming deposits in your QuickBooks Online. Let us assume that we received an invoice from a customer. The first thing to do is to click on the **create tab** at the top right side of the screen. Here click on the **receive payments option**

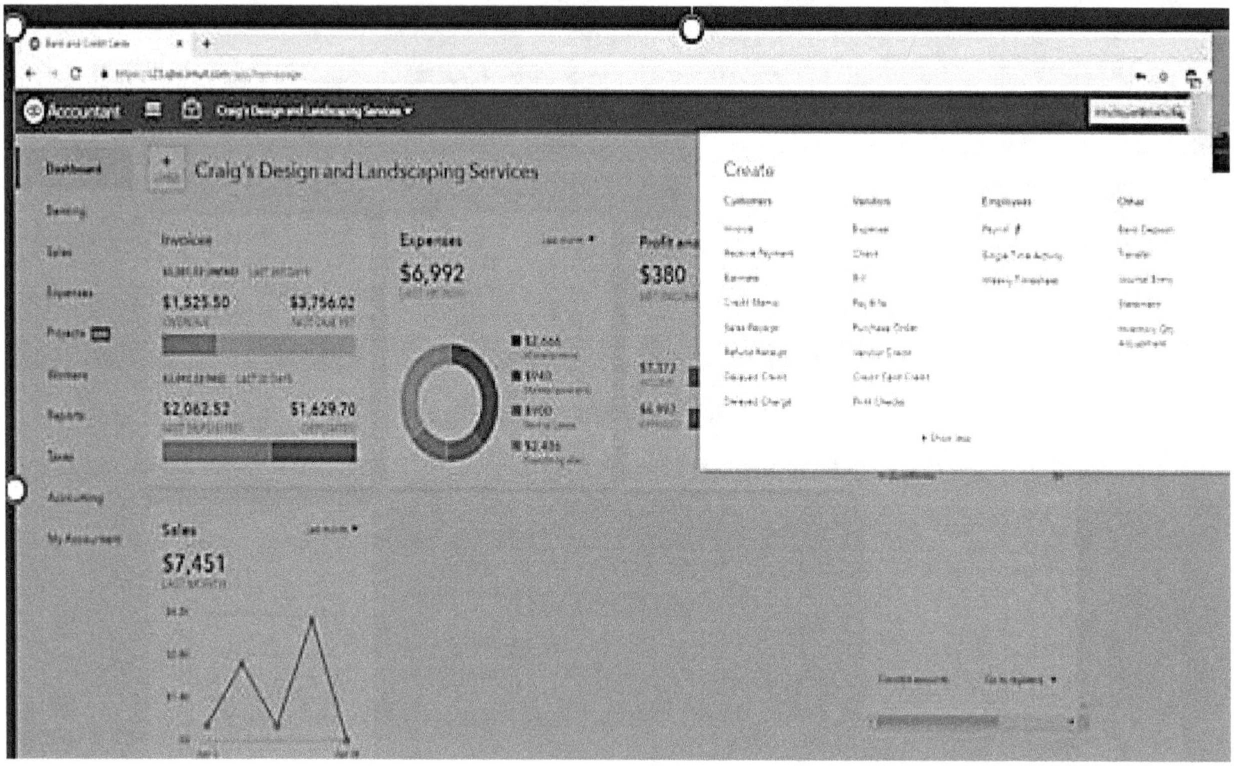

If the deposit is a cheque, input the cheque numbers and other details. You can also select **undeposited** if the cheque will not be taken to a bank.

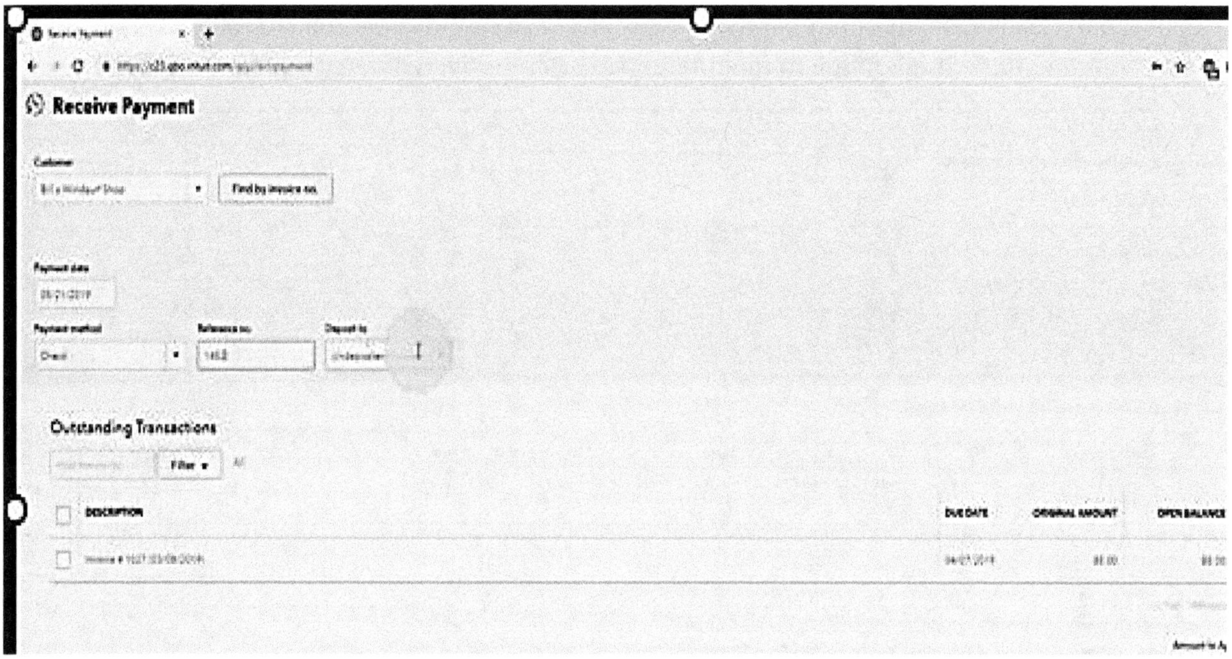

You can receive more deposits and save them in this undeposited account until you pay a visit to the bank for a deposit of your income. This is just a holding account to safely secure the funds until the actual bank deposit.

1. However, you can decide to input the data directly into the bank. To do this, navigate back to **create the menu** and choose the **Bank deposit** option.

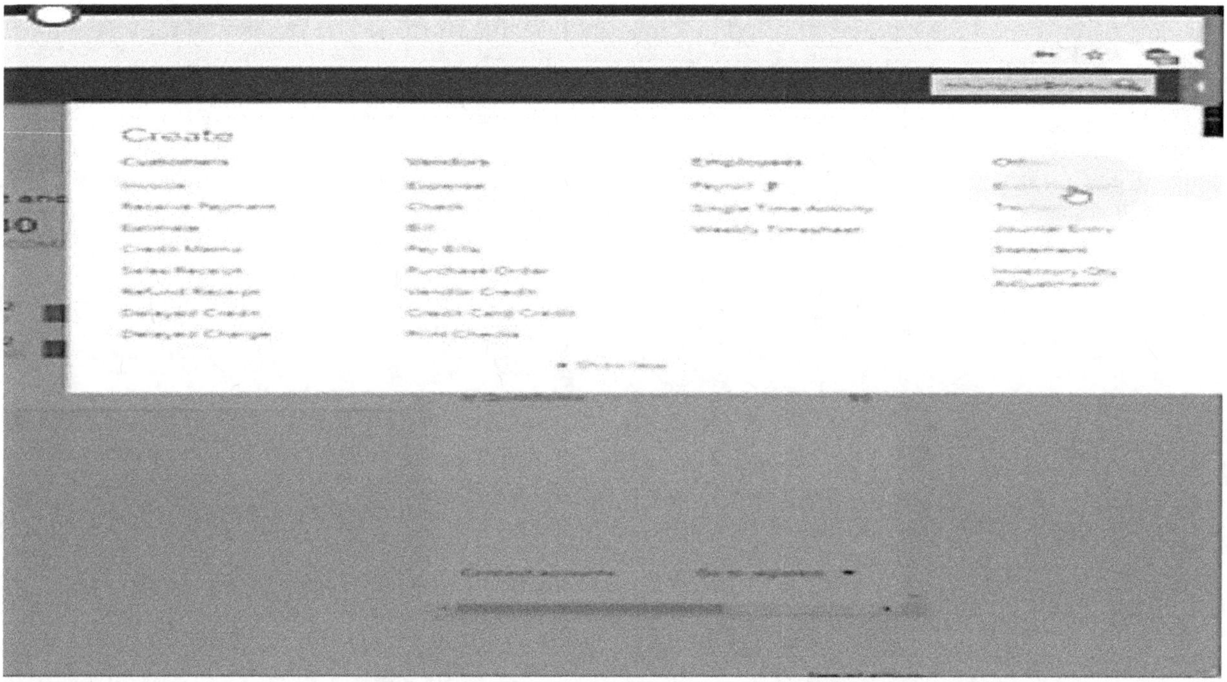

2. In the bank deposit option, you can input the required information from the cheque. At the bottom, there is an option to input refunded cash for overpayment from customers.

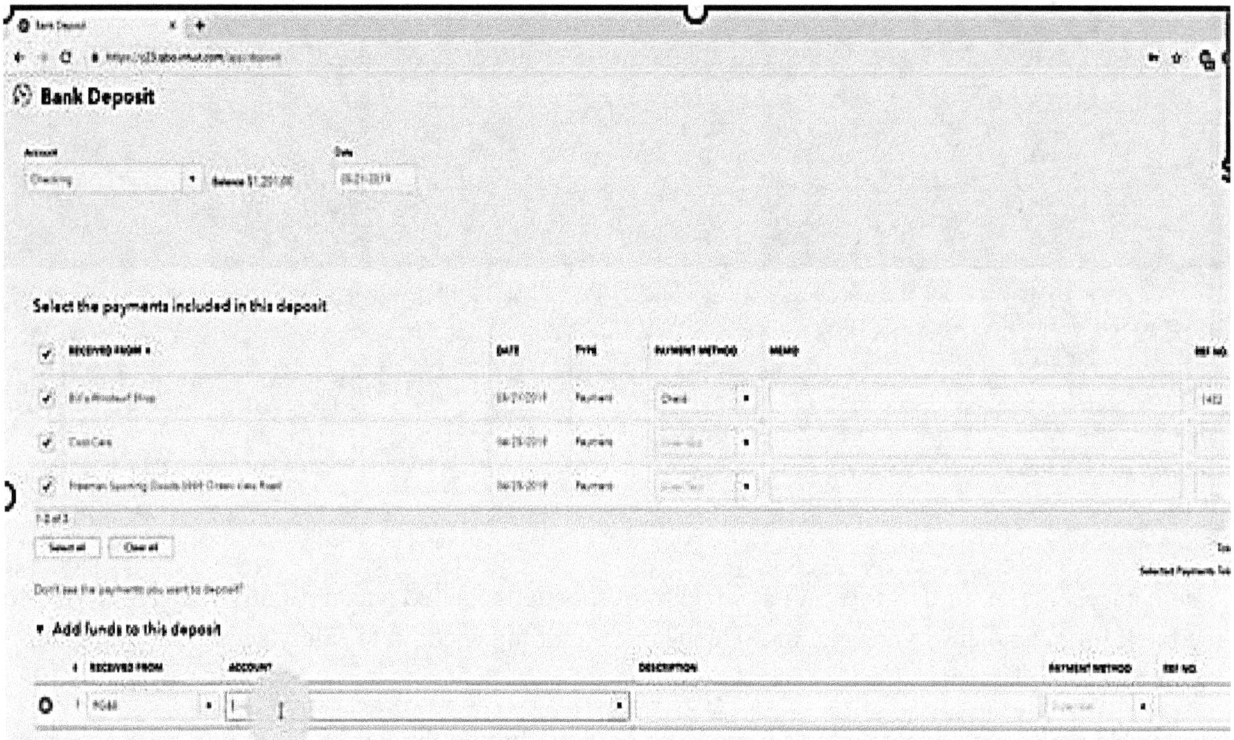

This refund will be put directly against utilities.

1. After the details have been filled in, click on the **Save button.** The funds will move from the undeposited to the **bank deposit.**

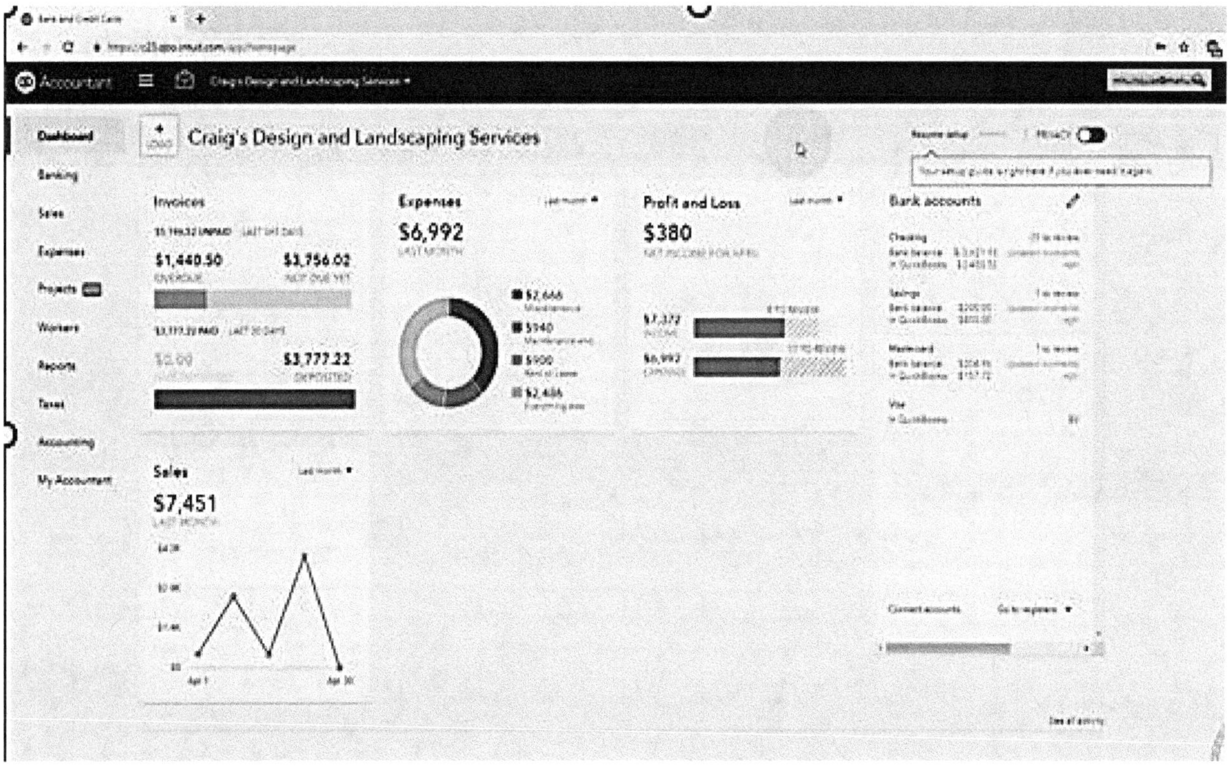

2. Next, go to your **chart of accounts.**

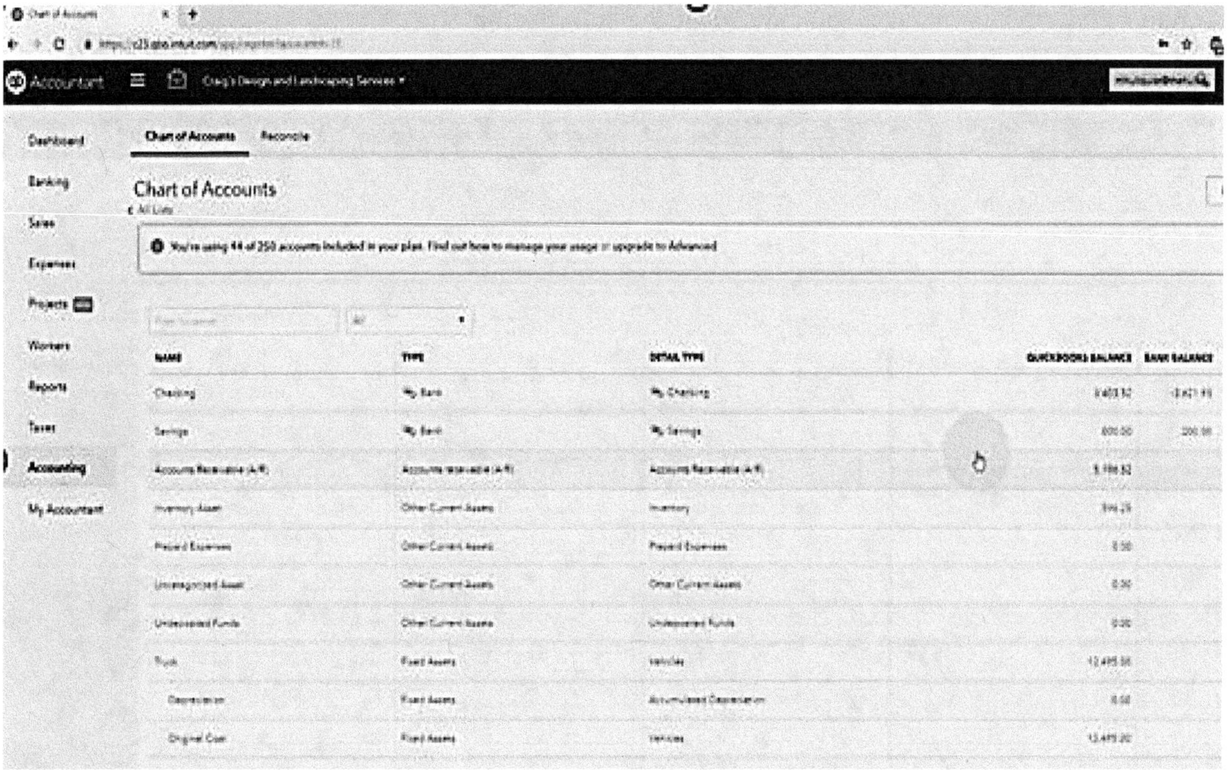

3. Click on the checking account.

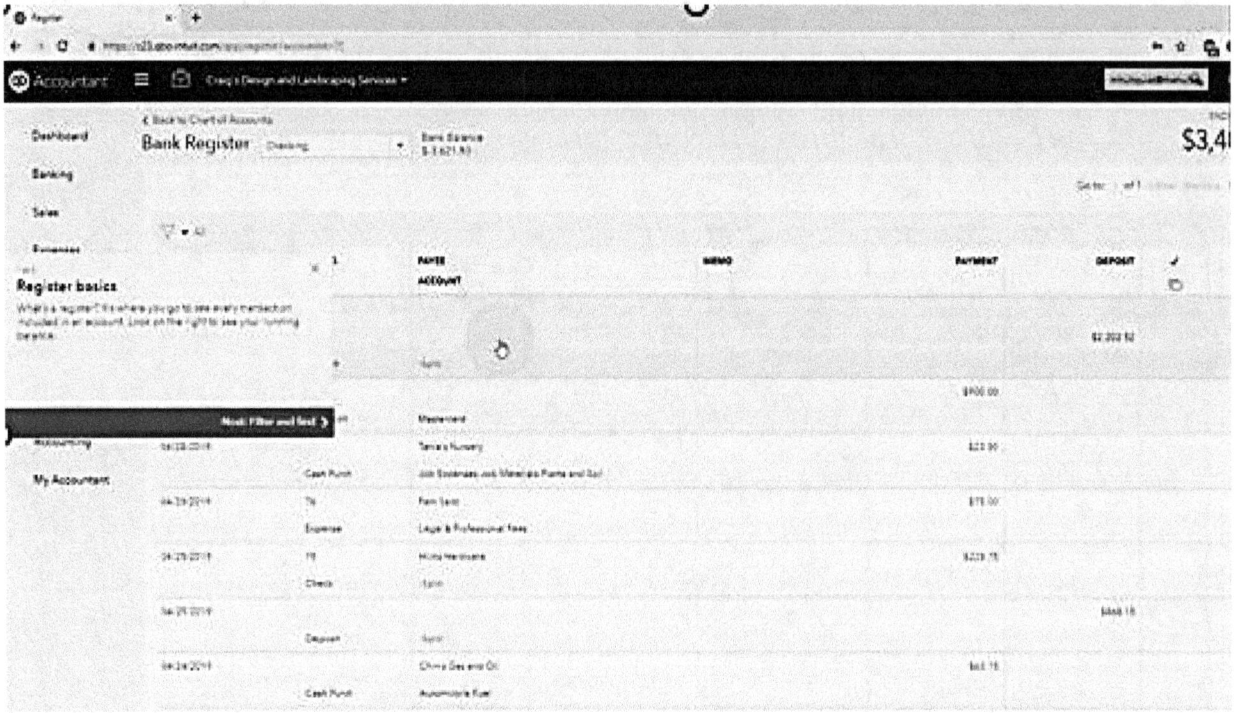

Here, you will be able to view the deposit. If it is multiple deposits and you intend to split it in bits, simply right-click on the deposit and choose the **split option.**

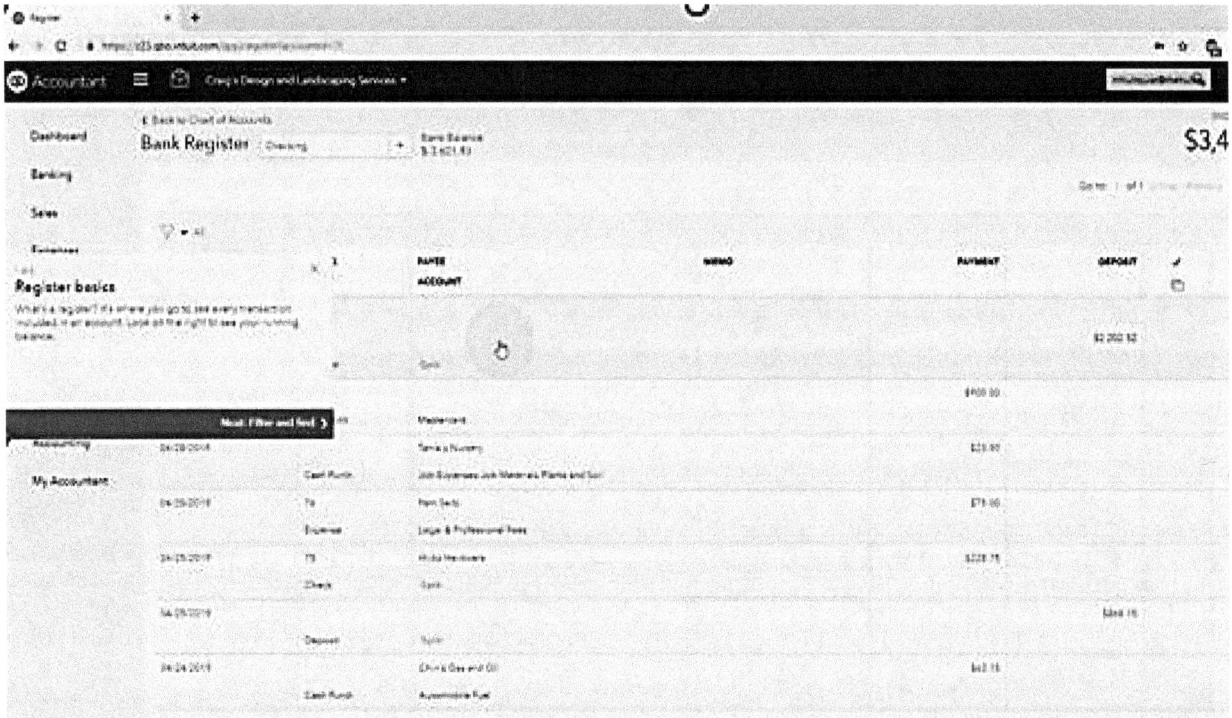

Setting up Sales Tax

QuickBooks helps you to keep track of how much sales tax to charge customers. In a bid to use this feature, you should know how much you need to pay when you file state and local taxes.

To set this feature up in your QuickBooks online;

1. Click on **taxes** in your dashboard.

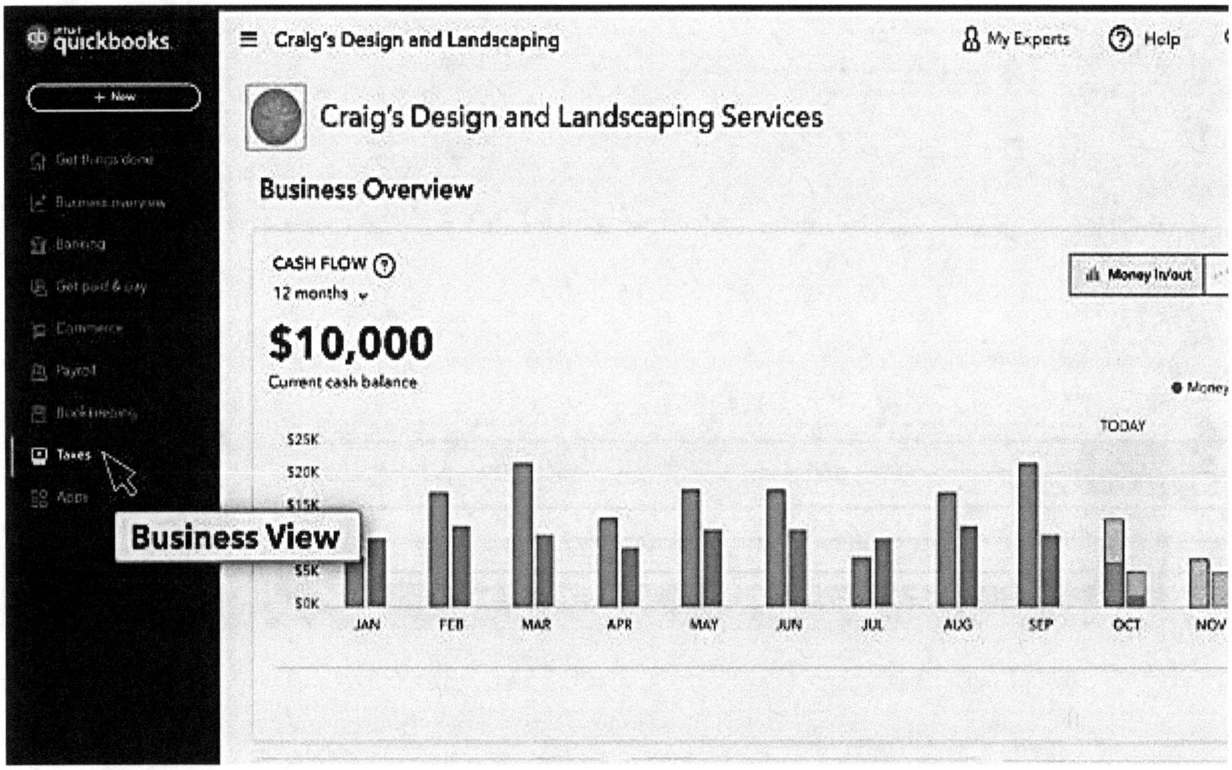

2. Click on the **green tab** to begin the set-up process.

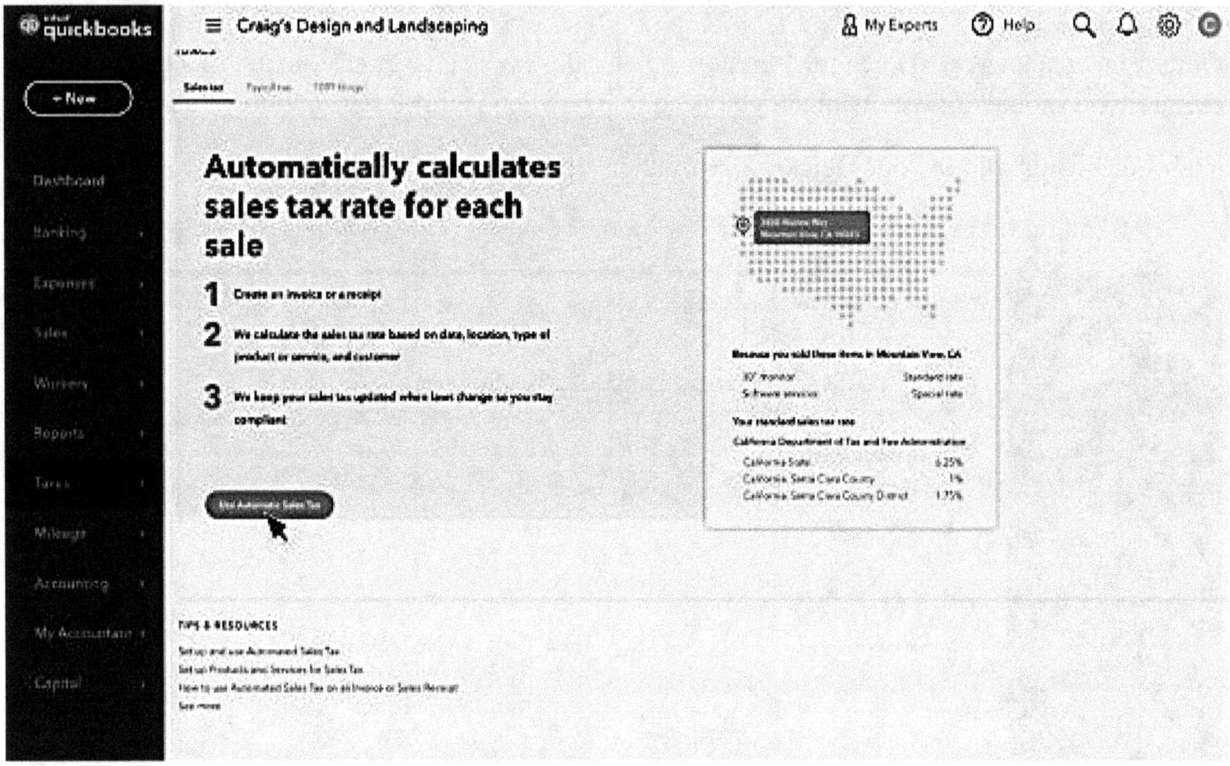

3. Enter your business address and click on **next.**

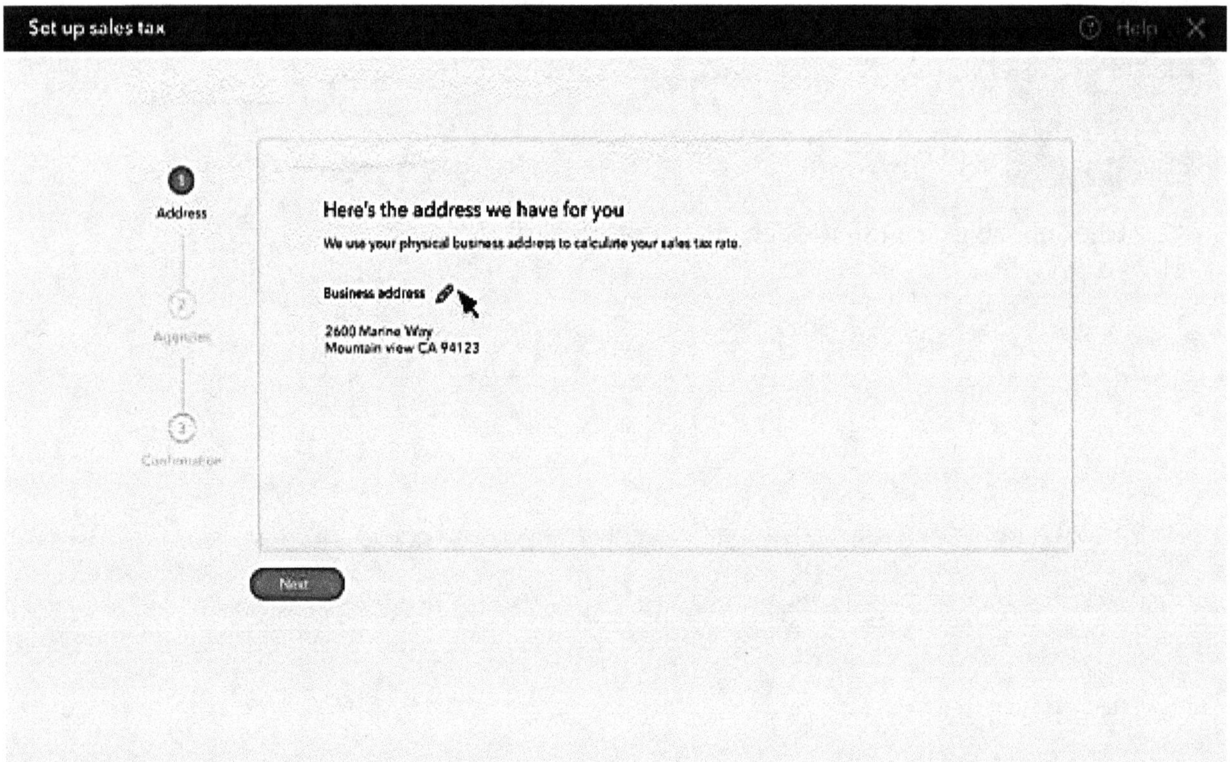

4. There will be an option to click **yes or no** if your business receives sales tax from outside your geographical location.

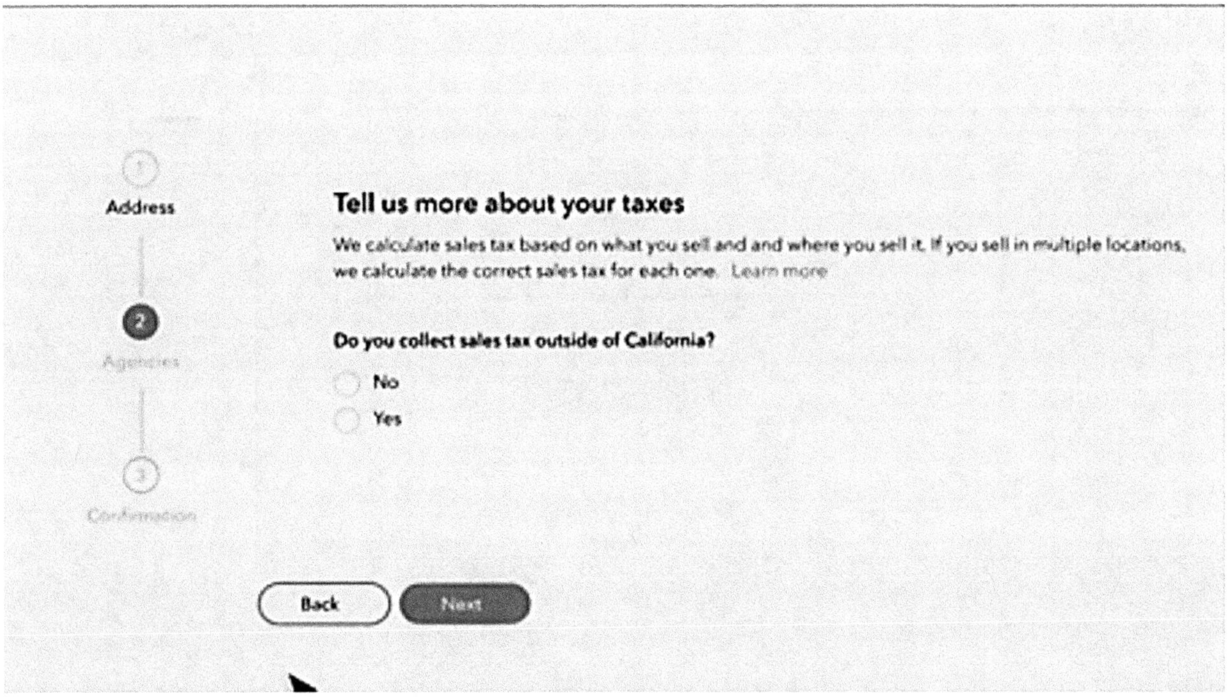

5. If you choose the **yes** option, choose the category of people or agencies you intend to send the sales tax to.

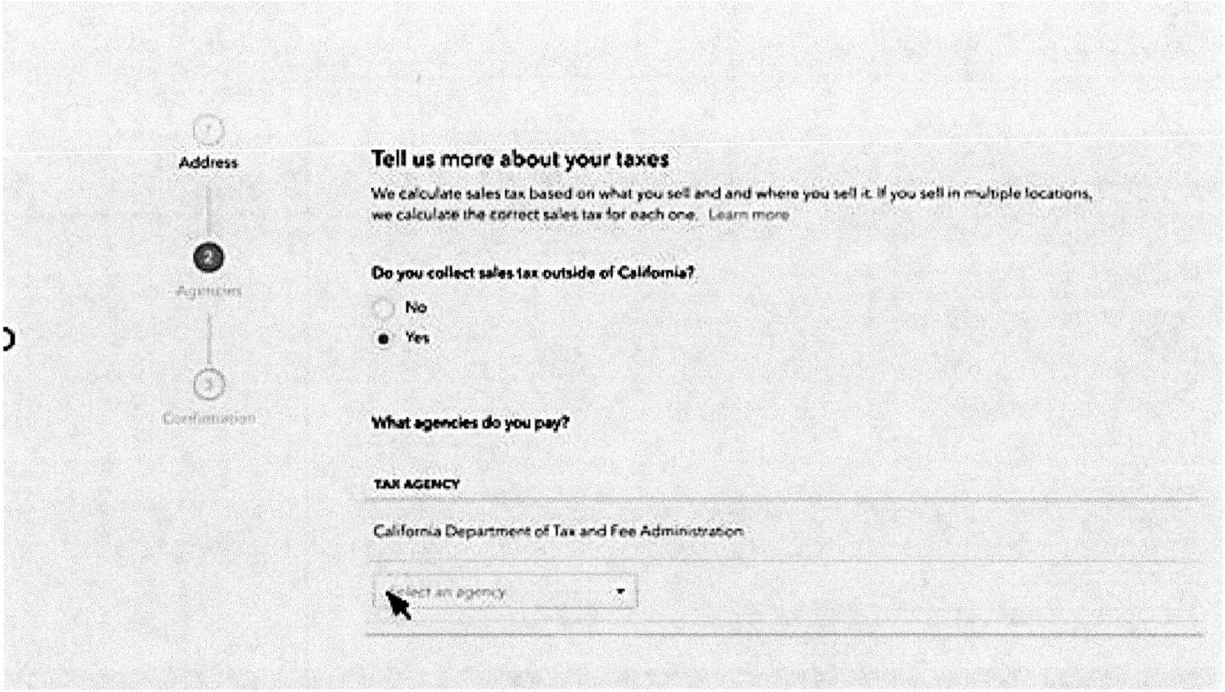

6. Next, click on the **create invoice** option.

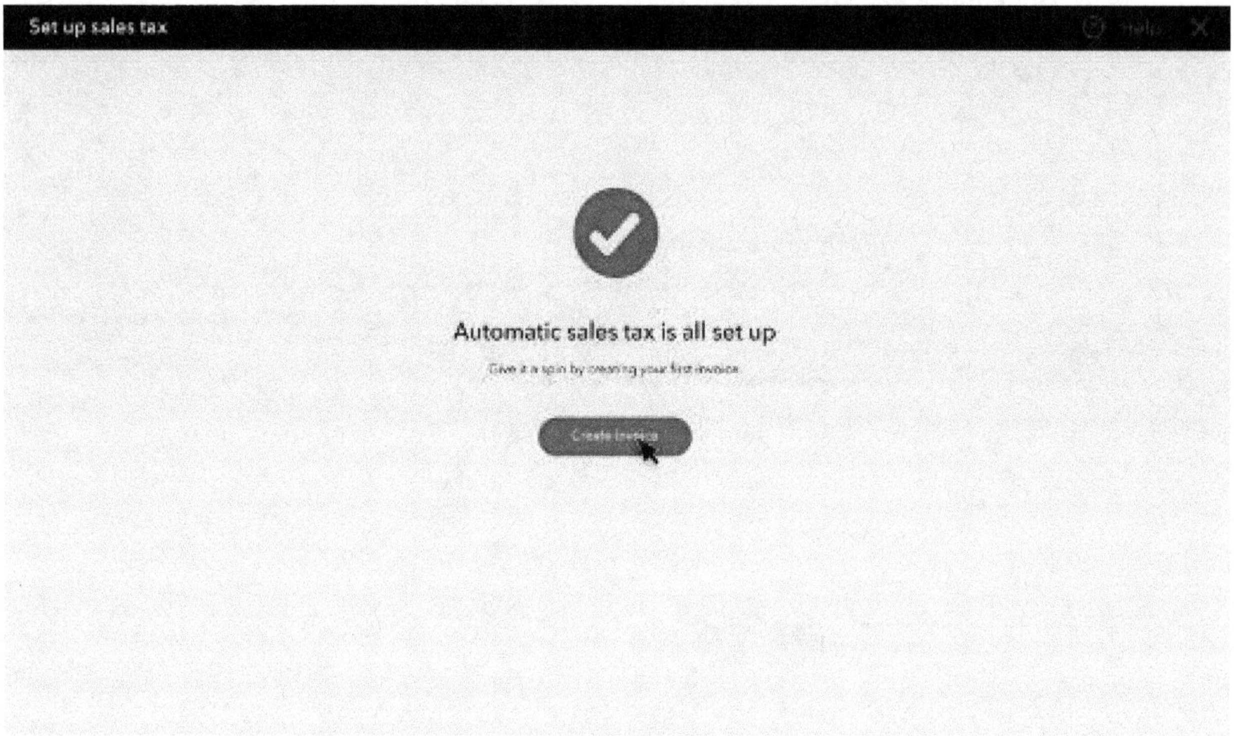

7. You can create a schedule for sending out invoices to your customers.

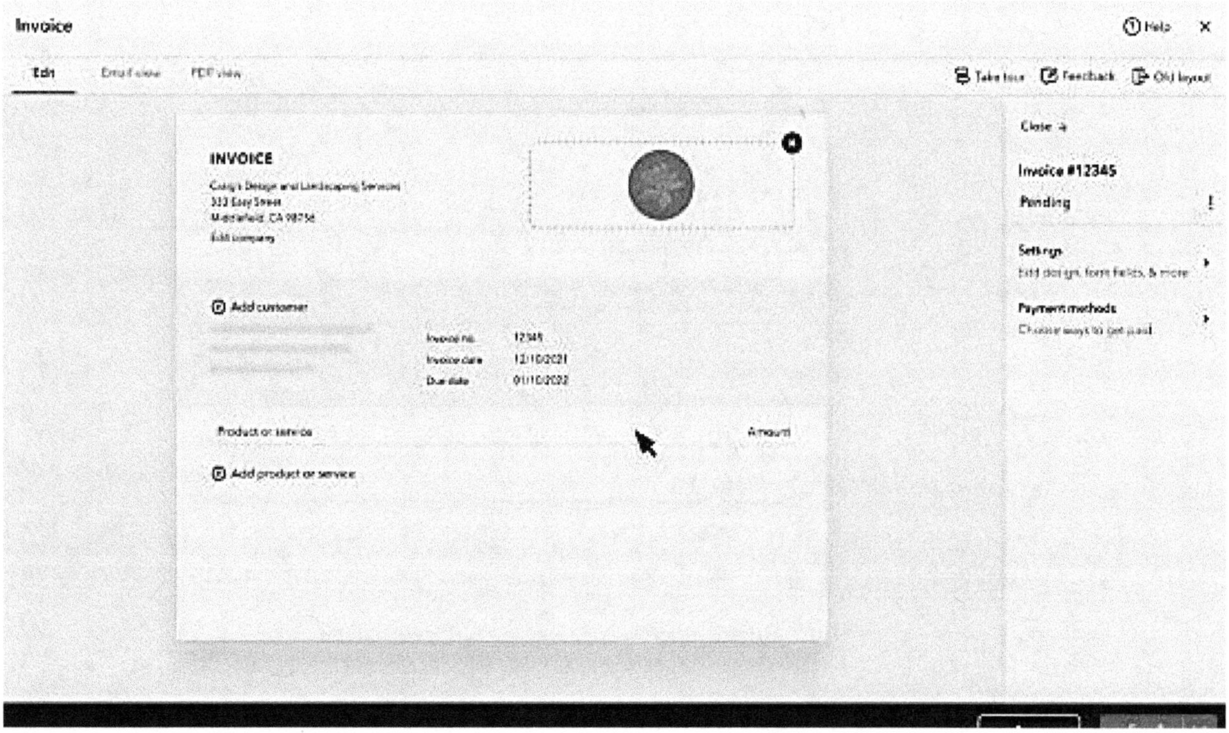

8. Different state has different sales tax filing policies. Select the filing frequency drop-down menu. Choose your preferred frequency for sending out the sales tax. When you are done, click on the **Save button.**

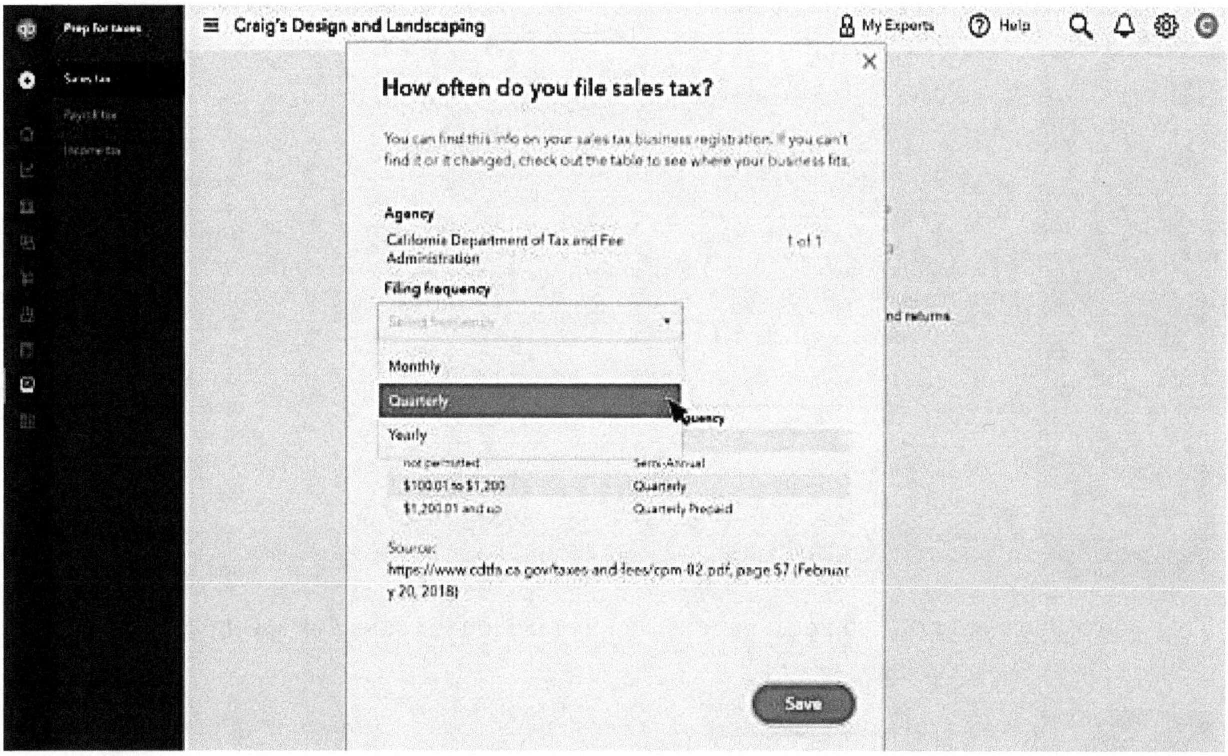

You can apply separate filing frequencies to each one of your entries.

1. When you are done, hit the **Save button.** Now you will be able to view where QuickBooks keeps track of the money you have collected from customers for sales you charged sales tax on.

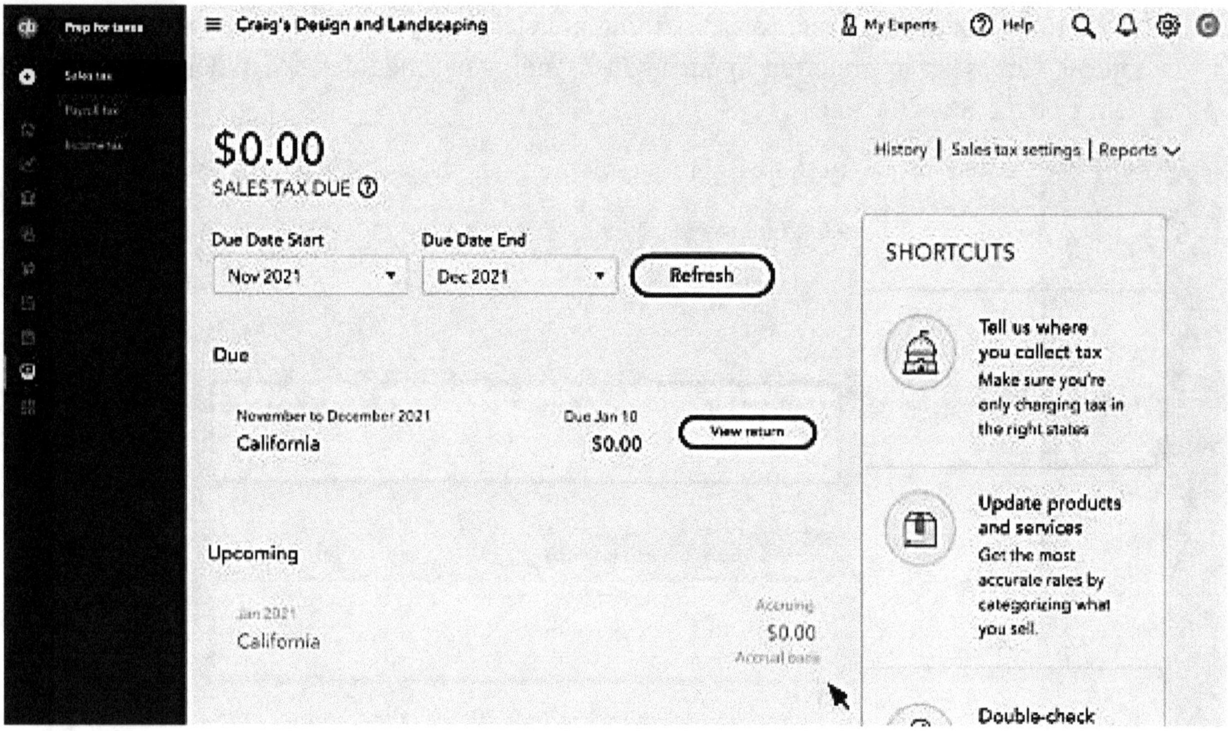

2. If you need to make some alterations, simply click on the **sales tax settings** at the top right side of your screen.

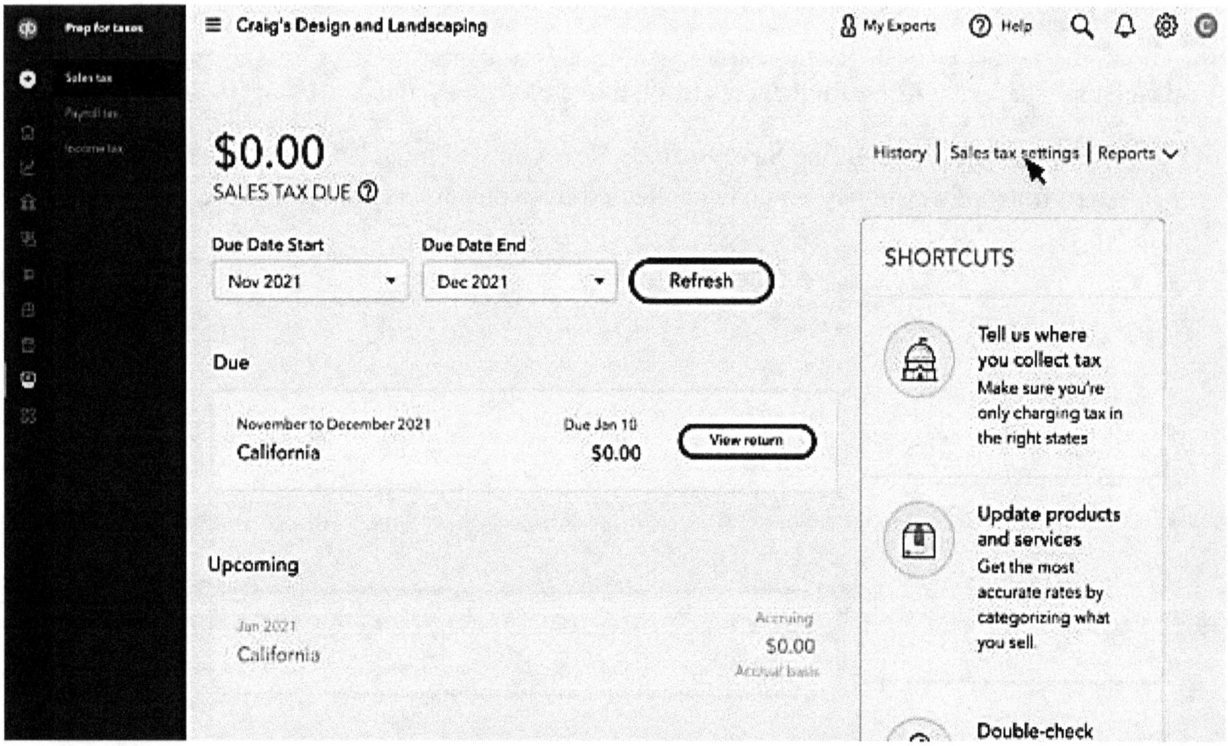

3. Click on add agency or edit tax agency.

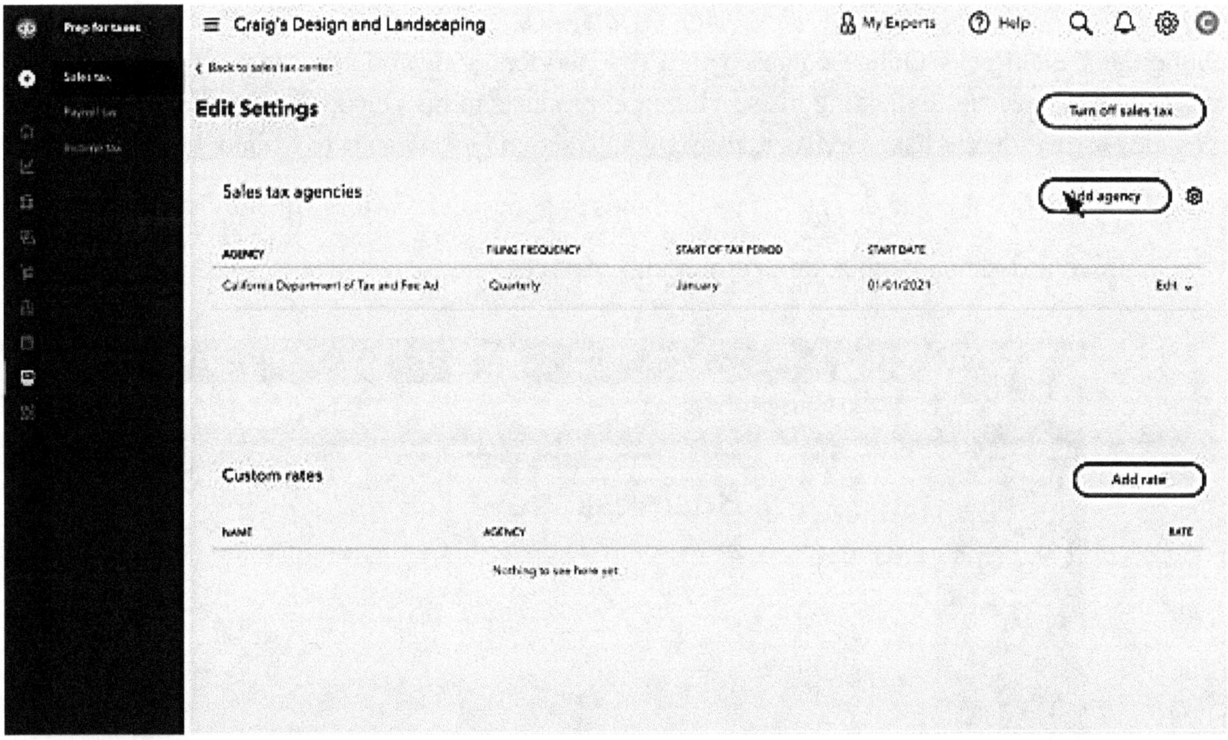

4. Fill in your preferred details.

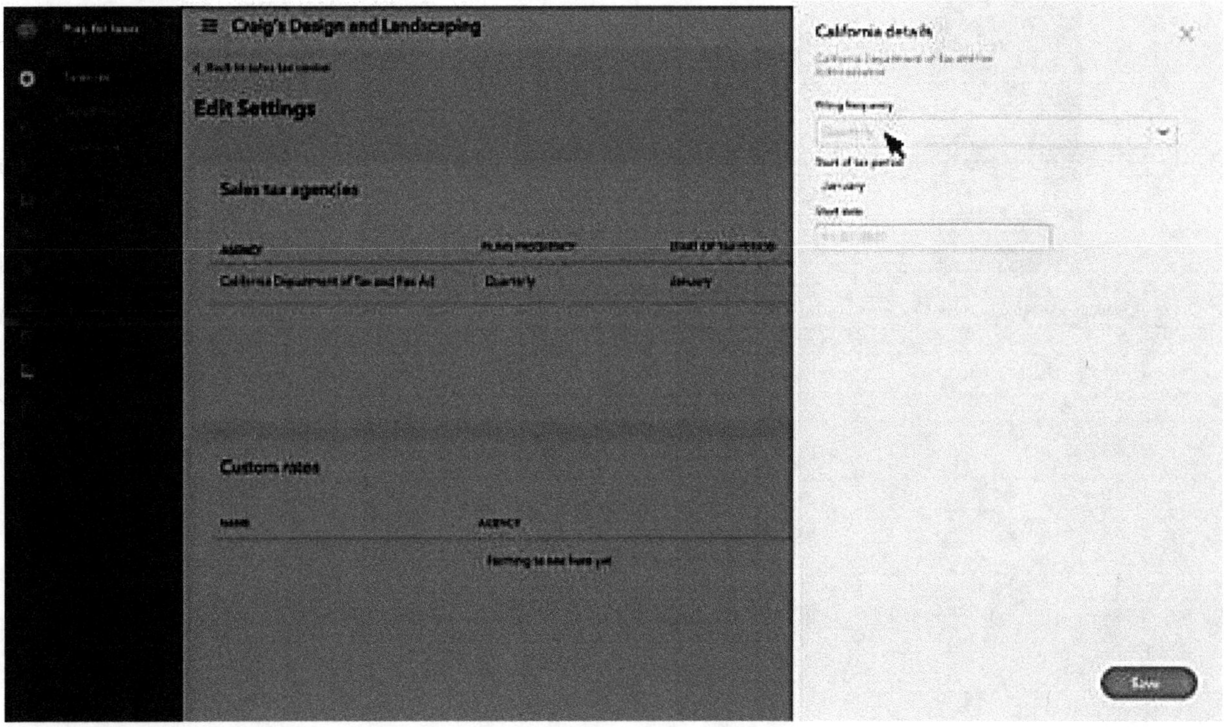

5. Click on **Save.**

Setting up Your Products and Services in QuickBooks Online

Although QuickBooks Online comes with a few services and products, the user is permitted to customize his account by adding his services and products to his QuickBooks account. This saves you ample time during usage. Also, it allows you to set up QuickBooks to fit into what you sell.

To do this, the first thing to do is to set up the kinds of goods and services you provide to customers.

1. In your dashboard, click on **product and services.**

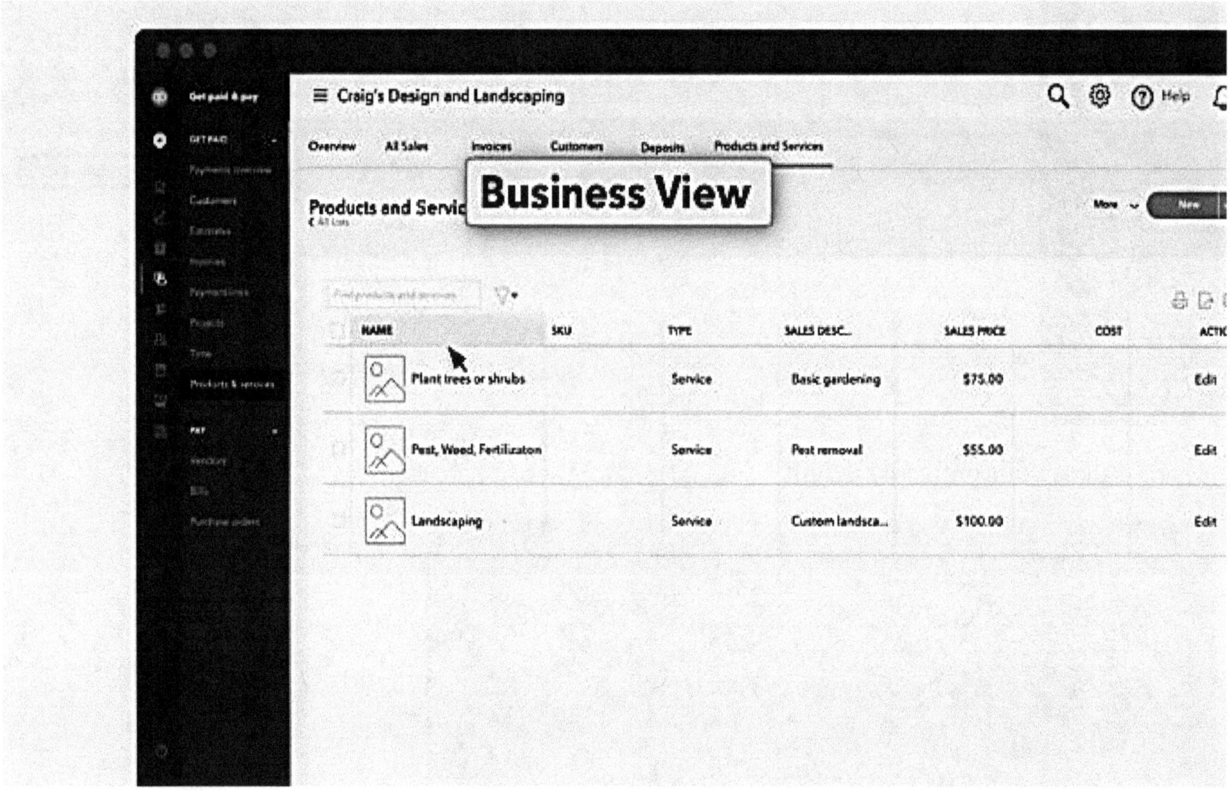

2. Select **New.**

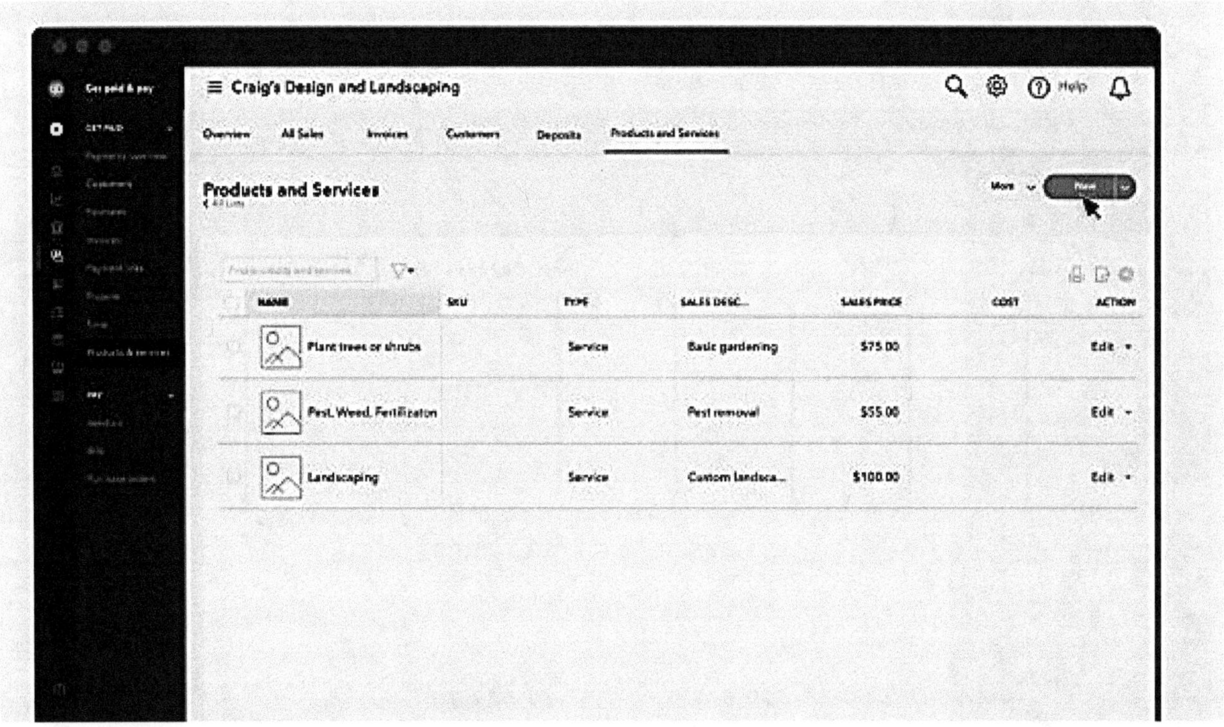

This method applies to the **Business view** of your QuickBooks Online. If you are using the **accountant view;**

1. Click on **sales** in your dashboard and select **products and services.**

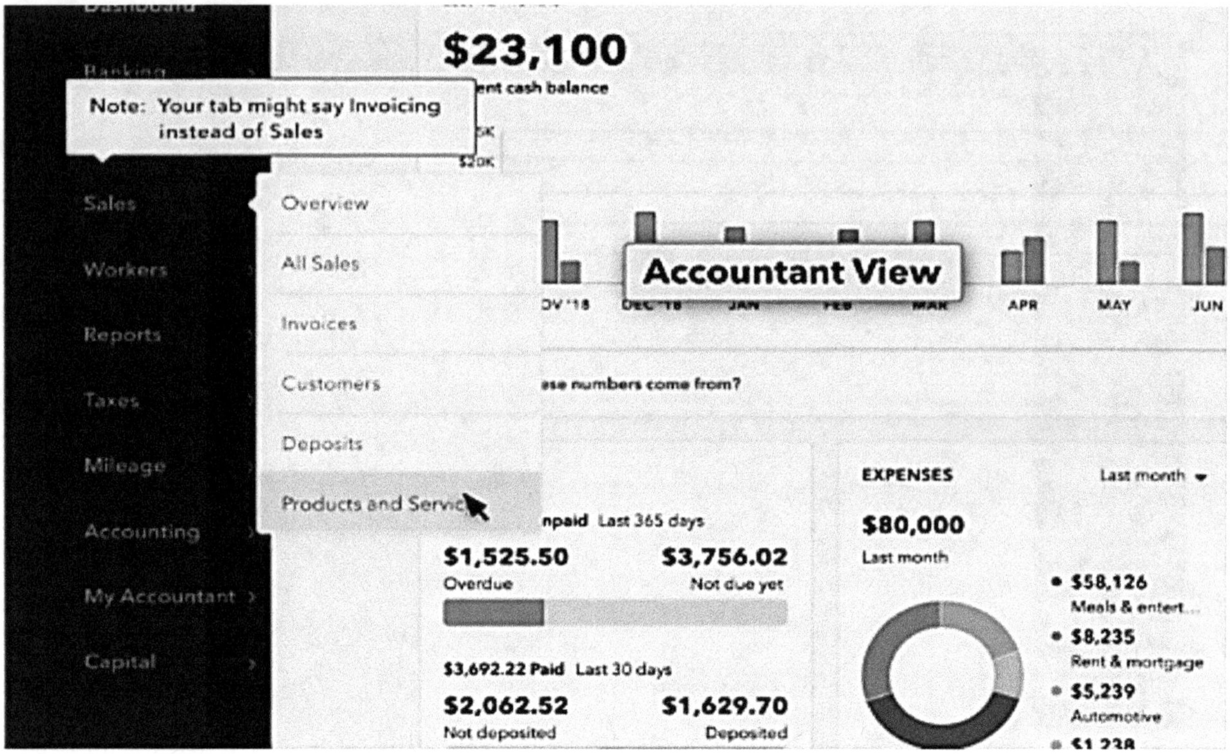

2. Afterwards, click on **new,** and choose the type of products or services you want to record.

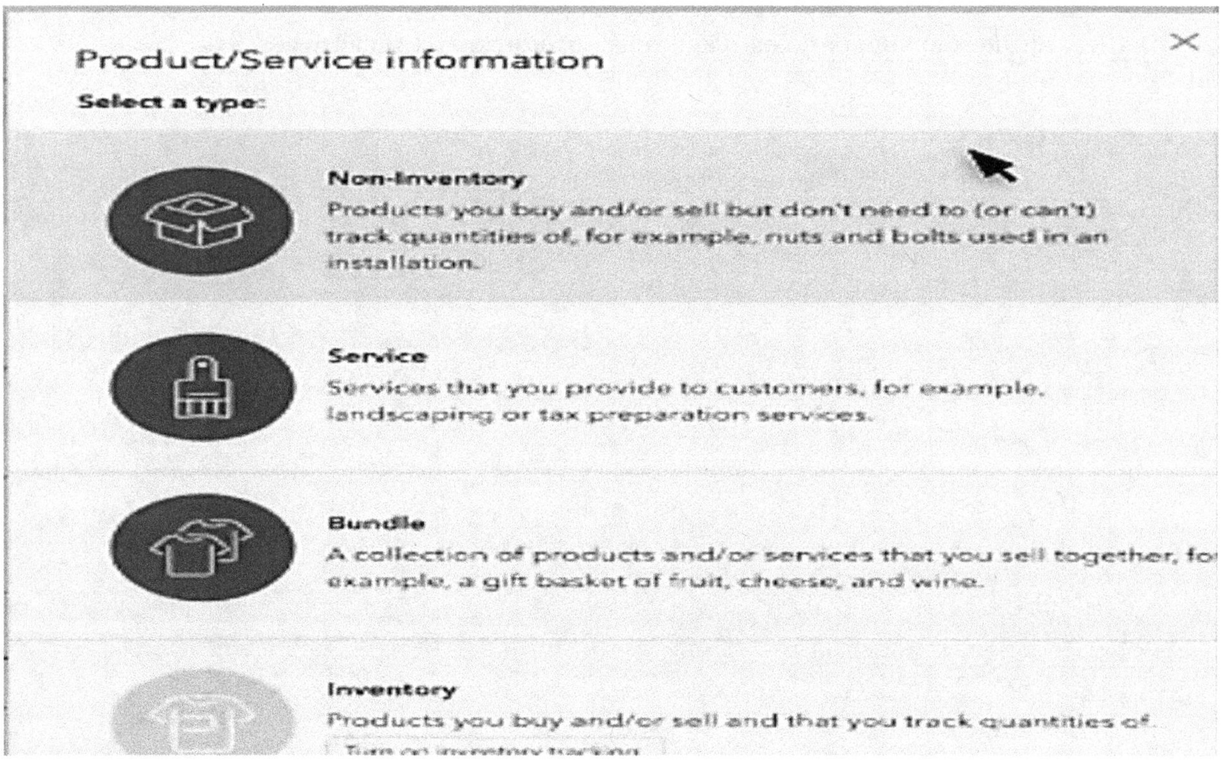

Non-inventory products are the products you sell that you do not keep track of how many of those products you have.

1. Here, we are going to choose the **services** tab.

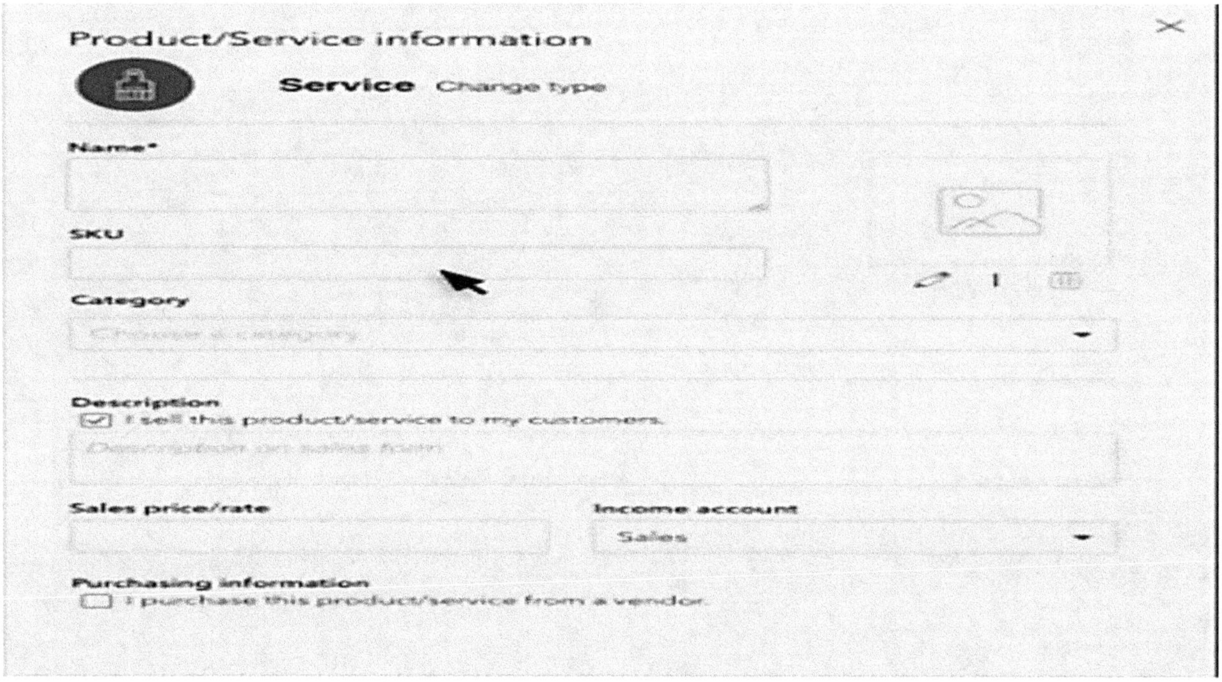

2. Fill in your details as required and hit the **save button** when this is done.

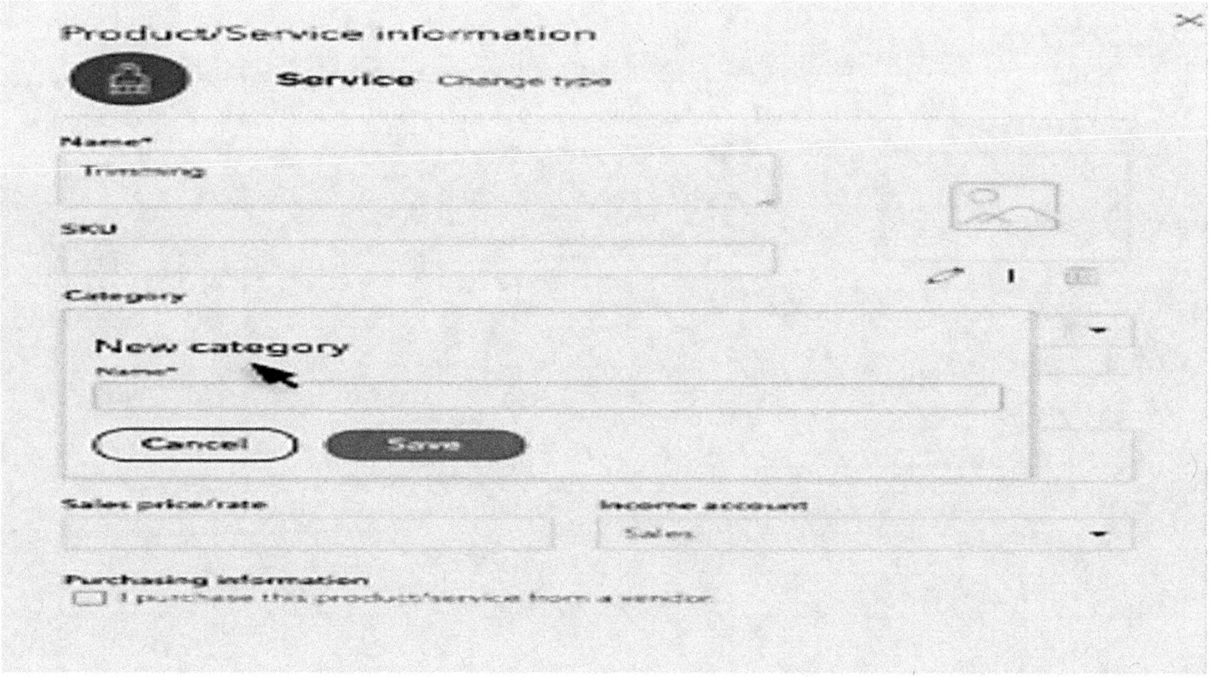

3. If you want to attach an image to this, click on the small box on the right side of your screen to upload the image.

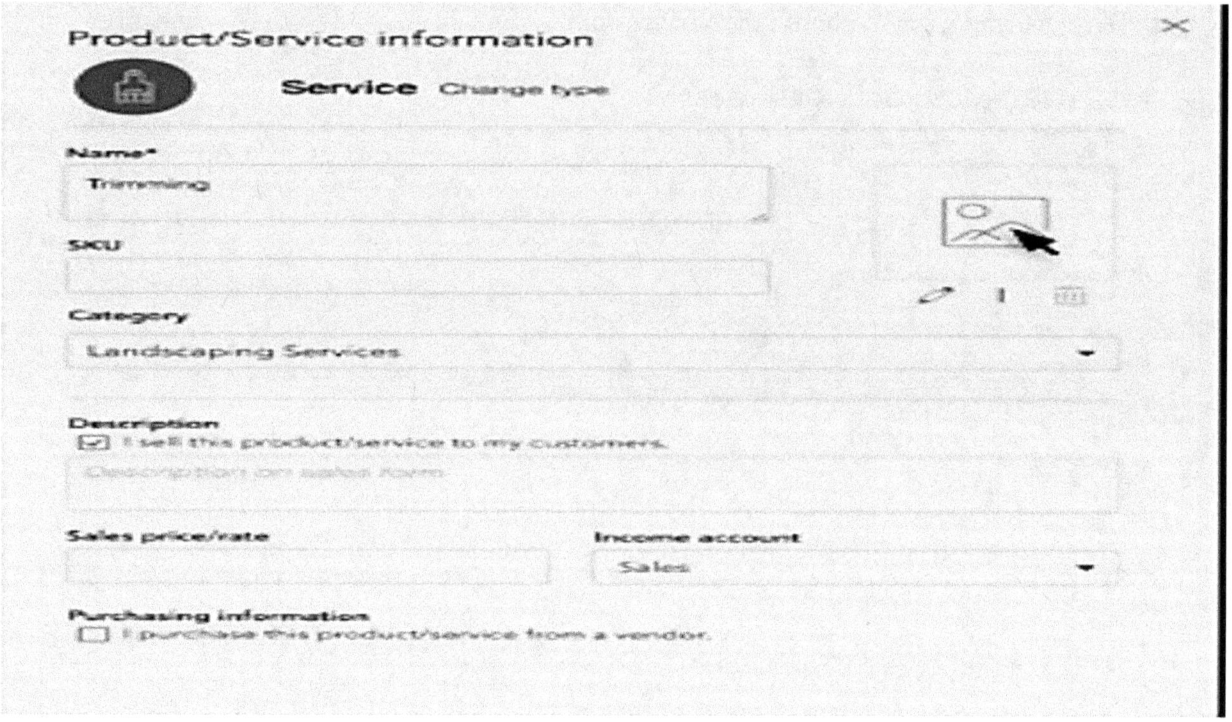

4. Input a description of the product in the description box.

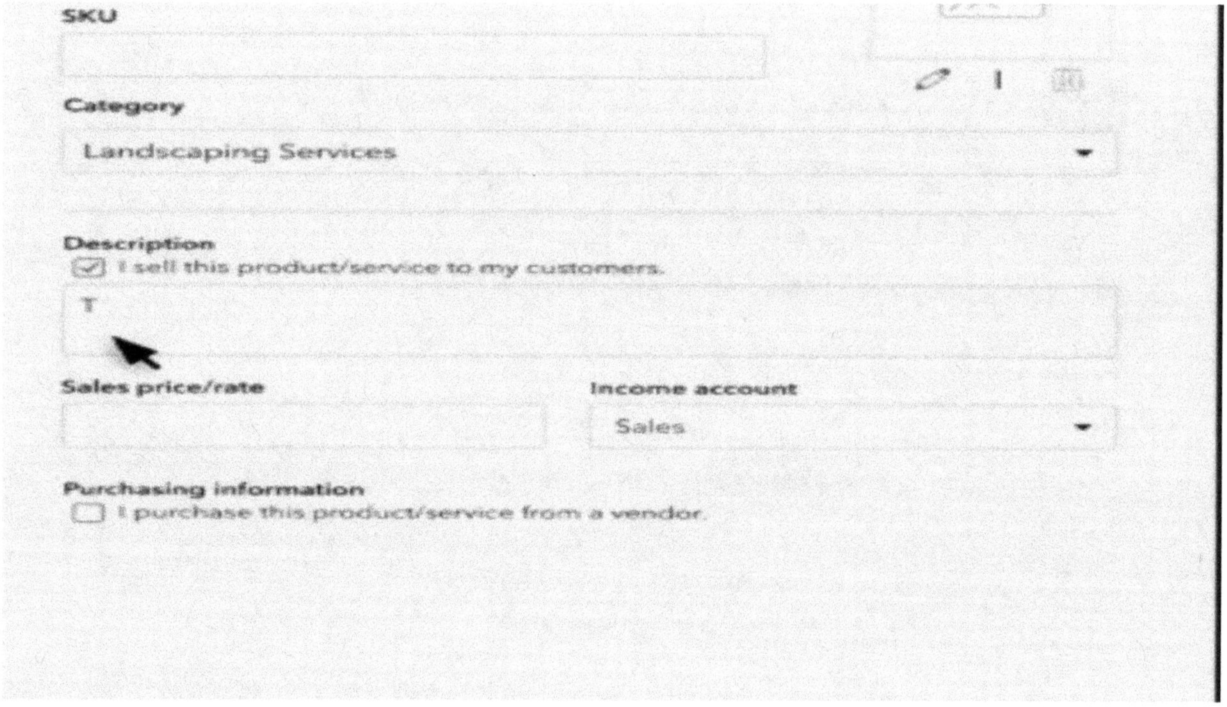

5. Click on the arrow beside the **sales option** to choose the account type under **income account.** To add a new account, from the underlined options in the image, select **add new.**

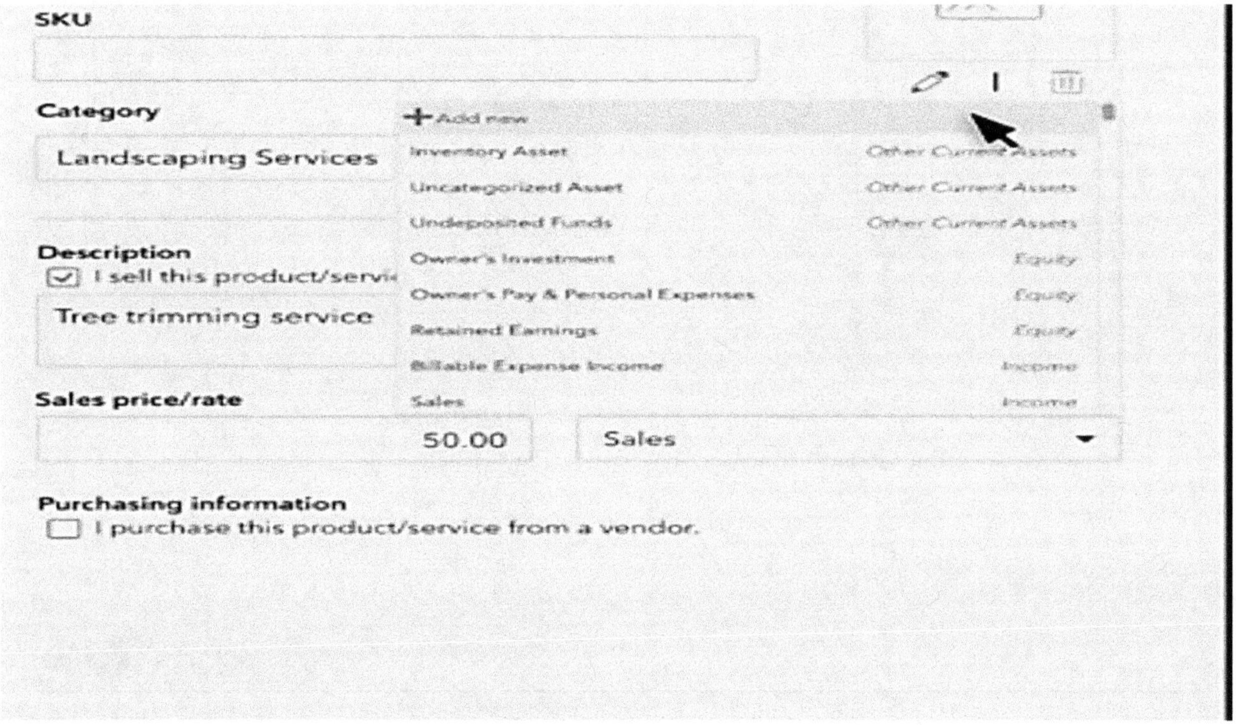

6. In the detail type, choose the **other primary income** option.

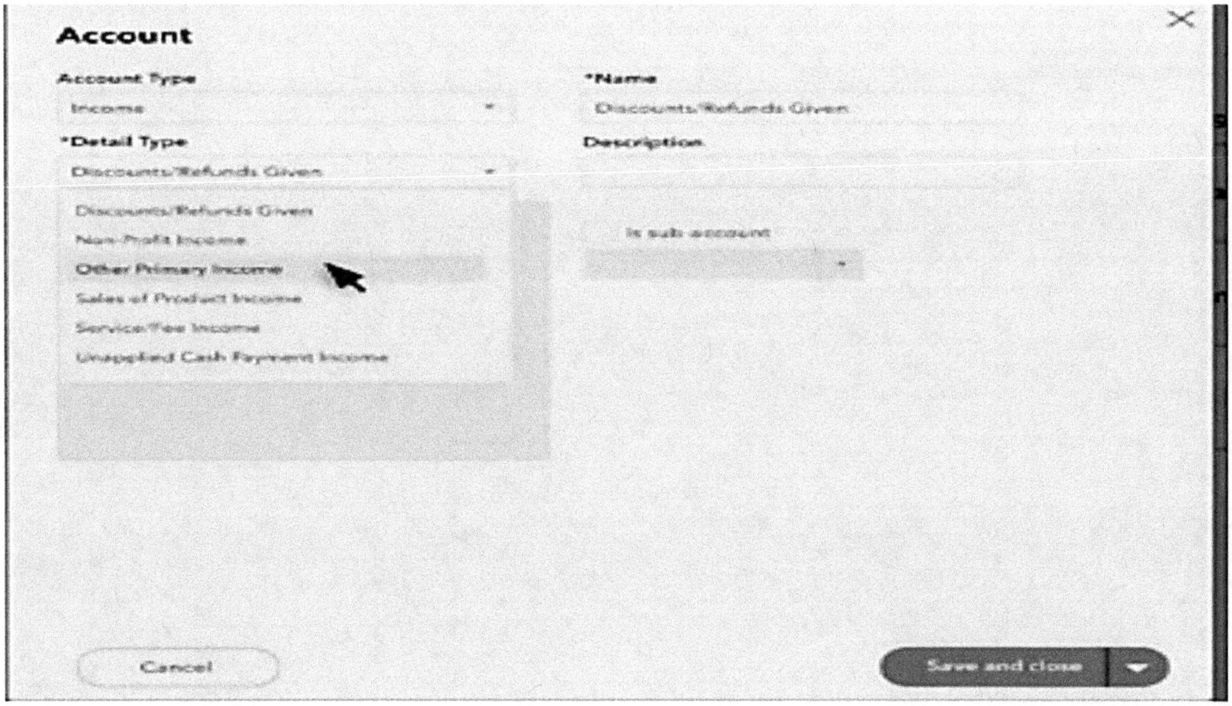

7. Under the **name option,** write the account you want the income to go into. When this action is completed, click on **save and close.**

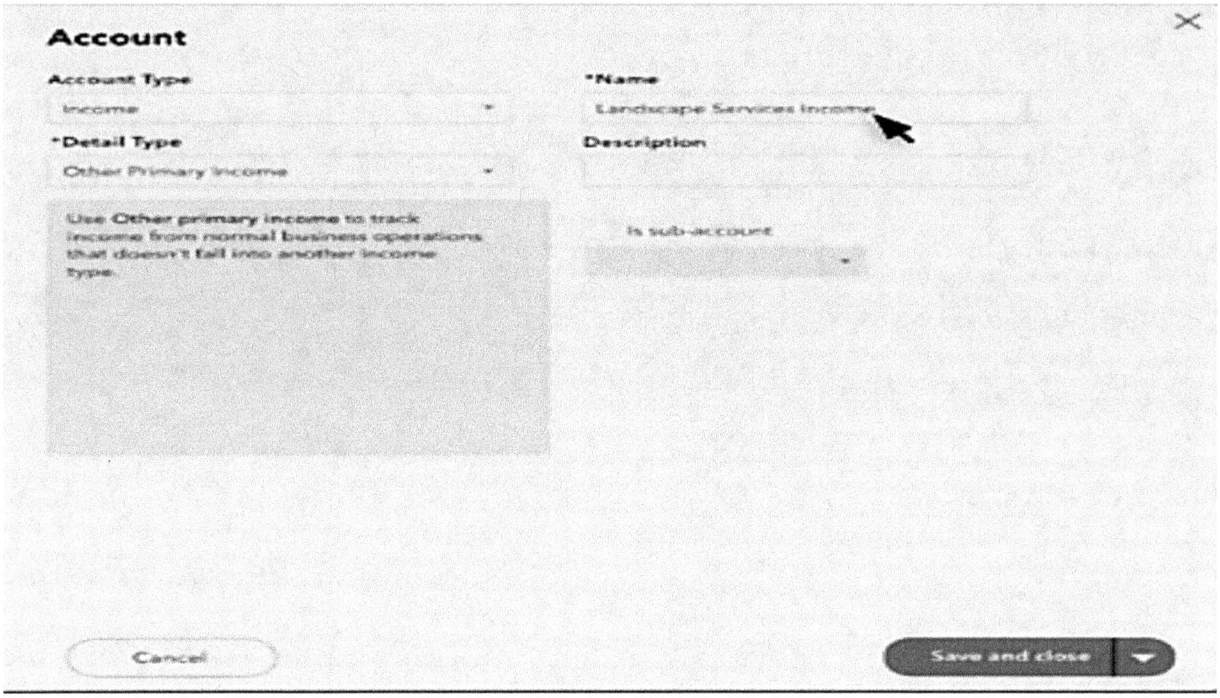

8. If you turn on the **sales tax** option, ensure that you indicate your service charge type for your customers' to easily understand your charges.

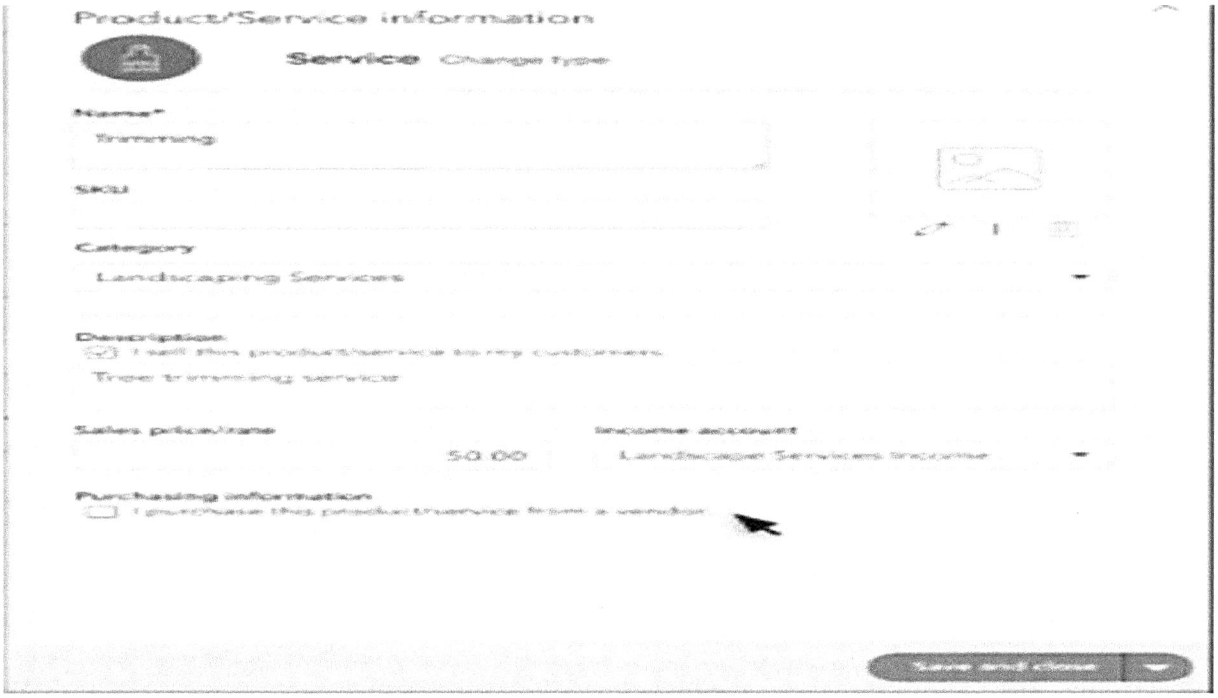

9. Now, we have the new service added to our list of services rendered.

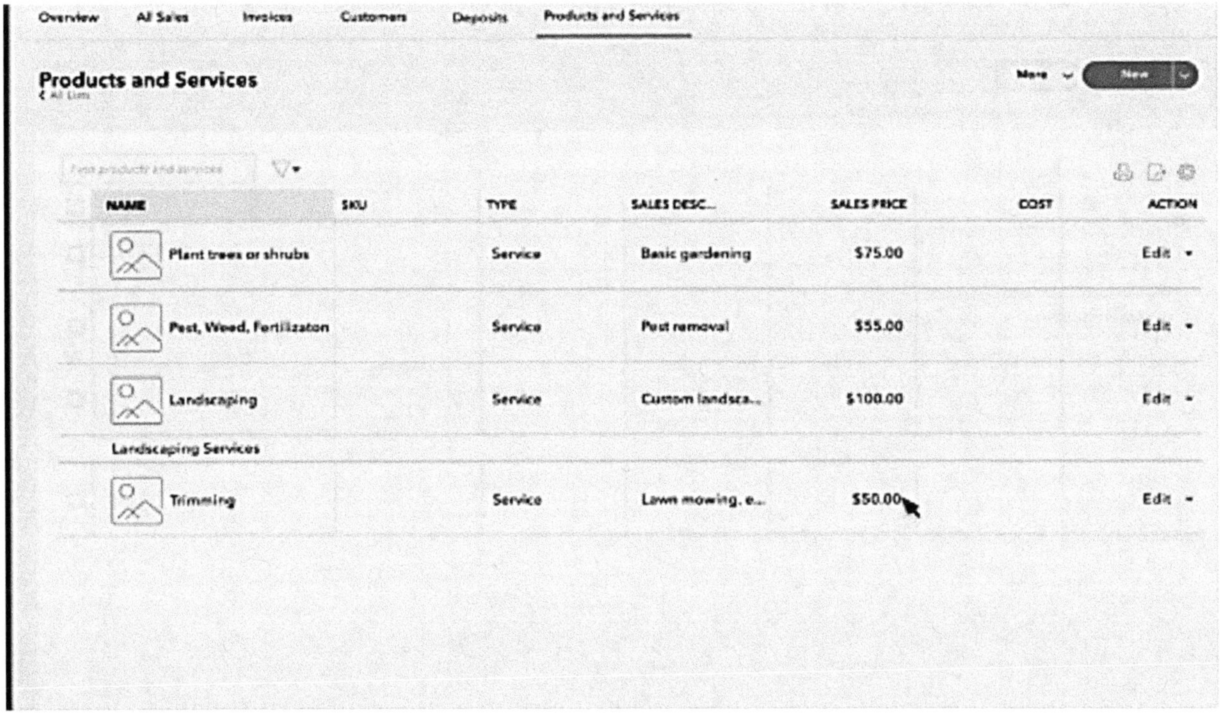

10. To import a list of vendors, click on the **import tab** at the top right side of your screen.

11. Click on the **browse option,** to upload the spreadsheet of the list of vendors. Select **export** to commence the upload of the spreadsheet to your QuickBooks Online.

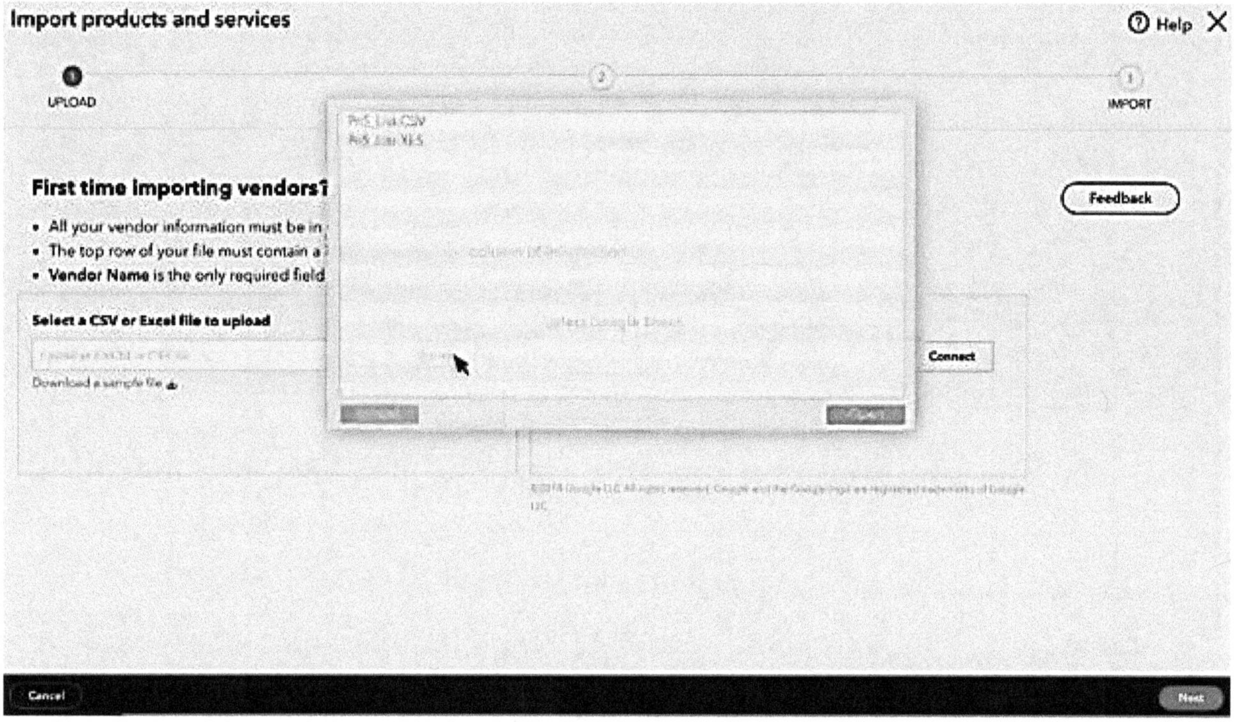

12. Now map out the fields you intend to use in your **QuickBooks Online.** Click on **Next.**

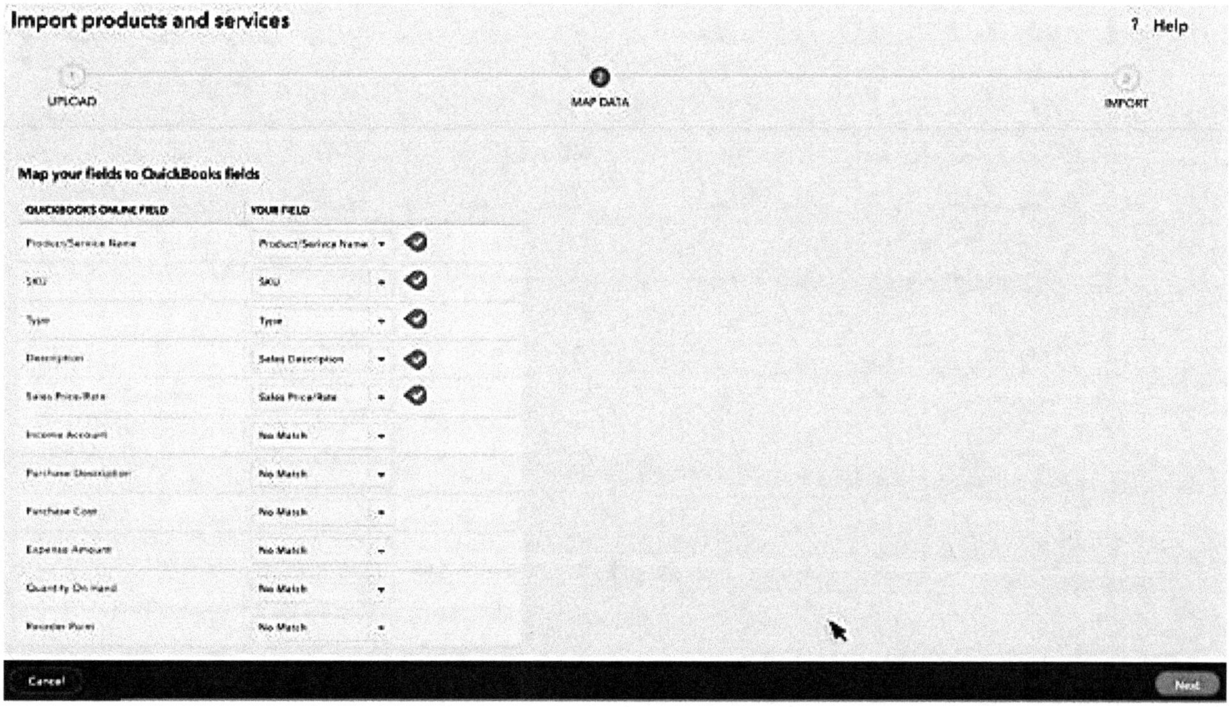

13. If all looks good, hit the **import button** to put all the items in your QuickBooks Online.

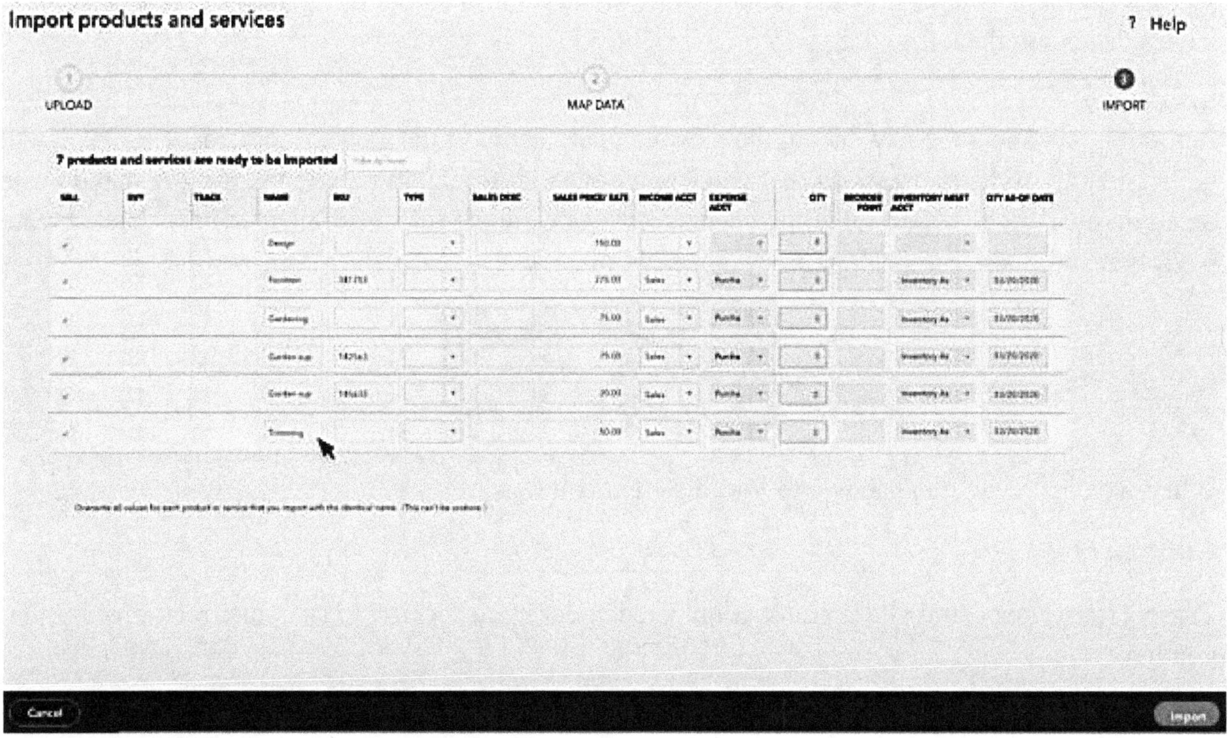

How to Get Around QuickBooks Online

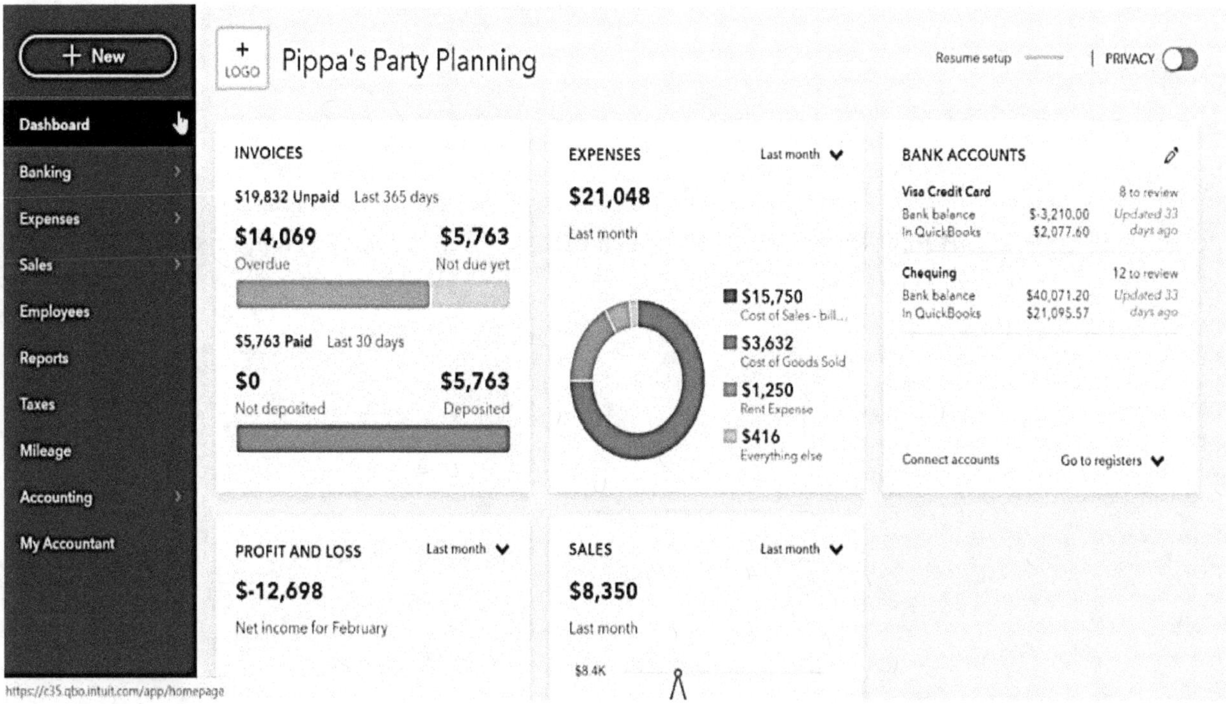

The above image is the QuickBooks starting window and it is known as the dashboard and you can see that on the left-hand side, the dashboard is the first thing on the navigation bar. Whatever you have selected on the left will display on the right side of the window.

New Menu

Let's first talk about the new menu; the new menu at the top of the navigation bar is where you will go to enter all of the transactions that you'll enter in QuickBooks. Whether you want to make a sale on an invoice, receive a customer payment, create an estimate for a customer, write a check, create payroll etc. all these can be done from the 'new' menu.

When we click new, it expands into four different columns;

Customers

There's 'customers' and all the transaction listed under it are specific to customer relationships that you have.

Vendors

The 'vendors' deal with suppliers that you may purchase goods and services from (subcontractors etc.).

Employee

'Employees' are those who work for you.

Other

'other' are several different transactions and tasks that you may have to accomplish over a variety of different circumstances in QuickBooks.

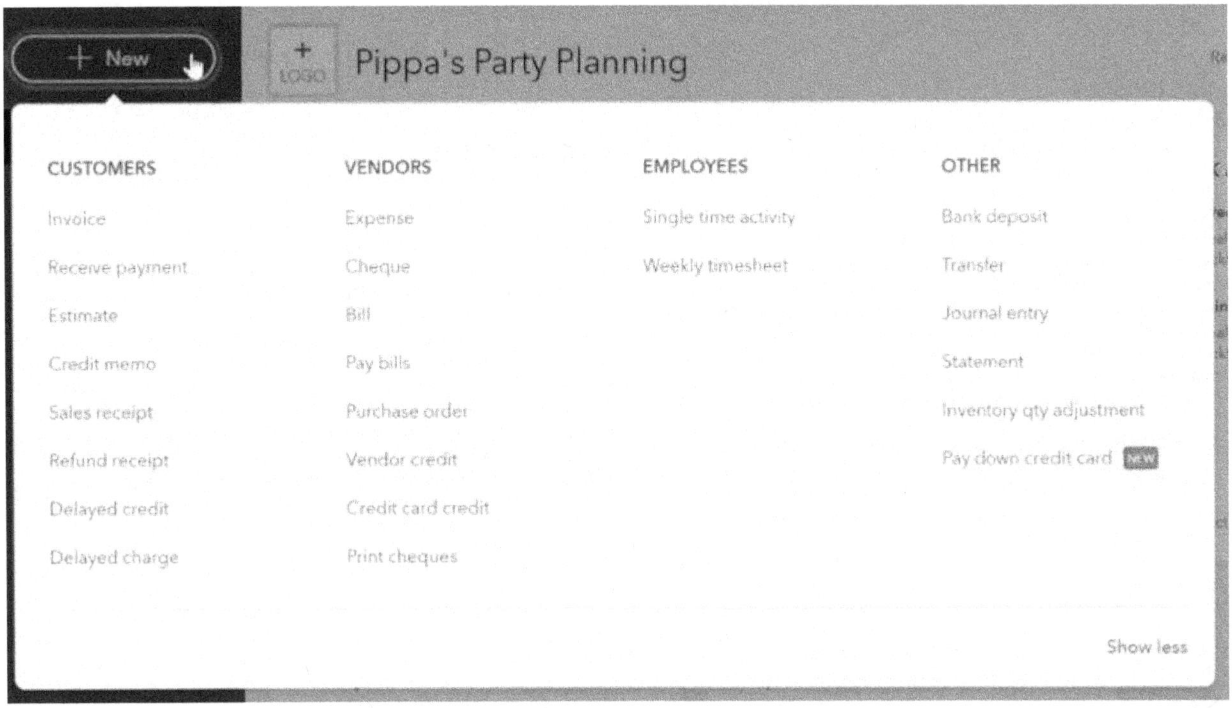

Always use the new menu when it comes to creating any new transactions in QuickBooks.

Navigation Menu
The second option on the left pane is the navigation bar and as we toggle down and hover over any of the title there, QuickBooks will display the appropriate list items contained within each of them.

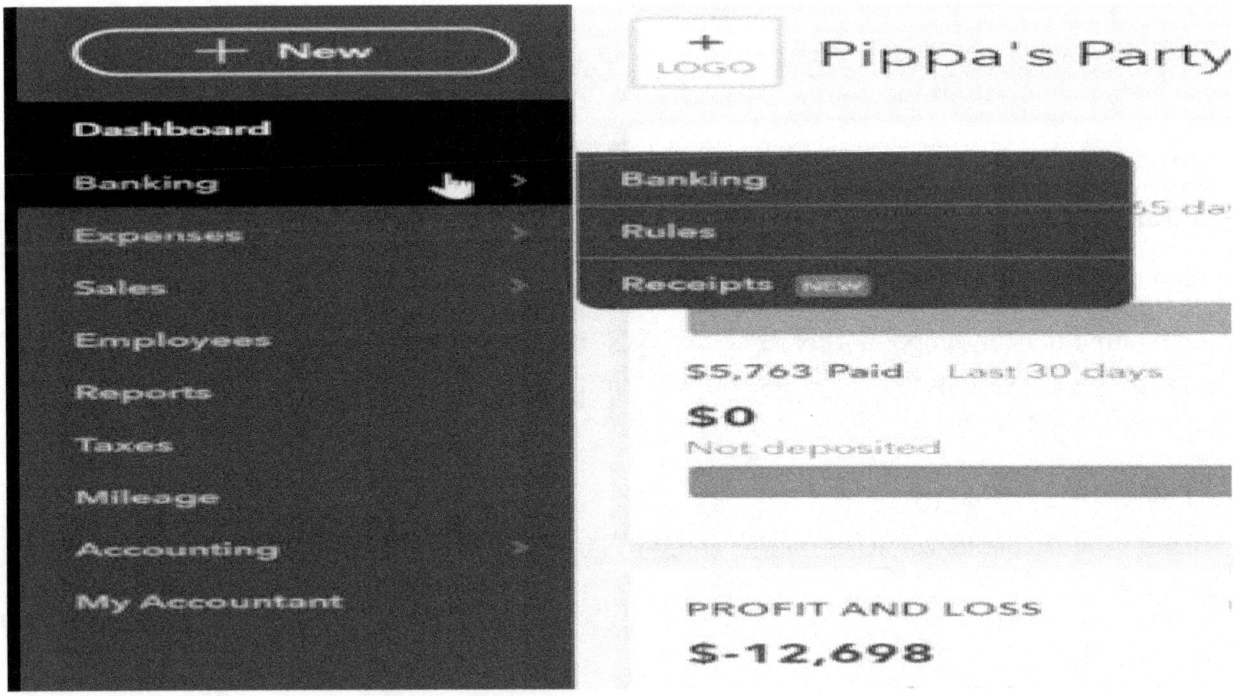

Tabs in the navigation menu;

Banking

In the navigation bar, we'll see 'banking' and this is where we're going to set up our online banking.

Expenses

'Expenses' is where we're going to enter our expense transactions; credit card entries, debit card entries and we'll also find our vendors there.

Sales

Next you'll see 'sales' and this is going to be where we deal with all of our sales transactions in QuickBooks. This is where we're going to create invoices, find our customers and we're going to have an opportunity to review our products and services.

Employees

'Employees' is just about employees and writing payroll checks.

Report

'Reports' is going to be something we'll talk about later but this is where you're going to find a wide variety of preset reports available for you to create at any time to give you information about your business.

Taxes

Next, we'll see 'taxes' and this is where we're going to find sales taxes as well as payroll taxes, both can be found under this menu.

Mileage

Mileage is where you track mileage

Accounting

Accounting is really important for us in this book because we're going to learn about the chart of accounts and how important it is in getting set up the right way and making sure that you get the information out of QuickBooks after you put it in.

My account

Finally, my accountant is where we're going to go to invite our accountant to participate in our accounting.

Always look to the navigation bar when you're dealing with various people in your business whether it's a customer, a vendor, or an employee because that information can be easily found on the navigation bar.

Gear Menu

If we look up in the top right corner, there is a gear menu that is going to contain a variety of things related to your company.

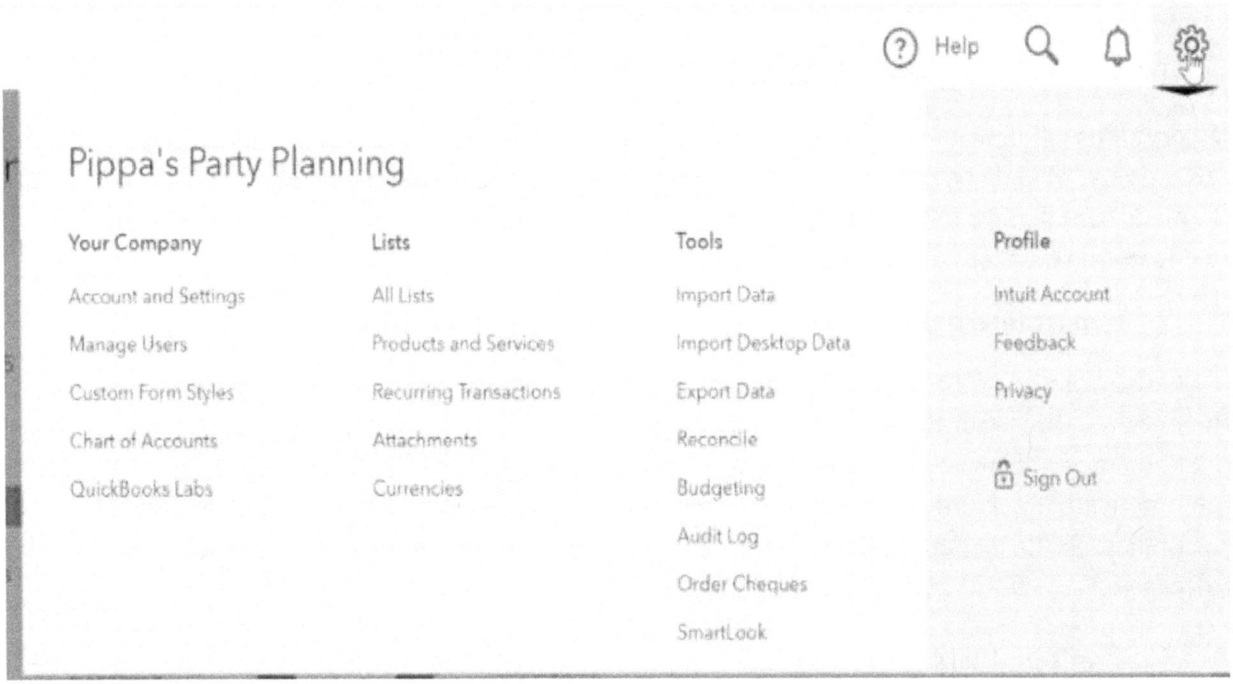

Your Company

This is where you're going to find your account and settings, you'll set up new users here and you'll also find your various forms in your company under custom form styles.

List

You'll also find a wide variety of lists that we will deal with, things like; products and services or transaction lists

Tools

Under tools, we'll be able to do things that are really important for our business, things like; budgeting, reconciling your bank accounts.

Profile

Under profile, we'll see the details about our intuit account, our QuickBooks subscription.

The new menu, navigation menu and the gear menu are the three primary ways to get around; we'll see them in action as we go throughout this book.

Why Use QuickBooks Online?

What are the benefits and why should we use QuickBooks online? And what is QuickBooks online going to do for us?

Let's review some of the importance of QuickBooks online;

1. **Tracking business transactions**

Every transaction that goes into your business must be tracked, QuickBooks online helps us do that effectively. Whether you're creating invoices for customers or writing checks to vendors, we want to make sure that we track all business transactions and QuickBooks allows us to do that easily once we learn the first few steps of data entry.

2. **Report internally for performance and position of our business**

We also want to report internally for the performance of our business and also the position of the business, so we want to have reports to know how profitable we are, we want to know our best customers, we also want to know how much debt we have, our liabilities and our assets. QuickBooks automatically tracks all of this information for us and it's ready whenever we want to create a report; its preset reports that are built as you go. So that's another benefit and power that QuickBooks will offer you.

- **Profit and loss:** In this specific section, we're going to review the profit and loss report; we'll talk about what it means to create a profit and loss or income statement as we often refer to it
- **The balance sheet report:** This is going to give you information about the position of your company; you'll know how much debt you have, what your assets are and so on.
- **Other financial reports:** There are other great reports that will help you find information about your business at any point in time and help you make decisions.

3. **Report externally to bodies like the CRA, minister of finance**

We also need QuickBooks to help us report externally. When we talk about external vendors and who we might report to, we're talking about things like; the CRA. The Canada revenue agency wants to know our sales taxes, they want to know our payroll taxes and QuickBooks helps us report externally to bodies like them. We might also report to people like; the minister of finance, workers compensation, there's a variety of people and organizations that we're going to report to externally and QuickBooks is going to help us do that efficiently and effectively in our business.

4. **Have data to help us make decisions**

Finally, we want to have data or information to help us make decisions. We need to know things about our business, we need to know the products and services we're selling, we need to know who our delinquent customers are, we need to know when our accounts payable is out of control and QuickBooks is automatically going to give us all of that information immediately when needed.

These are the reasons we're going to use QuickBooks online and why it's so important that we set it up in a way that's going to be helpful for our business.

Customizing QuickBooks for Your Business

We will go over how to change the look and feel of your invoices in this chapter. The custom format you create for your invoice can also be used for sales receipts and estimates, giving your business a unified and professional appearance.

Importance of Customizing Sales Forms

To make your business look professional and unique, I highly recommend customizing your invoices, receipts, and estimates. Many firms use the default QuickBooks forms, which are not particularly professional looking. With a well-designed logo on a one-of-a-kind invoice, you can increase brand visibility and name recognition.

How Can You Customize an Invoice in QuickBooks Online

Follow these five steps to modify the look and feel of your QuickBooks Online invoice:

1. Click on the gear icon,
2. Pick Account and settings in the first column, and then click on Sales to go to the Sales tab under Account and settings.
3. To make a new invoice template, click the green Customize appearance and feel button,
4. Then select Invoice from the drop-down arrow next to New Style.
5. Choose the layout, logo, colors, and font for your new invoice template.

Navigate to the Sales Tab in Account and Settings

In the sales area of your company settings, you may customize the look of your invoices. Click the gear button in the upper right corner of the QuickBooks Online page and select Account and settings in the first column to find the sales tab:

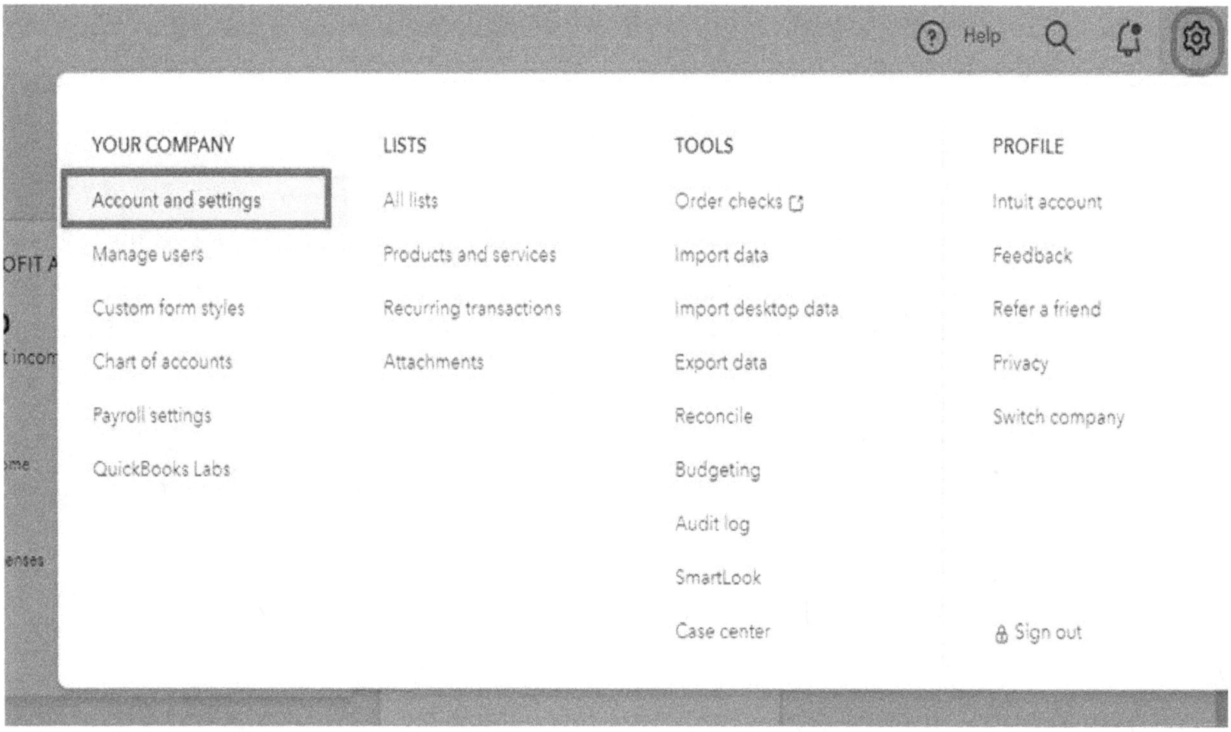

1. In QuickBooks Online, go to Account and settings.
2. Click Sales in the left menu bar from the Accounts and settings screen:

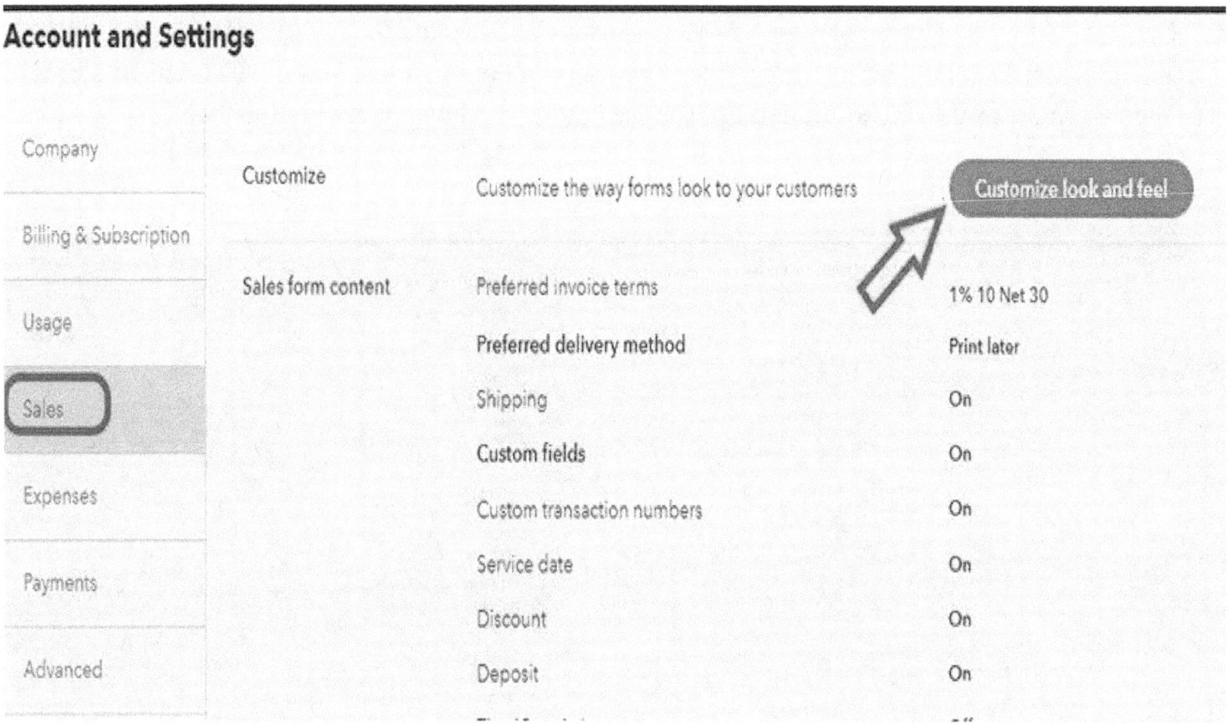

There are nine locations on your sales forms, which include invoices, receipts, and estimates, where you can adjust the options and defaults.

In the upper right corner of the sales tab, click the green Customize look and feel button.

Create A Custom Invoice

- **The default template titled "Standard" is the only form style accessible if** this is a new company. You can tweak the default template by selecting **Edit** on the far-right side of the line if you only want to make minor changes. However, for the purposes of this lesson, we will create an invoice from scratch.

Select Invoice: from the drop-down arrow next to the **New** style button in the upper right corner.

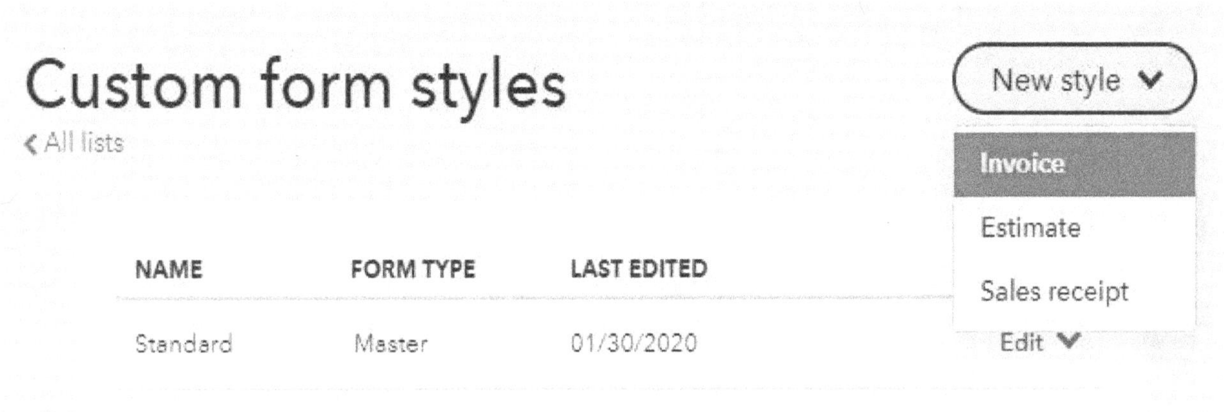

On the next screen, on the right, you may see a preview of your invoice. Design, Content, and Emails are the three tabs in the upper left corner. The Design tab will be covered in this book:

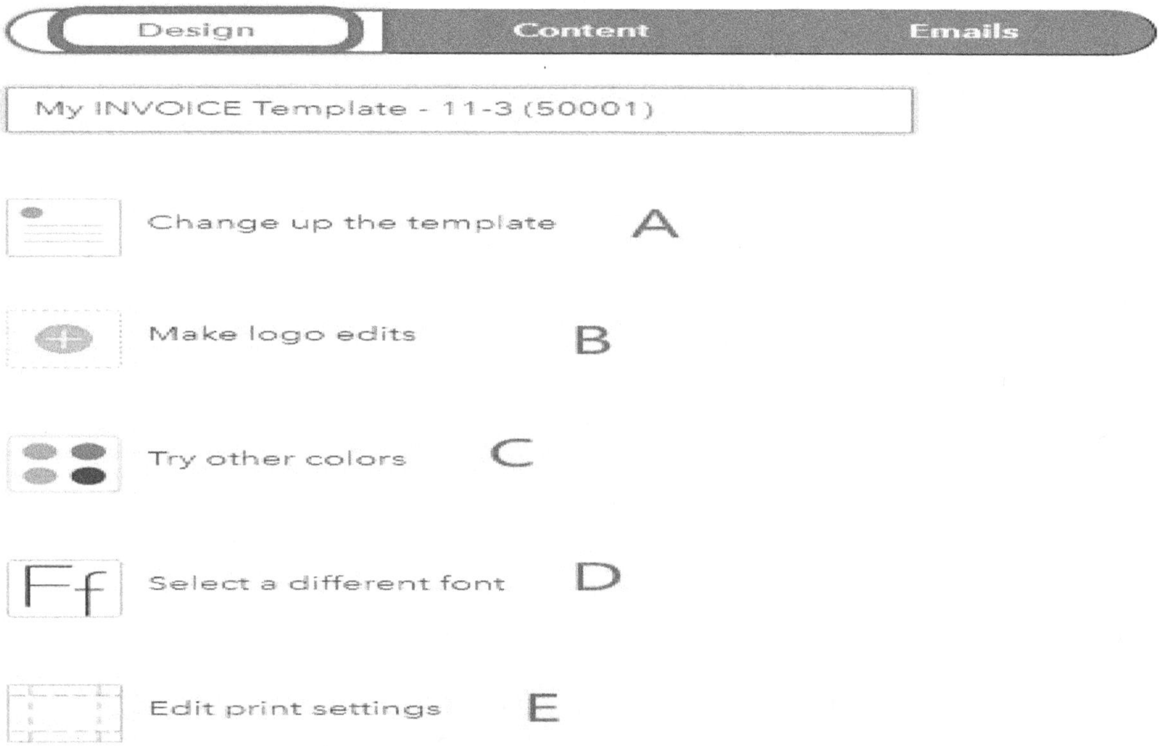

The design tab is solely concerned with the appearance of your invoice. Your invoice can be designed in five different ways. The preview of your invoice on the right part of the screen will refresh as you make new selections.

- **Preview your invoice:** The size of your screen effects the space between elements in the invoice preview on the right side of the screen. To preview how your invoice will appear, go to the bottom right corner of the screen and select Preview PDF.

A. Change Up the Template

You can choose from six different templates after clicking Change up the template under the design tab:

To see a preview of each template, click on it. Choose the template that best represents your company's image.

B. Include Your Own Customized Logo

You can personalize your invoice by using a photograph or logo. Your logo must be saved on your computer as an image file. To import your logo into QuickBooks Online, follow these steps:

1. Click the green plus sign under Add a logo, then click Add your distinctive logo. When you first click on Add your distinctive logo, you will notice that the button's description changes to **Make** logo edits:

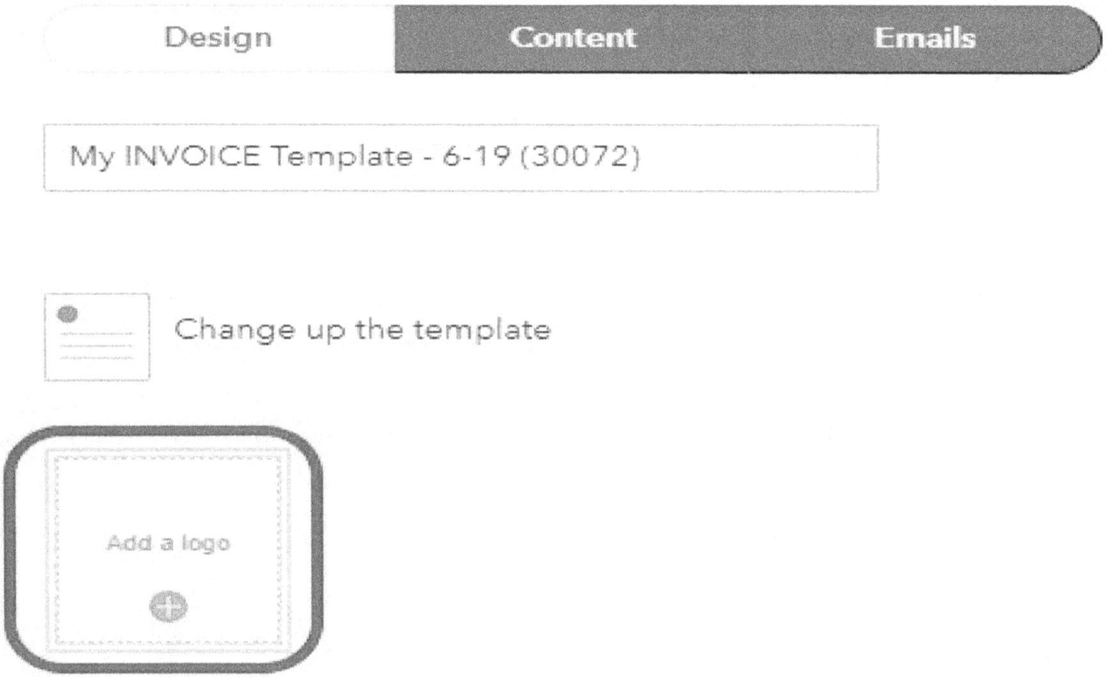

2. You will see all the logos you have already added to QuickBooks Online on the next screen. If you already have a logo, you may choose to include it in your invoice template by clicking on it. For new companies, or if you do not see your preferred logo, click the blue + sign:

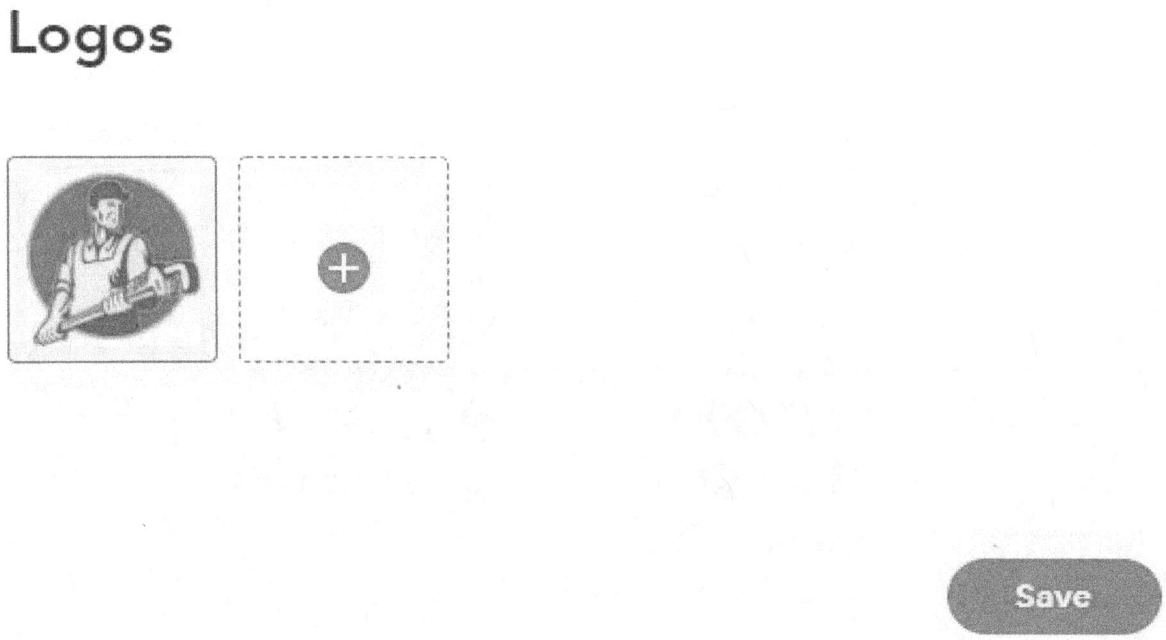

3. QuickBooks displays a window where you can explore your computer and pick the logo image file. After selecting the image file, click Open to return to the previous screen, where your new logo is displayed as a thumbnail.

The logo has now been saved in your QuickBooks Online account, and you may use it to customize additional forms without having to reload it. Make sure the logo you wish to use on your invoice is highlighted, then save it.

4. Your logo now displays in the Design tab, where you may modify the size and position it on the left, center, or right side of your invoice

The logo can only be placed at the top of the invoice, unfortunately. Play with the choices until you find a way to display the logo that you like. If you do not want the logo to appear on your invoice, select Hide logo.

C. Experiment with Different Colors

The color of your template is the next option under the Design tab. You can choose from 16 colors after clicking Try other colors:

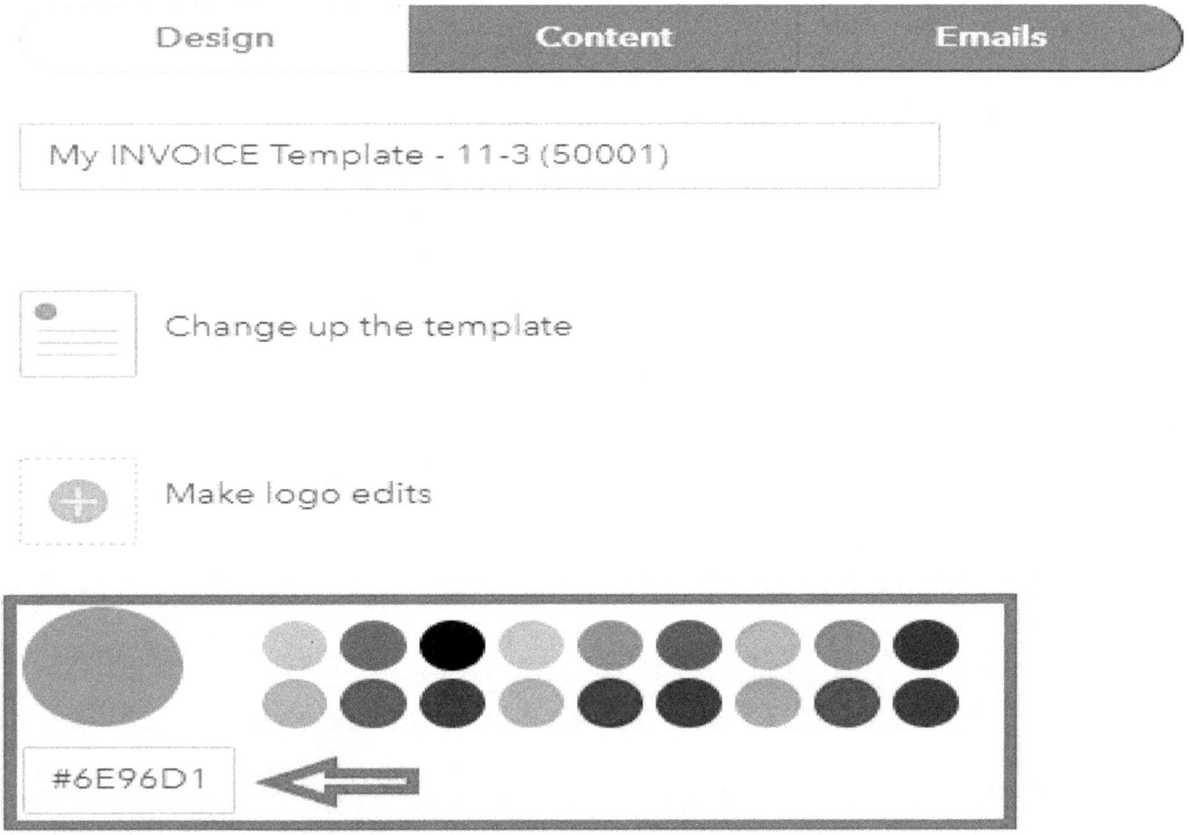

The invoice heads' text and highlight colors will be affected by the color choices. Some templates are more colorful than others, so you might want to reconsider your template choices. Try the "bold"

template, which shades the full backdrop of the invoice for maximum color. Colors can be customized: The 16 predefined colors are not the only ones available. The text box beneath your color choice is an HTML color code, which you can manually enter for an almost unlimited number of color options.

D. Choose Your Font Carefully

The next step in the Design tab is to select a font. To view a selection of four fonts and three sizes, click Get Choosy with Your Font (or Select a different font if you have already clicked there).

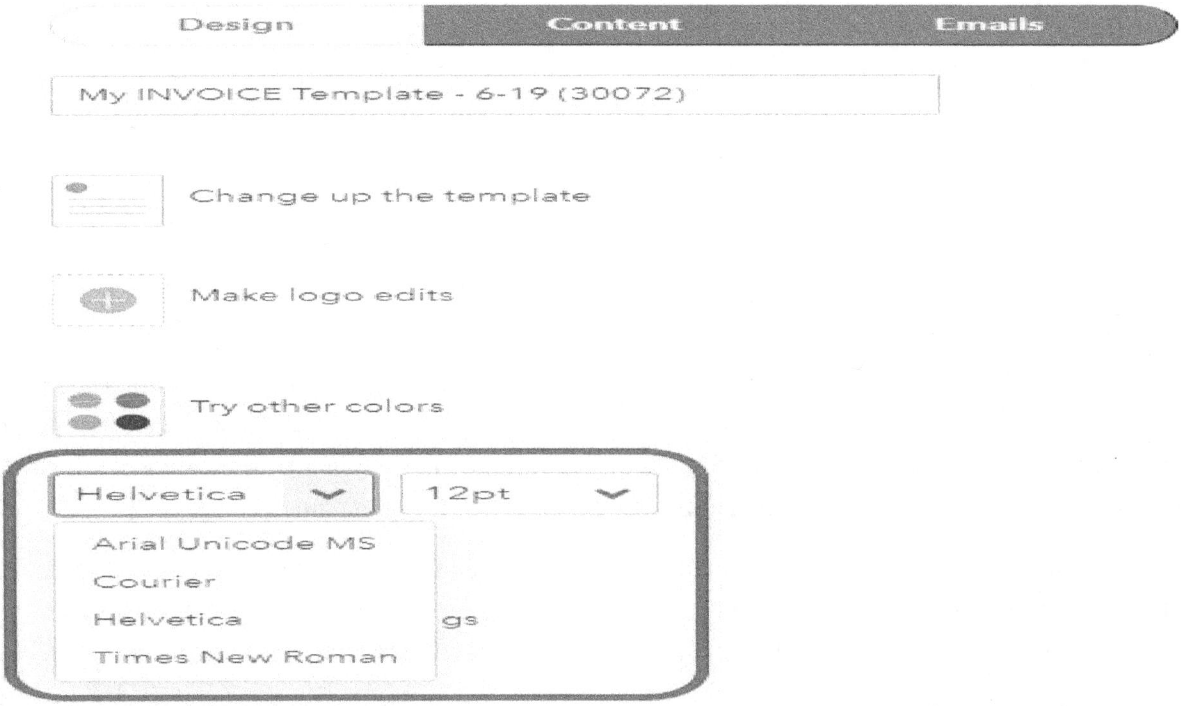

E. If You Are Not Sure, Print It Out

Setting your print selections is the final task under the Design tab. To examine options for printing your invoice, click When in doubt, print it out (or Edit print settings if you have already been there).

The Fit printed form with paystub in window envelope will print a dividing line on the top portion of your invoice, turning it into a payment stub, as well as the statement "Please detach top portion and return with your payment." This will assist you in matching payments to outstanding invoices, which is especially important if you send many invoices for the same amount.

The company name, address, and logo will be removed from the top of the invoice if you select Use letterhead paper. This allows you to include your business details and logo on emailed invoices, but you can instantly remove them when printing on corporate letterhead.

Click the green **Done** button in the bottom right corner of the screen when you are happy with the personalized design of your invoice. QuickBooks takes you back to the Custom form styles screen, where you can view your freshly created invoice template and its default name. By selecting **Edit** and then **Rename**, you may alter the name of your custom invoice:

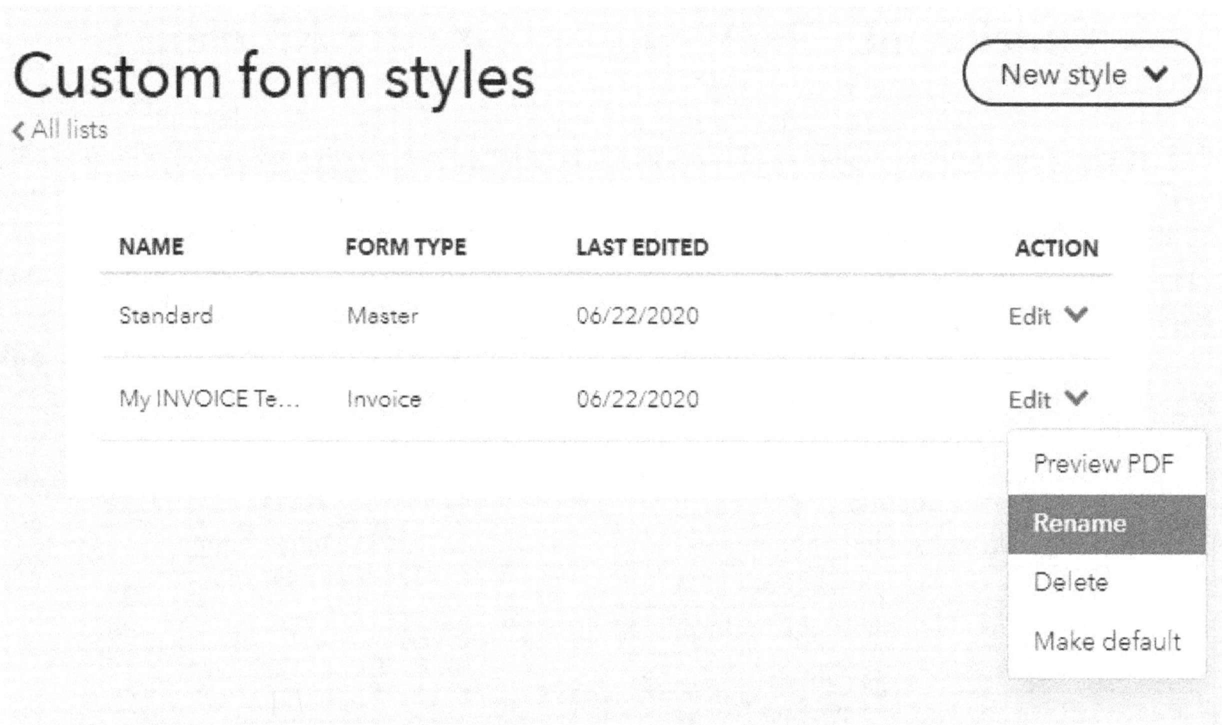
Custom form styles
New style
All lists
NAME
FORM TYPE
LAST EDITED
ACTION
Standard
Master
06/22/2020
Edit
My INVOICE Te...
Invoice
06/22/2020
Edit
Preview PDF
Rename
Delete
Make default

QuickBooks Shortcuts for Greater Efficiency

Keyboard shortcuts are a combination of keys for executing tasks without using the mouse. Using keyboard shortcuts are usually faster and speed up navigation when using QuickBooks. They can be used on both QuickBooks Desktop and QuickBooks Online. For QuickBooks Desktop, both MacOS and Windows are supported when using keyboard shortcuts. On the other hand, Internet Explorer, Chrome and Firefox works fine with keyboard shortcuts in QuickBooks Online. There are various categories of keyboard shortcuts ranging from general key shortcuts to dates keys, activity keys and editing keys. General key shortcuts are used to execute basic tasks within QuickBooks and they are:

Function	Keys
Launch QuickBooks without company file	Ctrl (while loading)
Suppress desktop windows	Alt (while loading)
Show QuickBooks version product information	F2
Close an active window	Esc or Ctrl+F4
Record (Save and Close, Save and New, OK)	Enter key
Record (always)	Ctrl + Enter key

Dates Key Shortcuts

These shortcuts are used to identify dates easily within QuickBooks. Each shortcut with its function is shown in the table below:

Function	Key
Next day	+ (plus key)
Previous day	- (minus key)
Today	T
First day of the Week	W
Last day of the week	K
First day of the Month	M
Last day of the Month	H
First day of the Year	Y
Last day of the year	R
Date calendar	Alt + down arrow

Activity Key Shortcuts

Activity shortcuts make task execution faster in QuickBooks. All activity shortcuts with their functions are shown in the table below:

Function	Key
Create invoice	Ctrl + I
Delete check, invoice, transaction or item from list	Ctrl + D
Find transaction	Ctrl + F
History of A/R or A/P transaction	Ctrl + H
Memorize transaction or report	Ctrl + M
New invoice, bill, check or list item in context	Ctrl + N
Open account list	Ctrl + A
Open Customer Center (Customers & Job list)	Ctrl + J
Open Help for Active Window	F1
Open list (for current dropdown menu)	Ctrl + L
Open memorized transaction list	Ctrl + T
Open split transaction window in register	Ctrl + R
Open transaction journal	Ctrl + Y
Print	Ctrl + P
QuickReport on transaction or list item	Ctrl + Q
QuickZoom on report	Enter key
Show list	Ctrl + S
Write new check	Ctrl + w

Editing Key Shortcuts

These keyboard shortcuts are useful for making changes and editing within QuickBooks. These shortcuts are listed in the table below alongside their functions.

Function	Key
Edit transaction selected in the list or register	Ctrl + E
Delete character to right of insertion point	Del
Delete character to left of insertion point	Backspace
Delete line from detail area	Ctrl + Del
Insert line in detail area	Ctrl + Ins
Cut selected characters	Ctrl + X
Copy selected characters	Ctrl + C
Paste cut or copied characters	Ctrl + V
Copy line in an invoice	Ctrl + Alt + Y
Paste copied line in an invoice	Ctrl + Alt + V
Increase check or other form number by one	+ (plus key)
Decrease check or other form number by one	- (minus key)
Undo changes made in a field	Ctrl + Z

Moving Around Window Key Shortcuts

These key shortcuts are useful for navigating within a window. They are outlined in the table below.

Function	Keys
Next field	Tab
Previous field	Shift + Tab
Report column to the right	Right arrow
Report column to the left	Left arrow
Beginning of current field	Home
End of current field	End
Line below in detail area or on report	Down arrow
Line above in detail area or on report	Up arrow
Down one screen	Page Down
Up one screen	Page Up
Next word in field	Ctrl + →
Previous word in field	Ctrl + ←
First item on list or previous month in register	Ctrl + PgUp
Last item on list or next month in register	Ctrl + PgDn
Close active window	Esc

Help Window Key Shortcuts

These keys can be used to access help when working in QuickBooks. They are as follows:

Function	Key
Display Help in context	F1
Select next option or topic	Tab
Select previous option or topic	Shift + Tab
Display selected topic	Enter key
Close Help window	Alt + F4

Customers: Quotes and Sales Management

This section is designed is to help you record all the sales transactions you made using various methods depending on the circumstances that surround your sales transactions, we will check different methods of recording payment from each of your customers and lastly how to raise credit memo and refunds your customer in some cases where the product or service does not deliver as expected. This section is deliberately made to consistently help you in tracking every money that comes into your business so sit tight and let us dive in together.

Recording Your Business Income

You can record the money that flows into your business using these two methods:

- Recording income with the sales receipt.
- Recording income with the invoice.

Recording Income with The Sales Receipt

This is the perfect method for recording sales transactions where sales of products and services take place immediately with the payment from customers. It means the customer will be paying immediately as they collect the product or enjoy the service. For instance, you open a saloon, customer drink and eat at your saloon and they pay you immediately after the service.

The following steps show you how to record sales transactions using a sale receipt:

1. Click the **New** menu at the top of the Left Navigation bar and choose **Sales Receipt** on the **CUSTOMER** column to access the sale receipt form.

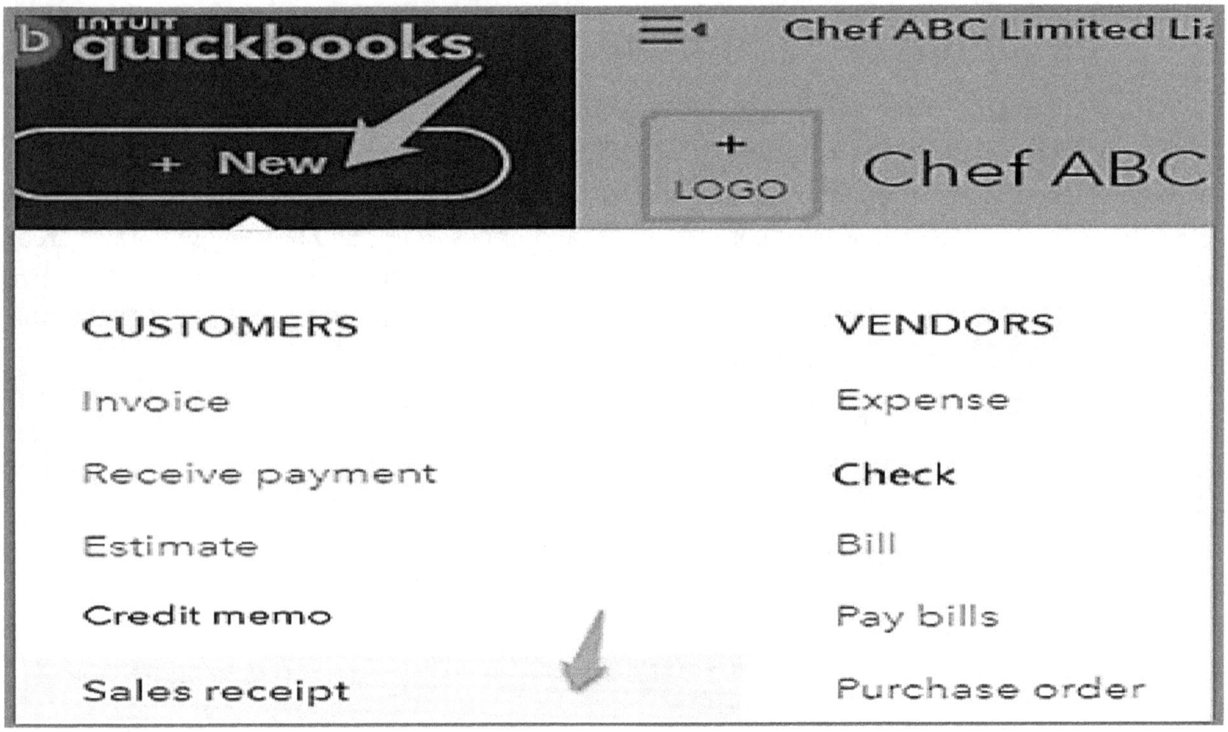

2. Supply the necessary information as they are related to the sales transaction, check below the description for directions:

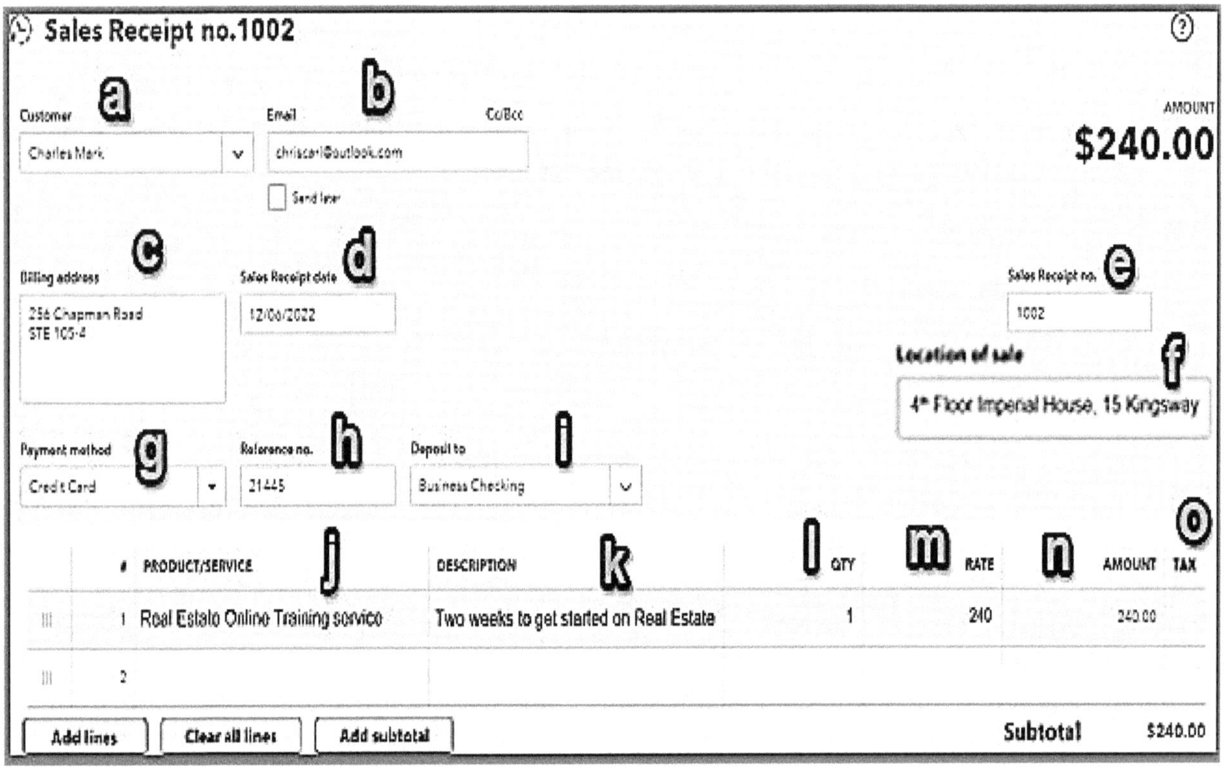

a. Customer: click the drop-down button and choose the customer that bought the product or service from you. If the customer is not on the list, you can enter the customer's name into the customer field.

b. Email: This field will be filled automatically based on the information you have entered when you are adding the customer to the list, if you see it empty, then fill the field with the customer email.

c. Billing address: This field will be filled automatically based on the information you have entered when you are adding the customer to the list, if you see it empty, get the customer billing address and supply it to this field.

d. Sales Receipt date: insert the date you made the sale into this field.

e. Sales Receipt no: the sales receipt number will be generated within QuickBooks automatically.

f. Location of sale: this field will be filled with the address you enter when you are entering the sales tax setup in the previous chapter. The address will be used for specifying the tax rate and filling criteria.

g. Payment method: click the down arrow and choose the payment method customer used on the drop-down list.

h. Reference no: (Optional) enter a reference number for the payment that was made by credit card or cash, if it was a check number, you will have to enter the check number.

i. Deposit to: click the down arrow and choose the bank account which you want to use to deposit the money.

j. PRODUCT/SERVICE: Click the drop-down and choose the product or service that you have sold to the customer. If you have not added the service or product to the product/service list, you will click **Add New** and supply the following information to add it to the list:

- Product or Service name
- Description
- Category
- Rate: rate of the quantity.
- Account: this is the account that you will use to record the product or service like Sales of product income

k. DESCRIPTION: This field will be filled automatically based on the information you have entered when you are adding the product or service to the list. If you haven't written any description, you can do it right from this place.

l. QTY: insert the quantity of the product which you have sold or the minutes/hours of the service rendered into this field.

m. RATE: this field will be filled automatically based on the information you have entered when you are adding the product or service to the list. If you haven't made a setting for the rate you can do it right from this place.

n. AMOUNT: the amount you are having here is the multiplication of the quantity sold by the rate of the quantity **(QTY x RATE**).

o. TAX: place a mark on this field to mark the product or service as taxable if it is a taxable product or service.

The above sales transaction will affect your business income and statement account and balance sheet. The total asset side will increase by $240 as a result of the increase in the business checking account while the total income side will also increase as a result of the $240 sales transaction you have made.

Recording Income with The Invoice

This is the perfect method for recording sales transaction whereby sales of products or services and payment does not occur at the same time. It means payment for the product or service is postponed until the future time. For instance, the payment may be net 30 days or 60 days this indicates the period when the payment of that product or service will be due for payment.

The following steps show you how to record sales transactions using an invoice:

1. Click the **New** menu at the top of the Left Navigation bar and choose **Invoice** on the **CUSTOMER** column to access the Invoice form.

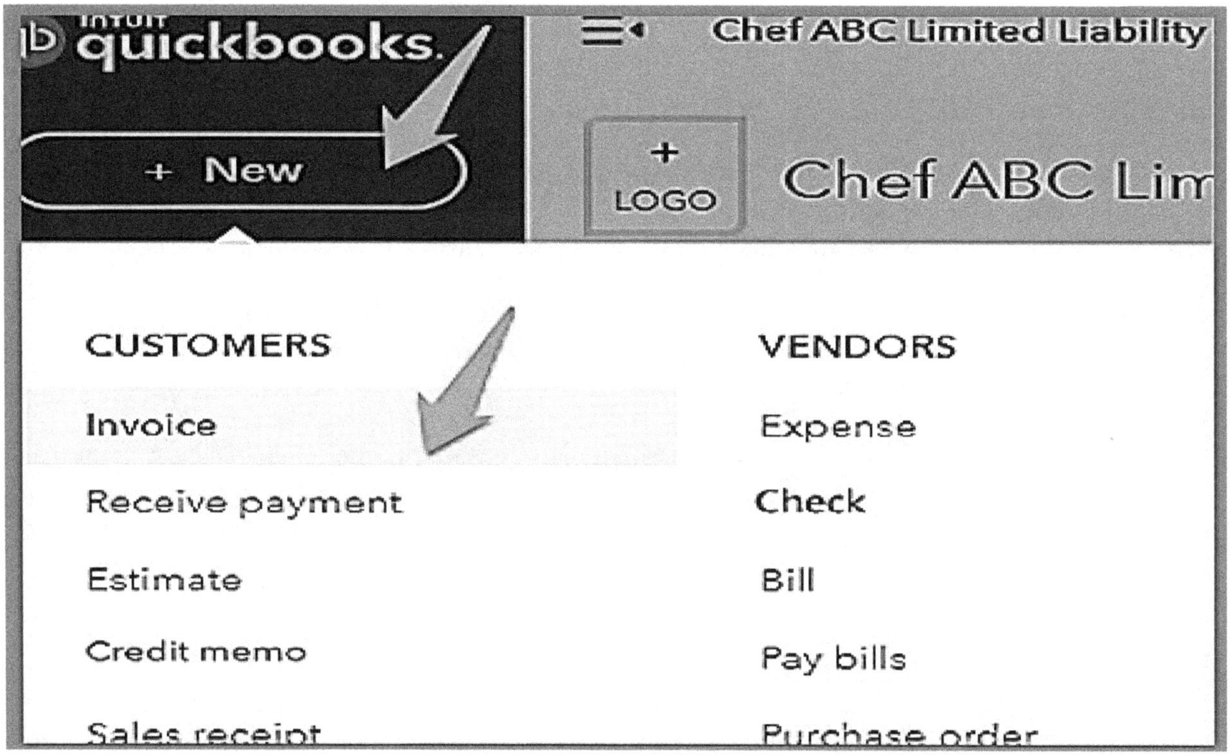

2. Supply the necessary information as they are related to the credit sales transaction, check below descriptions for directions:

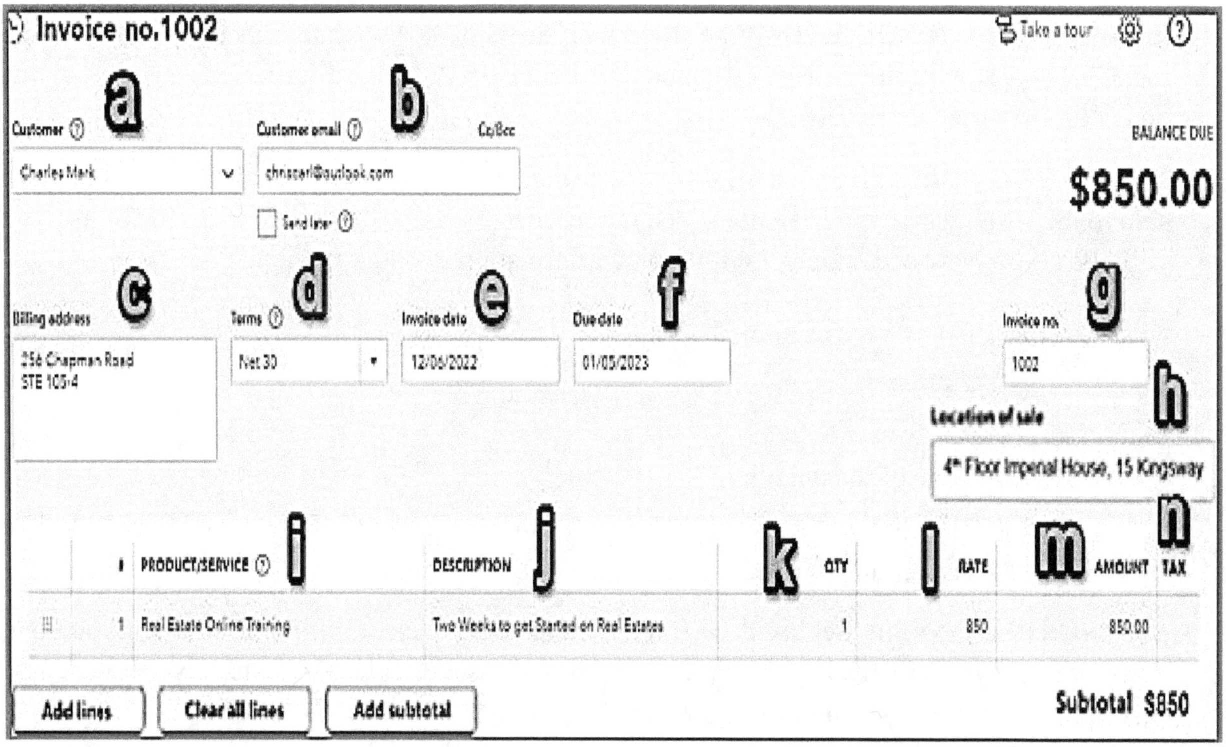

a. Customer: click the drop-down button and choose the customer that bought the product or enjoys service on credit. If the customer is not on the list, you can enter the customer's name into the customer field.

b. Customer email: this field will be filled automatically based on the information you have entered when you are adding the customer to the list, if you see it empty, then fill it with the customer email to enable you to send the invoice to the customer.

c. Billing address: this field will be filled automatically based on the information you have entered when you are adding the customer to the list, if you see it empty, get the customer billing address and supply it to this field.

d. Terms: this field will be filled automatically based on the payment term you have programmed when you are adding the customer to the list, if you haven't made settings for customer terms of payment, kindly click the down arrow and select term pf payment from the drop-down menu like Net 30 or Net 60.

e. Invoice date: insert the date you made the credit sale into this field.

f. Due date: this field will be filled automatically with the due payment date in which the customer is expected to make the payment based on the payment term you have set for the customer like Net 30 or Net 60.

g. Invoice no: the invoice number will be generated within QuickBooks automatically.

h. Location of sale: this field will be filled with the address you enter when you are entering the sales tax setup in the previous chapter. The address will be used for specifying the tax rate and filling criteria.

i. PRODUCT/SERVICE: Click the drop-down and choose the product or service that you have sold to the customer. If you have not added the service or product to the product/service list, you will click **Add New** and supply the following information to add it to the list:

- Product or Service name
- Description
- Category
- Rate: rate of the quantity.
- Account: this is the account that you will use to record the product or service like Sales of product income

j. DESCRIPTION: this field will be filled automatically based on the information you have entered when you are adding the product or service to the list. If you haven't written any description, you can do it right from this place.

k. QTY: insert the quantity of the product which you have sold or the minutes/hours of the service rendered into this field.

l. RATE: this field will be filled automatically based on the information you have entered when you are adding the product or service to the list. If you haven't made settings for the rate you can do it right from this place.

m. AMOUNT: the amount you are having here is the multiplication of the quantity sold by the rate of the quantity (QTY x RATE).

n. Tax: place a mark on this field to mark the product or service as taxable if it is a taxable product or service.

The above sales transaction will affect your business income and statement account and balance sheet. The total asset side will increase by $850 as a result of the increase in the account receivable which is the money owed by the customer while the total income side will also increase as a result of the $850 sales transaction you have made.

Receiving Payments from The Customers

Whenever customers pay you for the products or services they bought on credit based on the terms that you and the customers must have agreed on, you will then assign the payment against the outstanding sales you made with the invoice to cut down the account receivable balance.

The following steps show you how to record the payment you receive from your customer:

1. Click the **New** menu and choose "**Receive payment"** on the **CUSTOMERS** column to access Receive Payment form.

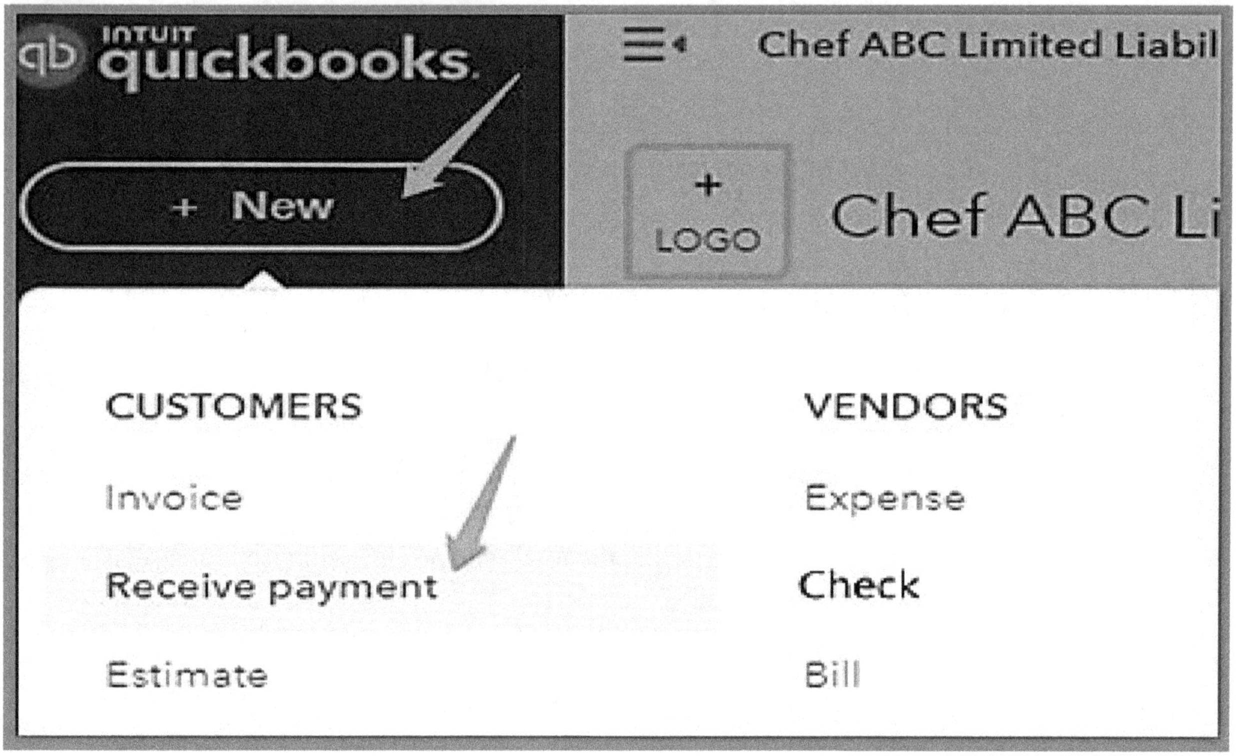

2. Supply the necessary information into the receive payment form as shown below:

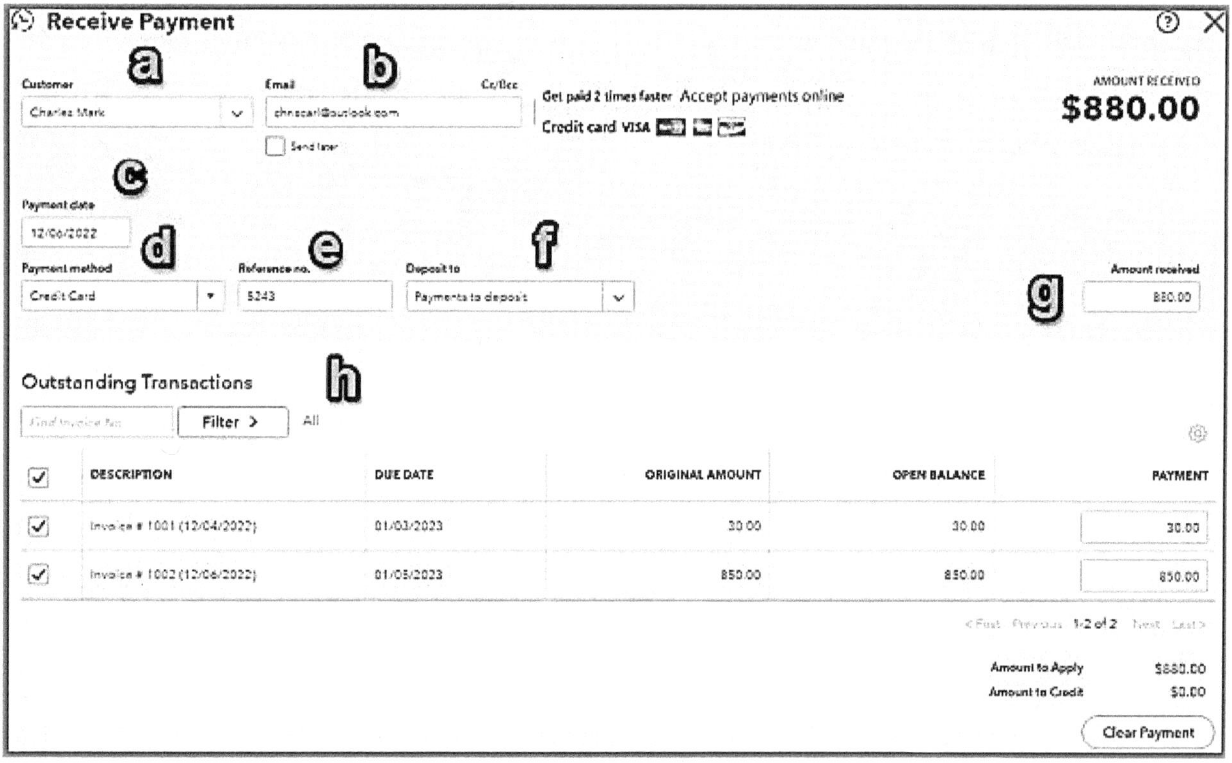

a. Customer: Click the down arrow and choose the concerned customer.

b. Payment date: Insert the date you received the payment from the customer.

c. Payment method: Click the down arrow and choose the payment method that the customer use in paying you like cash, check, or credit card.

d. Reference no: (Optional) enter a reference number for the payment that was made by credit card or cash, if it was a check number, you will have to enter the check number.

e. Deposit to: click the down arrow and choose the bank account which you want to use to deposit the money. Generally, it should be paid to the deposit account.

f. The amount received: put the amount you received from the customer into this field.

g. Outstanding transaction: the unpaid invoices will be listed in this section after which QuickBooks must have matched the payment amount that you have received. At times the payment received might be for a different invoice remove the mark from the invoice number that QuickBooks select and place a mark on the actual invoice that the payment money is meant for.

Here the payment will only affect the balance sheet, the income statement will stay untouched because the transaction has been recorded already in the income statement when the invoice was made.

The $880 made to the **"payment to deposit"** account will cause the assets side to be increased, decrease in the account receivable which is the money owed by the customer will cause a decrease in the assets side with $880.

Understanding Payments to Deposit Account

Sometimes when customers make payments with sales receipts or invoices, the payment will be transferred straight to the business checking account which means the money goes straight to the bank account but most time businesses will like to gather all the money collected from the customers into the payment to deposit account and delay it for a while to collect remaining payment and later pay the money altogether to the bank.

As long as the money is not yet deposited into the bank, it will assume it remains in the payment to deposit account but immediately after the deposit is dropped into the bank, you should attempt to record the deposit in QuickBooks so that each side can balance.

Recording Bank Deposits
If you fail to post the money in the "**payments to deposit**" account into QuickBooks, the money will stay lifeless in the Payment to deposit account, this will affect balances in your bank account and QuickBooks.

The following steps show you how to post your deposit into QuickBooks as soon as those moneys drop into your Bank account:

1. Click the **New** menu and choose **Bank deposit** on the **OTHER** column to access the Bank deposit form.

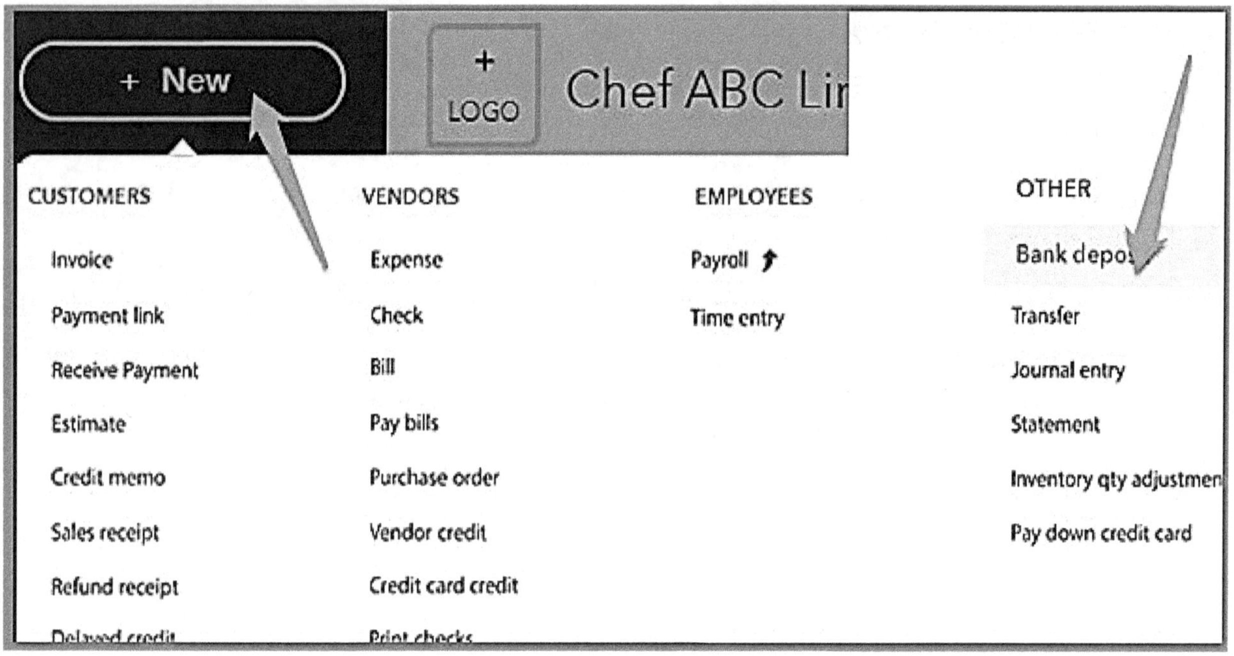

2. Click the **Account** drop-down arrow and choose the **account** where the deposit should go and choose the date when you want to post the deposit in the Date section.

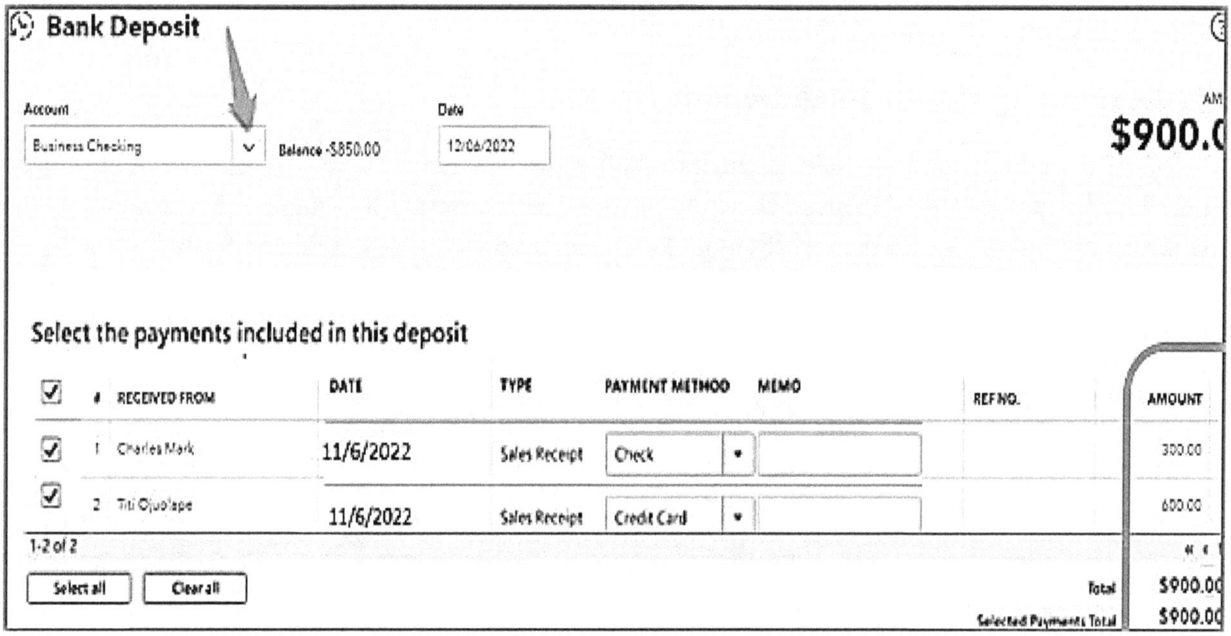

3. Move to "Select the payments included in this deposit" and place a mark on the payment that should be included in the deposit.

4. Click the Save button to validate the posting from the "payment to deposit" account to the real account.

The deposit you made to QuickBooks will affect the balance sheet side report alone. The Business checking account will be increased with the amount you deposited while the payment to the deposits account will be decreased with the amount of deposit made.

If you forget to post the amount in bank deposit into QuickBooks, you will always have an issue when you are reconciling with your bank accounts.

Returning Money to The Customer
Sometimes, you may have to refund customers for the money received from them, this may arise when there are one or more problems with the products sold to them or services rendered to them.

In such a case, you can resolve the issue either by issuing a credit memo that will stand against future invoices or issuing a refund receipt if the issue warrants you to refund the payment immediately.

Recording A Credit Memo
Credit memos cut down the outstanding balance or future balance of your customer. A credit memo can be entered similarly to the ways of entering an invoice.

Check the below steps for creating a credit memo in QBO:

1. Click the **New** menu and select **Credit memo** on the **CUSTOMERS** column.

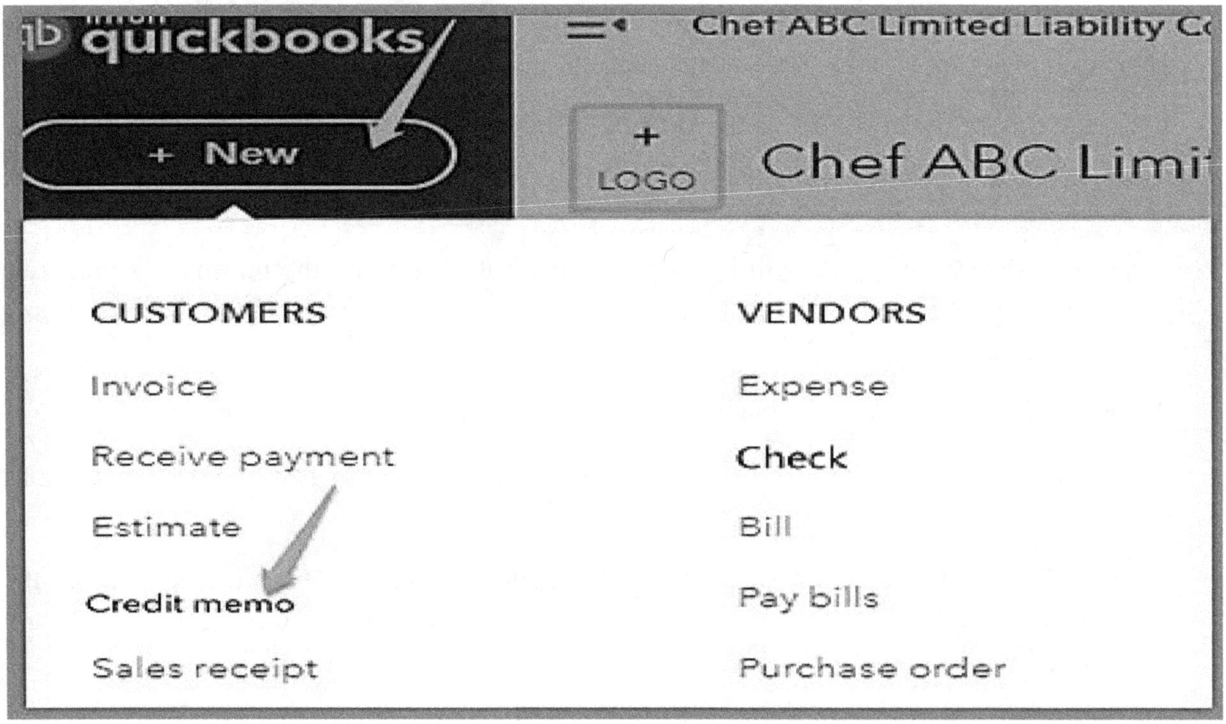

2. Supply the necessary information as they are related to the credit memo transaction you want to record, check below information for the description:

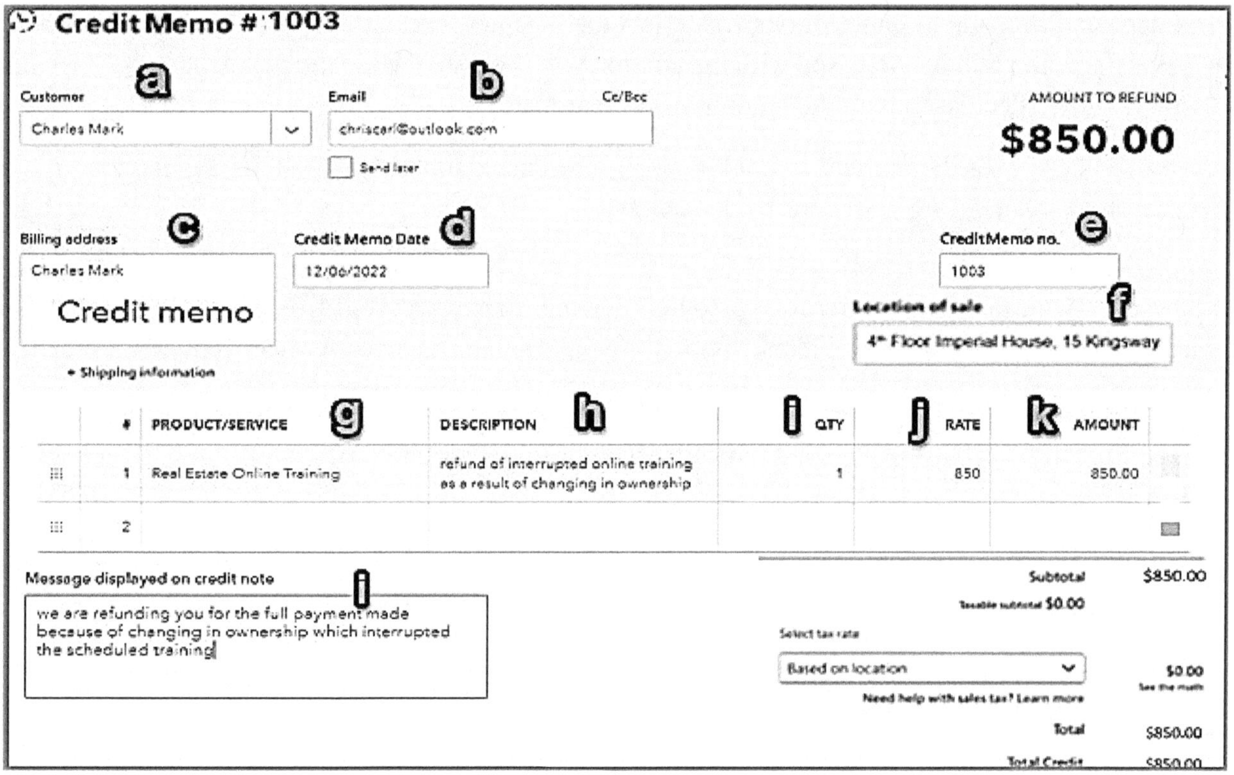

a. Customer: click the drop-down button and choose the customer which you want to refund. If the customer is not on the list, you can enter the customer's name into the customer field.

b. Email: this field will be filled automatically based on the information you have entered when you are adding the customer to the list, if you see it empty, then fill it with the customer email to enable you to send the credit memo to the customer.

c. Billing address: this field will be filled automatically based on the information you have entered when you are adding the customer to the list, if you see it empty, get the customer billing address and supply it to this field.

d. Credit memo date: insert the date on which you create the credit memo into this field.

e. Credit Memo no: the credit memo number will be generated within QuickBooks automatically.

f. Location of sale: this field will be filled with the address you enter when you are entering the sales tax setup in the previous section. The address will be used for specifying the tax rate and filling criteria

g. PRODUCT/SERVICE: Click the drop-down and choose the product or service in question that necessitate a refund to the customer.

h. DESCRIPTION: this field will be filled automatically based on the information you have entered when you are adding the product or service but you have to edit by indicating the reason why you have to refund the customer, you also indicate the invoice number you used to bill customer at the first place.

i. QTY: insert the quantity of the product or minutes/hours that you are refunding to the customer.

j. RATE: this field will be filled automatically based on the information you have entered when you are adding the product or service to the list. If you haven't made settings for the rate you can do it right from this place.

k. AMOUNT: the amount you are having here is the multiplication of the quantity sold by the rate of the quantity (QTY x RATE).

l. Message display on credit memo: you can type any form of message that relates to the refund you are making like the reason for the refund, whether it is going to be a partial or full refund, and so on.

Note: This above credit memo will affect both your income statement and balance sheet reports. The sale is reduced so the total income on the income statement will reduce. The account receivable which is the amount owed by the customer will be reduced this will reduce the total asset on the balance sheet reports.

once you are done recording the credit memo for the customer refund, the customer invoice balance will reduce.

If the issue warrants you to refund the customer immediately, you can do that by clicking the New menu at the top of the Left Navigation and choosing refund receipt, then following the directions displayed on the screen.

Suppliers: Inventory and Invoicing Management

Inventory

Enabling Inventory in QuickBooks
Inventory tracking enables you to always know how much stock is on hand. Using the accounting software QuickBooks, you may monitor your inventory in real-time. This functionality is available in QuickBooks, but it is not immediately active when the software is installed. In actuality, you must activate the inventory option in QuickBooks. QuickBooks Enterprise, Premier, and Pro all provide inventory tracking as an optional feature.

1. Log in to QuickBooks using your administrator credentials. The inventory can only be activated by the administrator.
2. To access the "Edit" menu, click on it. Once the menu has opened, select "Preferences." This launches the Options window.
3. Select Items & Inventory" in the list of editable settings. Navigate to the "Company Preferences" section from there.
4. Mark the box next to "Inventories and purchase orders are active." Select the box by clicking on it.
5. Click the "OK" button to save your modifications. This enables inventory management in QuickBooks.

How to Create New Inventory Part Items
QuickBooks provides you with the opportunity to add inventory items as well as non-inventory items for the sake of managing your inventory. Things that are in stock at your company are referred to as inventory items. For example, if you manage an electronics store, you might keep track of the number of particular brands of television. Items that are not in stock include those that are specifically ordered or drop-shipped directly to the consumer. Before you can create inventory parts in QuickBooks, you must enable inventory tracking; however, you can create non-inventory parts without modifying the QuickBooks settings.

1. Open QuickBooks
2. Afterwards, select "Preferences" from the "Edit" menu.
3. Select the "Company Preferences" tab after clicking the "Items & Inventory" button.
4. To enable inventory tracking, check the "Inventory and purchase orders are active" box. Select "OK"
5. Select "Items & Services" on the Home pane, then click "Item," followed by "New."

6. Choose "Inventory Part" from the drop-down option labeled Type.
7. Fill out the "Item Name/Number" text box with the name of the item that is in the inventory. When you want to keep track of the revenue that this inventory item generates, select the account that you would want to utilize by clicking the "Income Account" drop-down option.
8. Select the "OK" option to create the inventory section after filling in the remaining required fields.

How to Create A Purchase Order

1. If you have not done so already, activate purchase orders:
    - Under Edit, select **Preferences.**
    - Choose **Items & Inventory**, followed by the tab labeled **Company Preferences**.
    - Ensure the Inventory and purchase orders are active box, then click **OK.**
2. Click Create Purchase Orders within the Vendors menu.
3. Select the vendor for whom you would want to place a purchase order from the Vendor dropdown menu. Additionally, you can select Add New to add a new vendor.
4. Fill out the remaining sections and add the things you wish to purchase.
5. Choose Save and Close.

Hint: Purchase orders are an integral component of the Accounts Payable (A/P) process.

How to Create Purchase Order Reports

You must generate two reports in order to compare the transactions and balances. This is how:

1. Select the Reports button.
2. Select Customized Reports.
3. Choose Transaction Detail
4. Click the button labeled Customize Report.
5. Update the report date in the Display tab.
6. On the same page, in the Columns section, click Paid.
7. Select the Filter tab.
8. In the Filter section, select Either from the options under Posting Status.
9. Select Transaction Type from the Filters menu, and then select Purchase Order from the drop-down menu.

10. Click Accept.

11. In the Total By drop-down, select vendor.

This report will display received or billed purchase orders. Use the Open Purchase Orders by Job page to view open purchase orders. Follow the below steps:

1. Select the **Reports button.**
2. Select **Purchases**
3. Select **Open Purchase Orders by job**
4. Click the button labeled **Customize Report.**
5. Select the Display tab.
6. Select Debit and Credit in the Columns section.
7. Click **Accept.**

How to Receive Inventory with A Bill

Each time you get an item from a purchase order (PO), we can transform the PO into a bill. The item's quantity will be added to the inventory (Products and Services) list in this manner. This is how;

1. Select the "+New" button.
2. Beneath Vendor, select **Bill.**
3. Click the drop-down arrow next to Vendor and then choose the vendor's name.
4. All existing purchase orders will be displayed on the left. Select the appropriate PO, then click **Add.**
5. Click **Save** and close when finished.

If you received the goods without a receipt, we can still alter the quantity and not record a transaction. In other words, we can match your inventory. I'll guide you how:

1. Select the "+New" button.
2. In the Other column, choose **Inventory quantity adjustment.**
3. Enter the date of the adjustment and choose the items to amend.
4. Click **Save** and then Exit.

Once the inventory modification is saved, QuickBooks automatically records the corresponding inventory account adjustments.

How to Enter Bills
After receiving a bill from a vendor, record it as follows:

1. First and foremost, choose + **New**.
2. Afterwards, choose Bill.
3. Choose a vendor from the drop-down menu labeled **Vendor.**
4. Specify the bill's terms from the drop-down menu labeled Terms. This is when your vendor anticipates receiving payment.
5. Input the Due date, Bill date, and Bill number exactly as they appear on the bill.
6. Input the details of the invoice in the Category details box. Choose the cost account you use to track spending transactions from the Category selection. Enter a description then. To itemize the bill, you can also specify individual products and services in the Item details area.
7. Enter the Amount with tax.
8. Choose the Billable checkbox and put the customer's name in the Customer field if you intend to bill a customer for the spending. Learn more about chargeable expenses.
9. When finished, select **Save** and Exit.

If you have many workplaces or business divisions, you may also choose locations from the Location drop-down menu.

Track and Pay Bills
If you don't also know how to pay bills in QuickBooks Online, entering your bills won't do you any good. Thankfully, the procedure is once again rather basic.

Using QuickBooks Online, you have the flexibility to pay your vendors directly from your bank account through free options like direct deposit or paper checks. Alternatively, you can opt for payment via a debit or credit card. Regardless of your chosen payment method, the following steps will guide you through the process of paying invoices in QuickBooks Online.

1. **Select the "Pay Bills" window.**

There are two locations on your Dashboard where the "Pay Bills" link can be found. The first location is in the shortcut's menu mentioned in the instructions for entering a bill.

The second method for initiating bill payment is to click the "New" button at the top of the page. You will next locate "Pay Bills" under the "Vendors" menu.

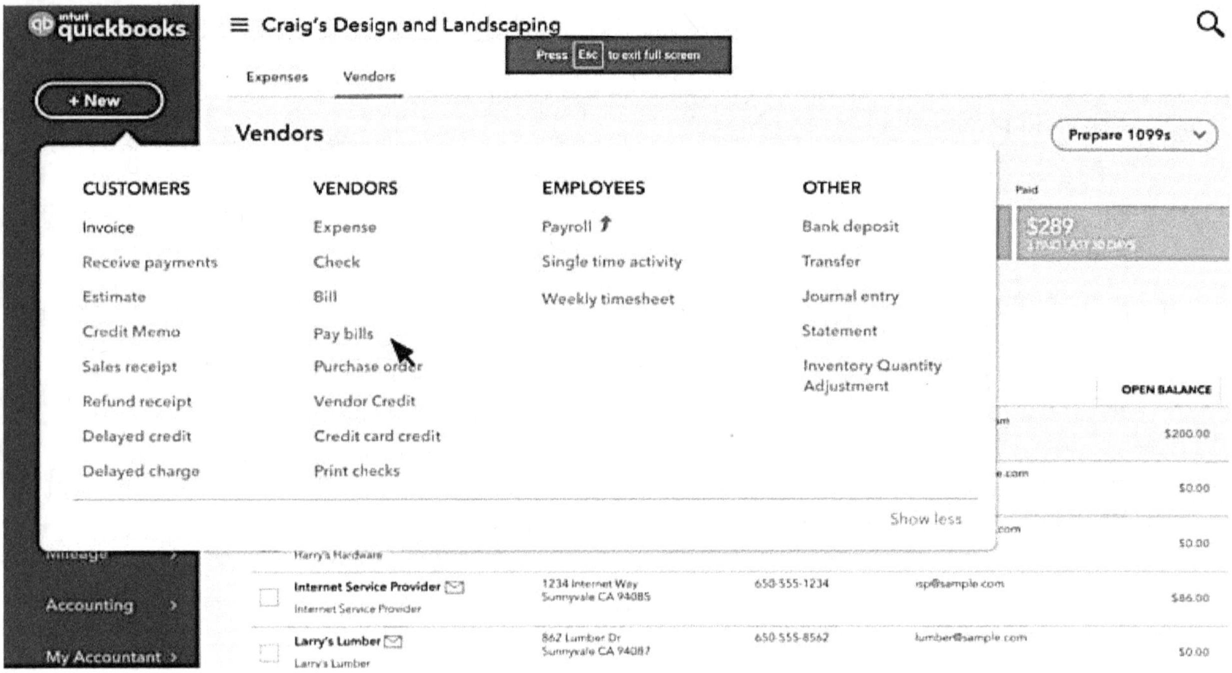

2. **Choose Your Bill**

Locate the bill that you wish to pay among your list of bills. Click the checkbox on the left and then choose "Online payment scheduling."

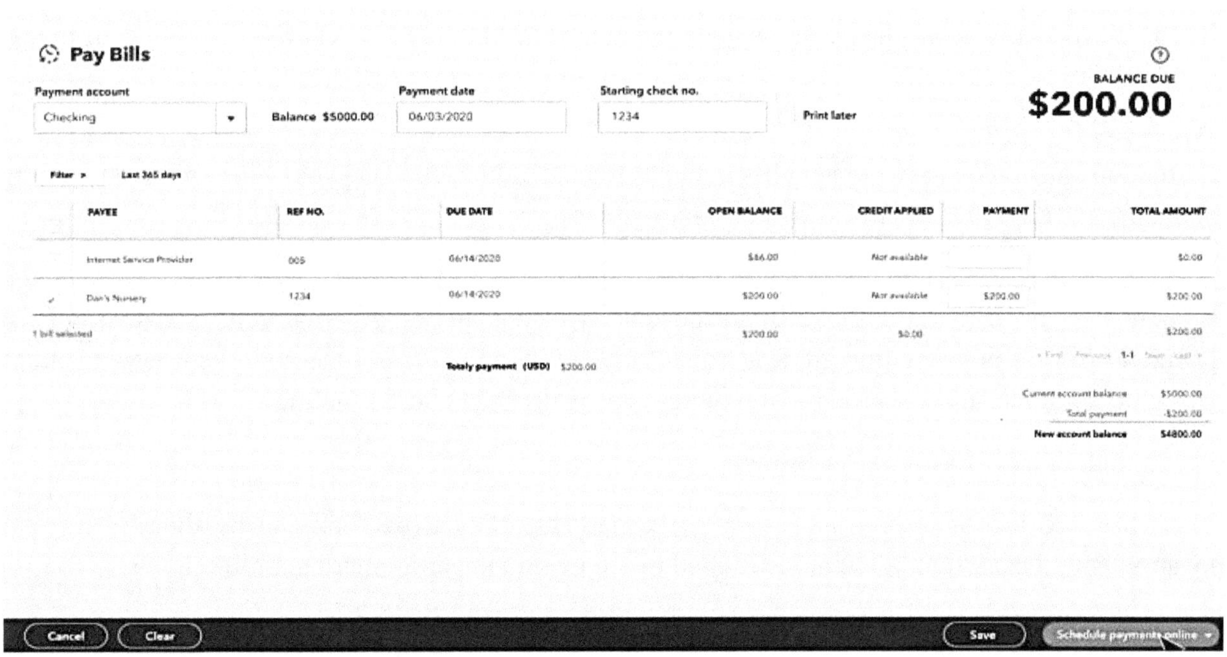

3. **Select Your Payment Method**

Next, you must select your payment method. Payments made via bank account (including paper checks) and debit card are entirely free. The credit card processing cost, however, is 2.9% plus $0.25 each transaction.

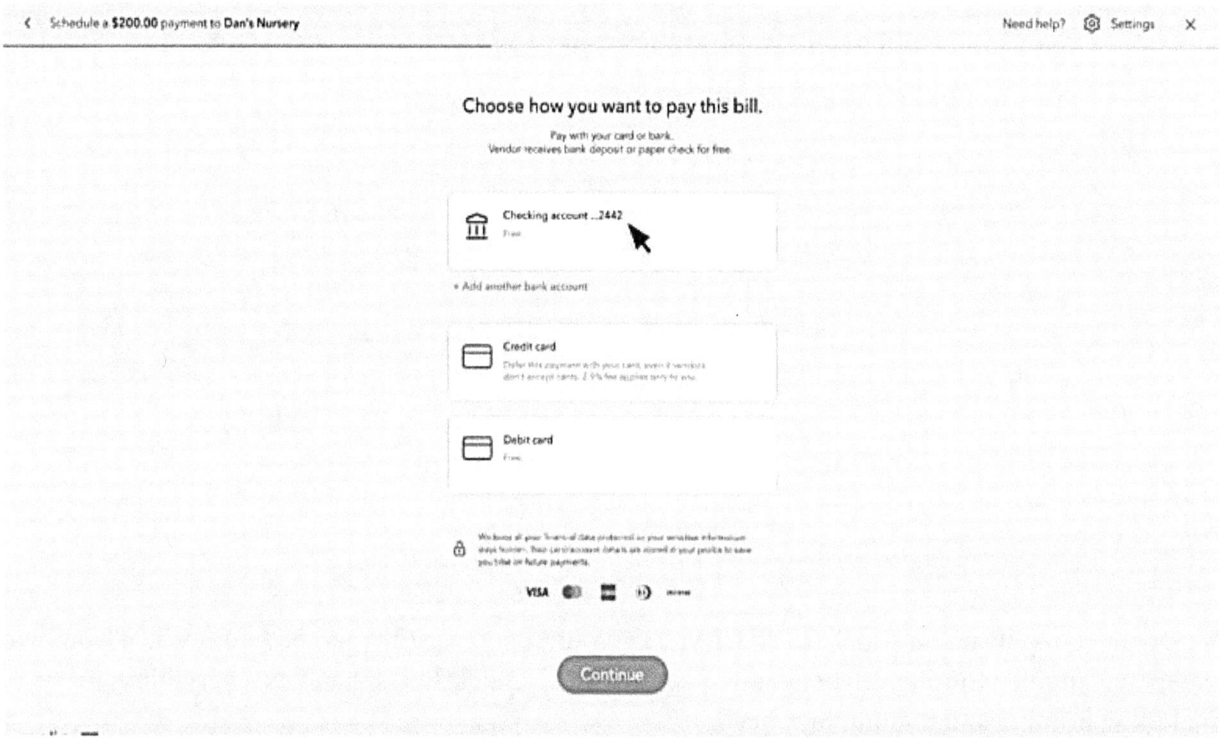

If you wish to pay with an unlinked bank account, select "Add another bank account" and follow the instructions.

4. **Decide Between ACH or Paper Checks for Bank Payments**

If you opt to pay bills directly from your bank account in QuickBooks Online, you will be presented with an additional screen where you can choose between direct deposit and a physical check.

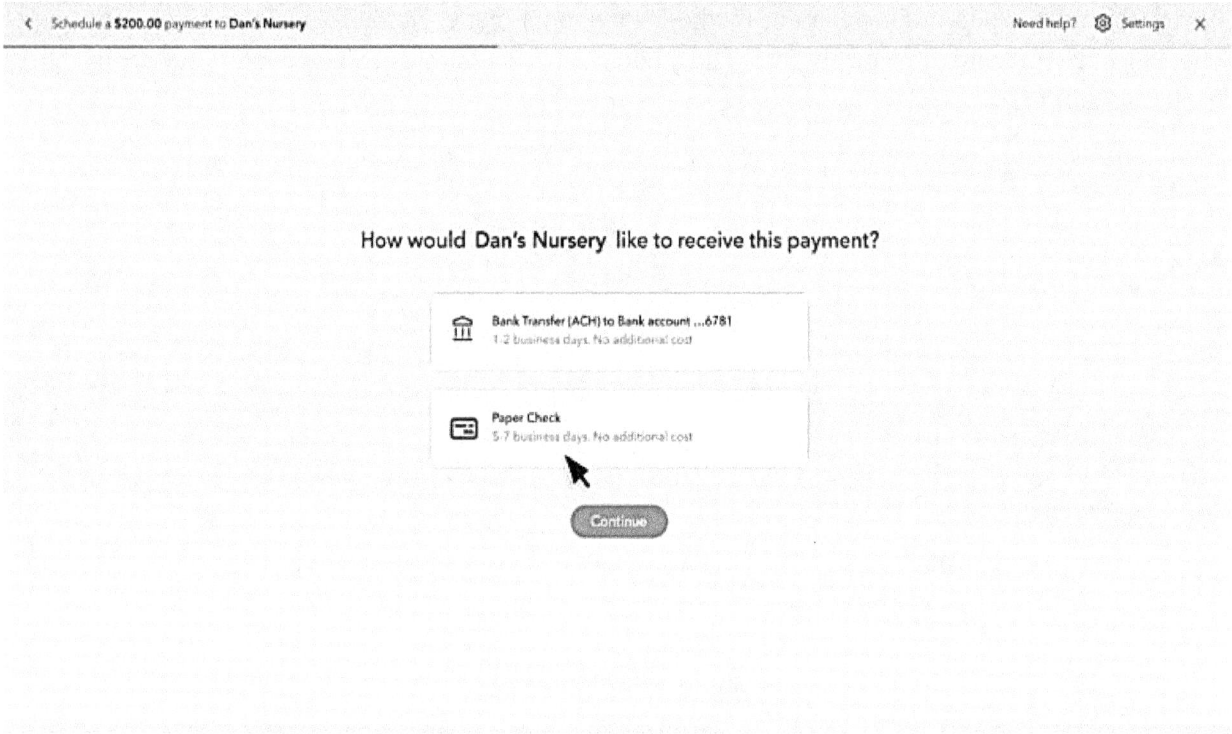

Yes, you can still send a paper check (if you or your vendor prefer this method) even if you plan payments online. Similar to bank bill pay services, QuickBooks handles everything for you, including printing and mailing the check.

Whether you choose ACH or a paper check has no effect on the price. Each option is free. However, paper checks normally arrive within 5 to 7 business days, whereas bank transfers typically arrive within 1 to 2 business days.

5. **Select Your Payment Date**

Next, a calendar will appear for you to choose the date on which you would like your payment to be processed. Remember that this is the intended date of payment, although it will arrive later. At the bottom of the scheduling calendar, the approximate arrival time of your bill will be displayed.

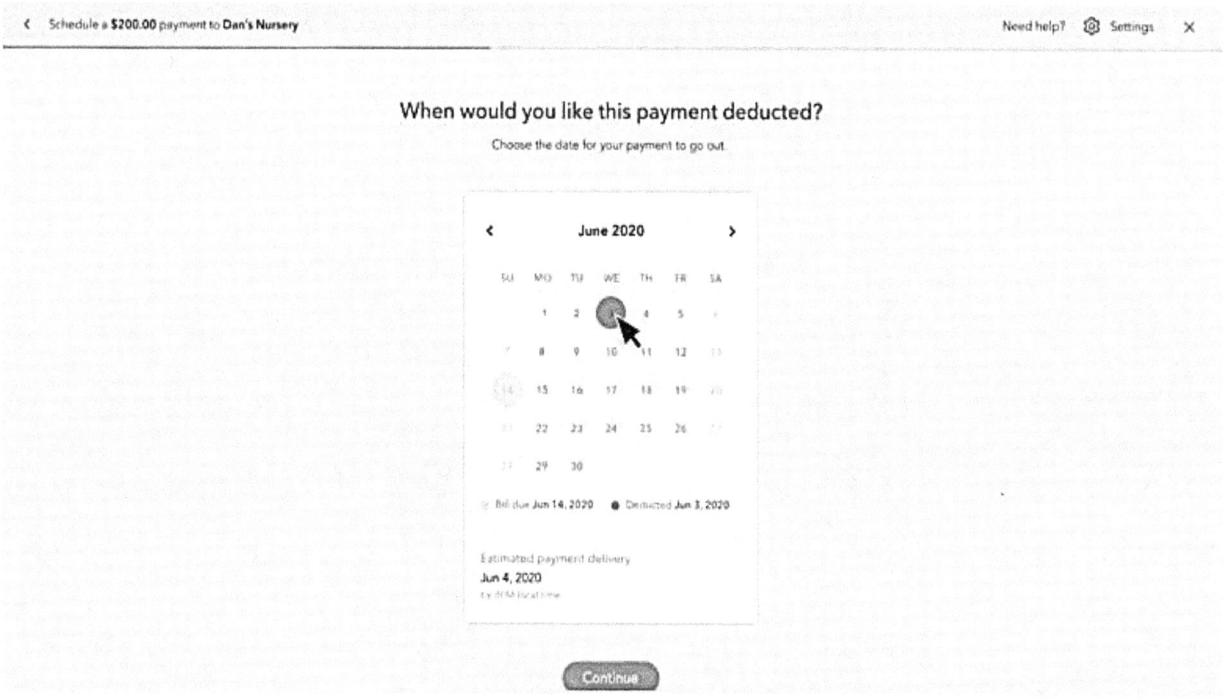

6. **Review and Confirm Your Payment Schedule**

After selecting your payment date, you are nearly finished. You will then have the option to include a note to your bill, if desired. Alternately, you may skip this step and proceed to the "Review & Confirm" screen.

Check the final details of your bill payment to ensure that everything is in order. If so, you can then click "Confirm and Schedule Payment."

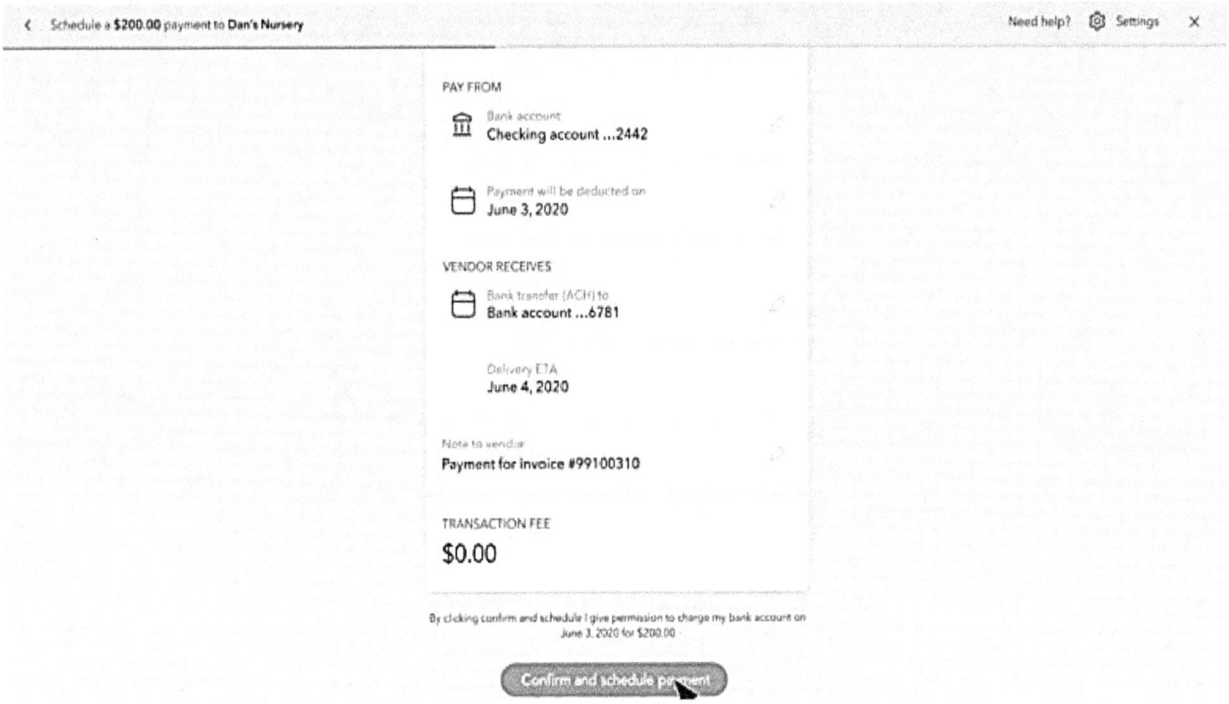

You have successfully scheduled your first bill payment in QuickBooks Online.

7. **Document your Bank Transaction**

Your job is not yet complete. After the transaction is complete, the bank payment is matched with your bill as the final step. To accomplish this, you must navigate to "Bank Transactions."

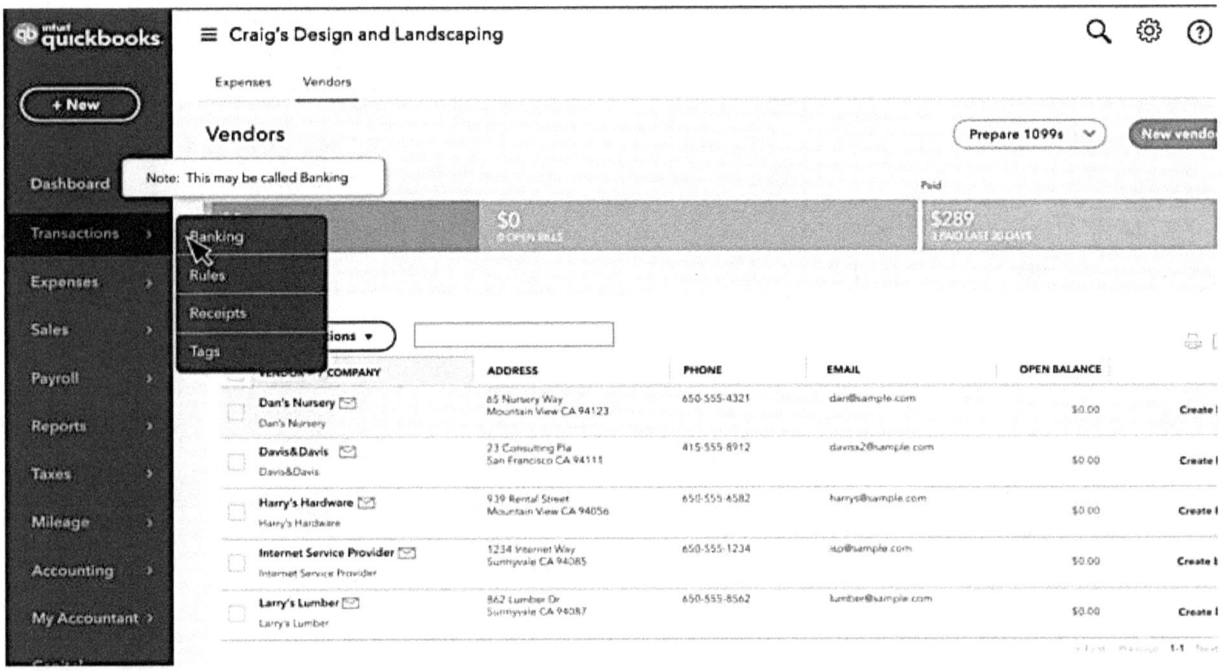

On this page, you'll see a list of all the transactions downloaded from your bank by QuickBooks. If one of your transactions is for the same amount as a recent bill, QuickBooks may identify a probable matching record and highlight this in a green book.

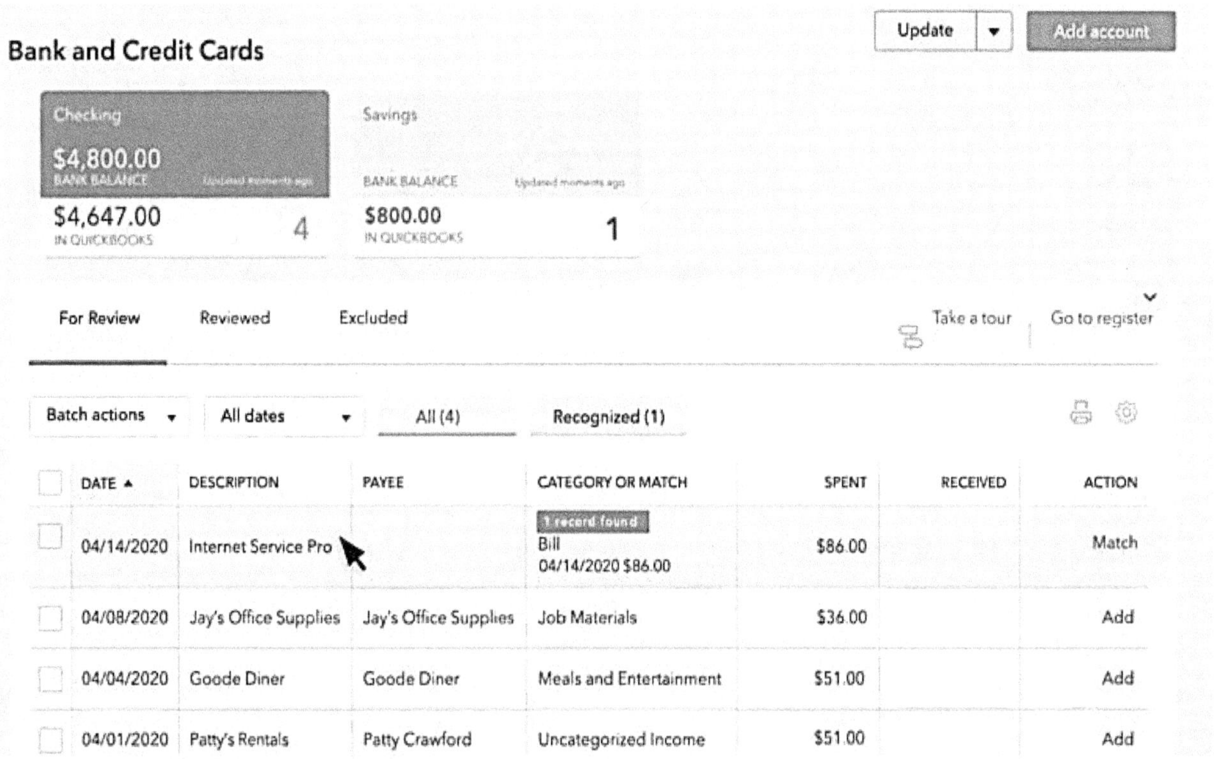

You only need to select "Match" from the "Action" tab on the right.

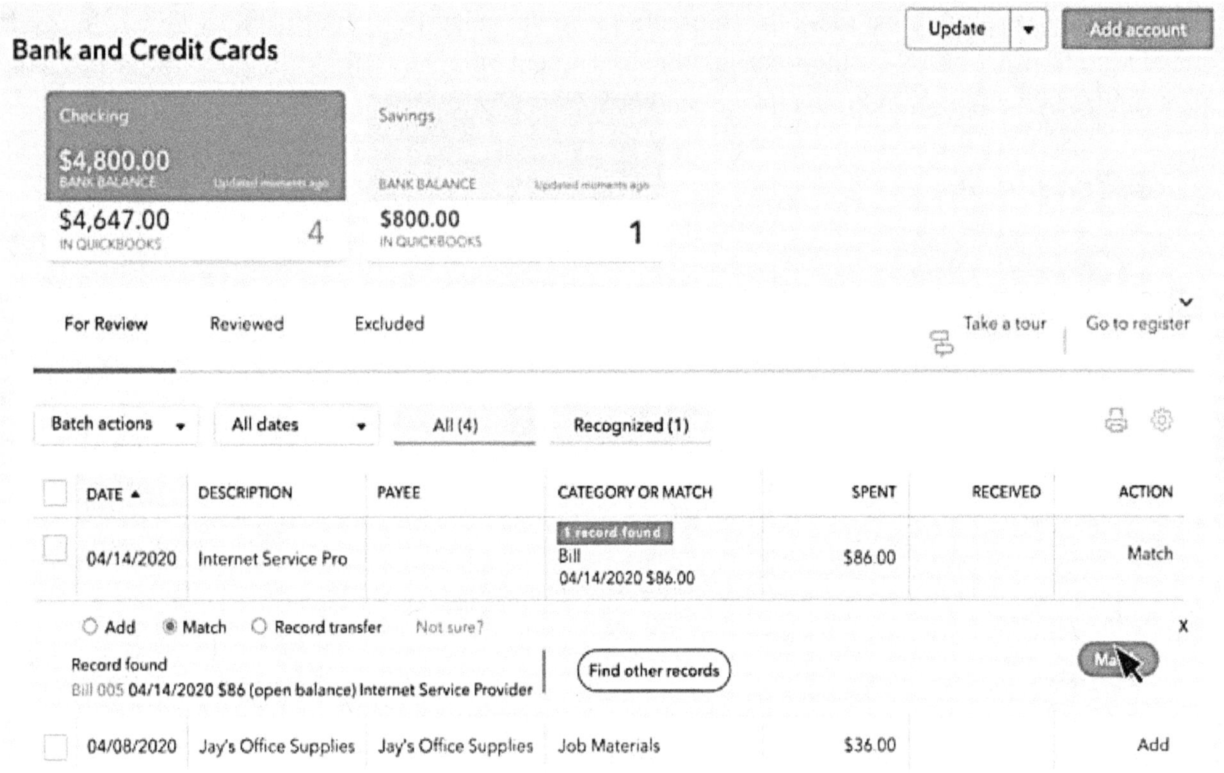

And that concludes it! You have just finished all the QuickBooks Online bill entry and payment processes.

How to Create an Item Receipt

In order to produce an item receipt in QuickBooks Desktop, you must add the relevant bills to your inventory. This allows you to conveniently record the amount due for the item receipt. To enter the bill for the item receipt, select Enter Bills against Inventory from the Homepage. When you access the Select Item Receipt screen, you may choose the vendor, enter the correct date for the invoice, choose the item receipt, and save details.

In QuickBooks Desktop, the creation of invoices against inventory is a standard A/P process. It is encouraged to review the list of vendor-related workflows and transactions.

1. To access the "Home" screen in "QuickBooks Desktop," navigate to the "Home" screen.
2. Then, choose the option to "Enter Bills against Inventory."
3. In the "Select Item Receipt" screen, choose the vendor's name from the "Vendor" drop-down menu.
4. Place a checkbox in the "Use Item receipt date for the bill date" box if the original date of inventory is being used.

5. Click on "Item Receipt" at this time. If there are multiple item receipts, ensure that each bill is converted separately.

6. Select the OK button. This turns your "Item Receipt" into an invoice.

After completing these procedures, you can proceed with bill payment. Thus, you may quickly create the item receipt against the inventory and pay the charge.

If you have previously recorded the item receipt, you can create an item receipt in QuickBooks Desktop by following these steps:

1. Select the "Vendors" button.

2. Afterwards, select "Enter Bill for Received Items". This will open a window titled "Select Item Receipt."

3. Now, choose the vendor using the drop-down menu labeled "Vendor."

4. QuickBooks will then display a list of item receipts from the chosen vendors (Merge Vendors in QuickBooks). Choose the "Item Receipt" that corresponds to your bill.

5. Select the OK button.

6. When the "Enter Bills" window opens, QuickBooks will automatically enter the details from the item receipt into the text area.

7. If the information entered by QuickBooks is incorrect, you can enter the "Date," "Bill Due," and "Amount Due" boxes manually.

8. Using the "Conditions" drop-down box, you can then examine payment terms and reference numbers to determine the vendor's reference number.

9. Add the memo description, if desired, in the "Memo" box.

10. Now, click the "Expenses" tab so that you can review the expenses represented by your bill.

11. Once complete, describe the items on the "Items" tab.

12. You can then click "Save & Close" or "Save & New" to save further bill and item receipt information.

If the item receipt has already been recorded in QuickBooks Desktop, you can enter the bills in this manner. Make sure that each field contains the correct information.

Create Sales Receipt and Deposit

Do you provide products or services to customers and receive immediate payment? Find out how to generate QuickBooks sales receipts.

1. Open Sales Receipt. Under Customers on the **Plus Sign Menu**, select Sales Receipt.

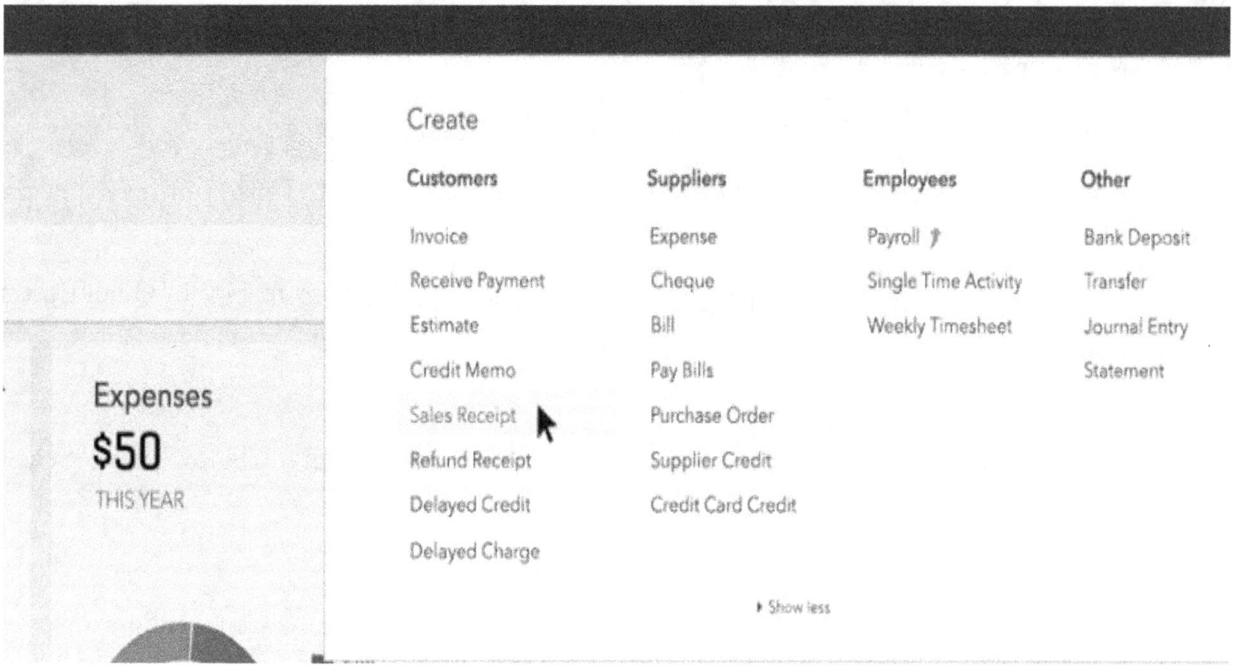

2. Enter the Name of the Customer. Enter the customer's name who is paying you. If the customer is new, click Save.

You can simply name them with a generic term like "Internet Sales."

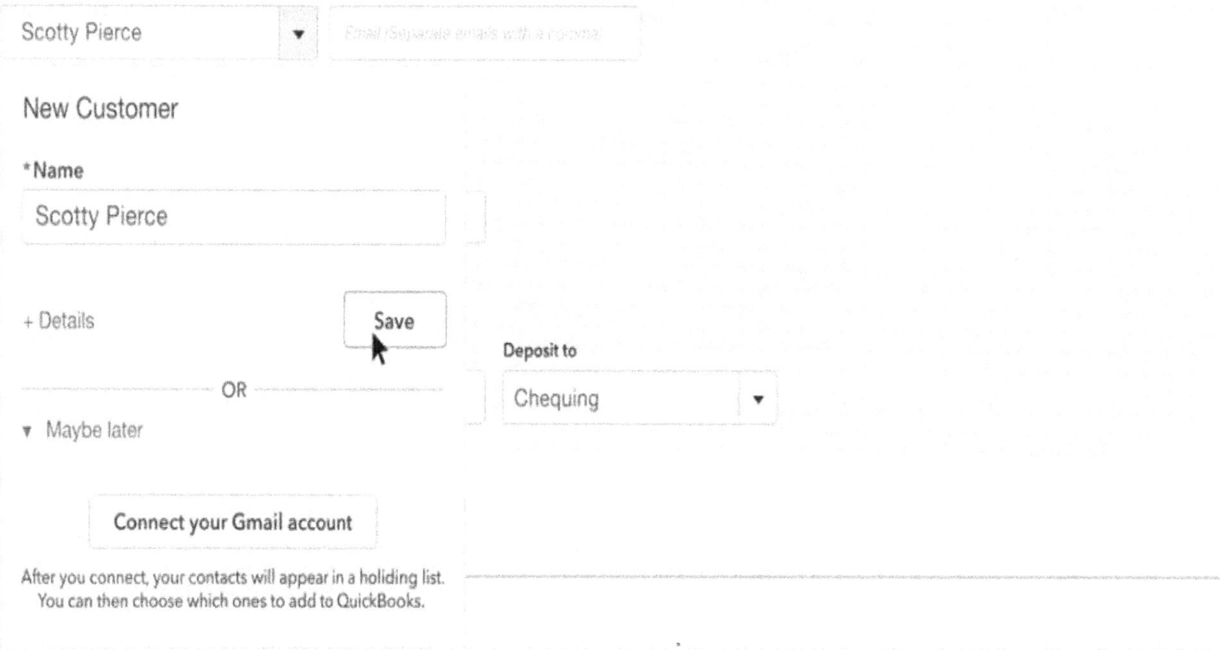

1. **Enter Goods and Services**

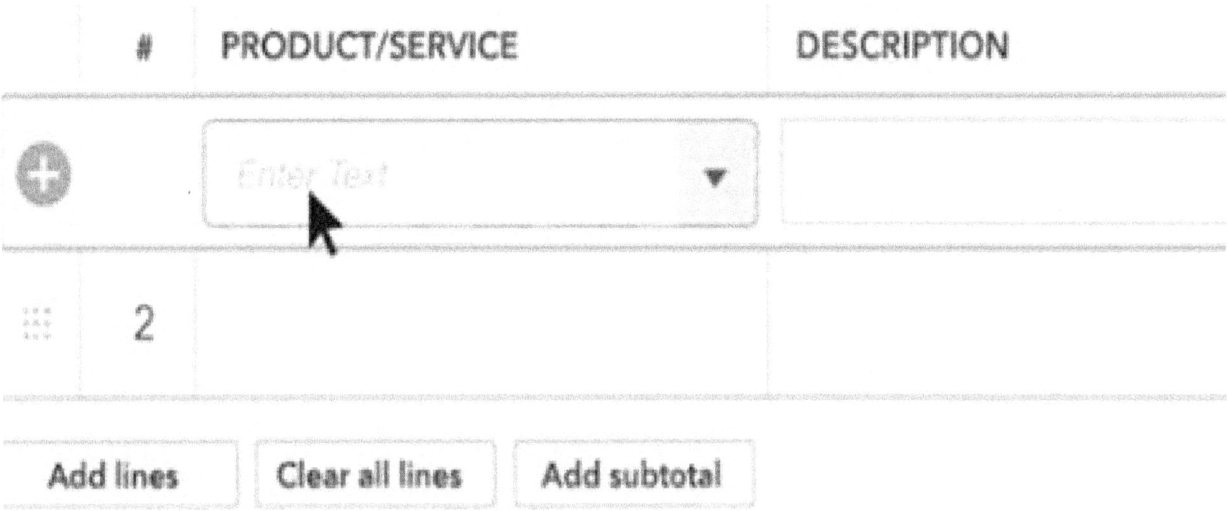

Enter the new product or service and click the Add button. Then, insert details regarding this product or service.

2. **Select a Revenue or Income Account**

Select the Income Account inside the Product or Service Information pane. This is an accounting account, not a bank account. This account grows with each sale of this goods or service. Select Save.

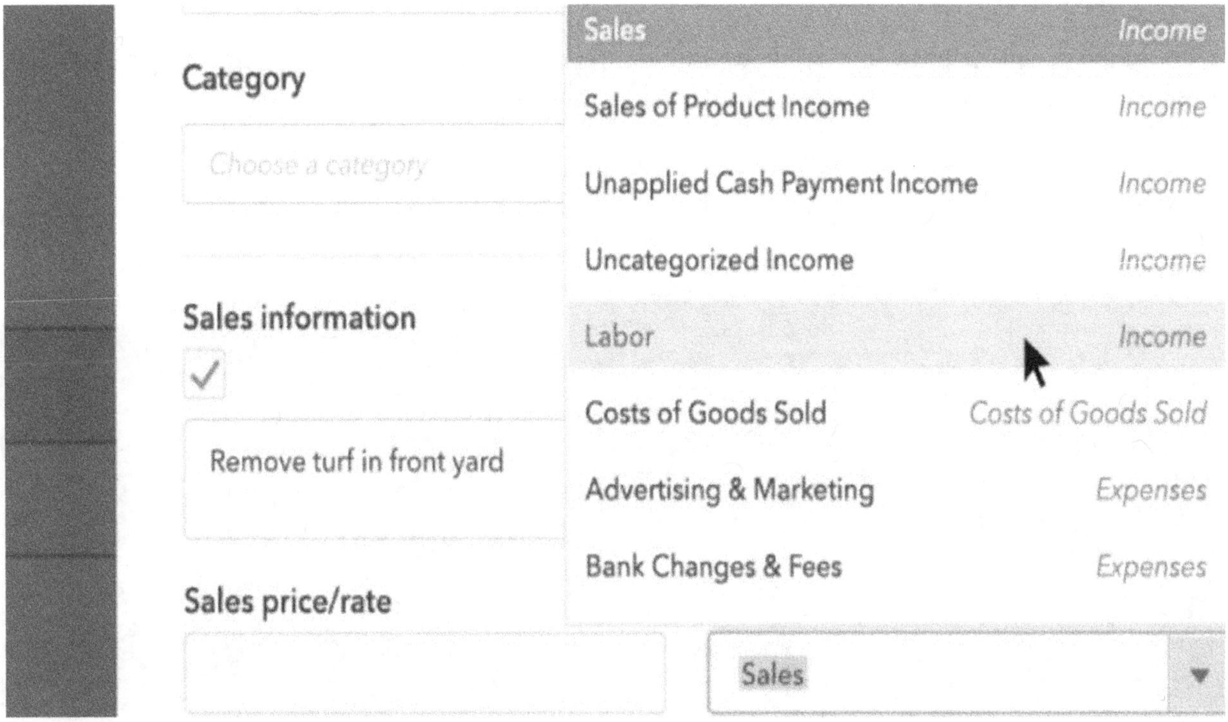

3. **Enter Payment Information**

Input the Payment Method used by the consumer to pay you. In the Reference No. field, enter the cheque number if the payment was made by check.

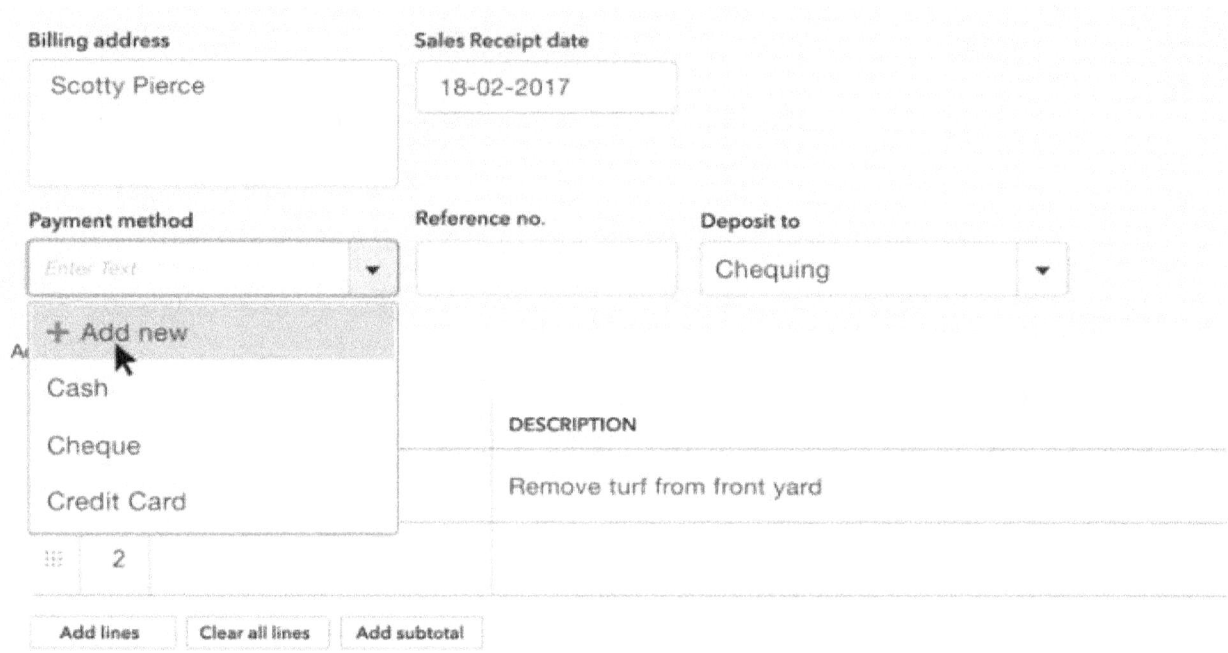

4. **Select Bank Account**

Choose the bank account you placed money into under Deposit To. If you are depositing this cheque alongside other cheques and cash, select **Undeposited Funds.**

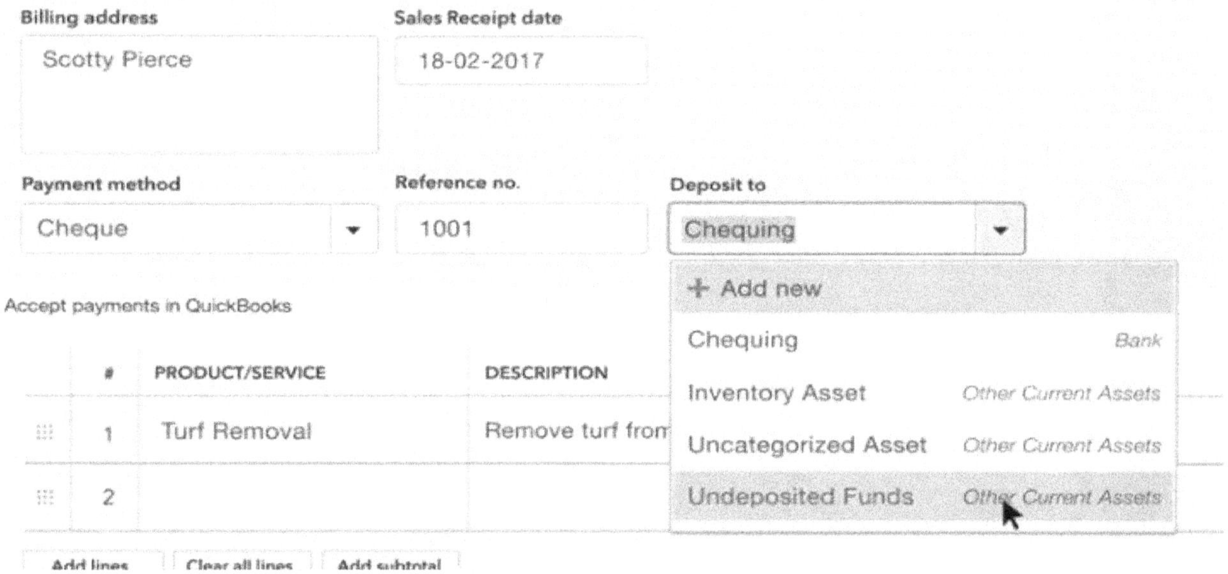

5. **Print preview and Printing**

To get a preview of the printed receipt, select Print or Preview at the bottom of the screen. If all is in order, you can print the receipt by clicking **Print** from the Print Preview.

6. **Saving for Later**

If you do not intend to print this receipt, click the arrow next to Save and submit. Select Save and then close.

7. **Document of the Deposit**

The group deposit must now be recorded in QuickBooks. Under Other on the Plus Sign Menu, select Bank Deposit.

Select the appropriate account, after which insert it under **Add New Deposits.**

How to Setup Advance Payments from Customers
Create a liability that is treated as a liability and holds the retainer or deposit. When you invoice the consumer and obtain payment, this liability will be converted into income.

This is how:

1. Navigate to Settings > Chart of Accounts.
2. Select New.
3. Select Current Liabilities from the Account Type drop-down box.
4. Select Trust Accounts - Liabilities in the Detail Type drop-down menu.
5. Provide a username for the account.
6. Click Save, then close.

Second, a non-inventory or service item must be created for the retainer. Let me guide you how:

1. Click the Sales tab, followed by Products and Services.
2. Select New.
3. Select Service from the Product/Service information screen.
4. Enter a name before selecting the Trust Liability Account in the Income account.
5. Click Save, then close.

Create a memo or invoice that will be attached to the newly created invoice. Thus, the invoice will reflect as paid. Follow the below steps:

1. Click the +**New button** at the top of the page.
2. Select the **Cash memo** or **Invoice option.**

3. Choose the Customer from the drop-down menu.
4. From the Deposit to drop-down option, pick the bank account you created for the trust responsibility.
5. Select the Retainer or Deposit item you configured in the Product/Service column.
6. Enter the amount of the retainer or deposit received.
7. Select **Save** and then close.

Setting Up PayPal

While QuickBooks can automatically integrate transactions from certain bank accounts, integrating a PayPal account to QuickBooks to track online transactions involves a bit more effort. Although automatic synchronization is not possible, it is still possible to manually export PayPal transactions into QuickBooks.

1. In your favorite web browser, access the PayPal website. Use the password and user name for your business account to log in. If you don't have a distinct PayPal account for your business, sign in using the credentials for your personal account.
2. Move the cursor over "History" on the "My Account" page to access the account history options menu. To access the download choices screen, choose the "Download History" option.
3. Click the "Last Get to Present" option if you are interested in downloading the entirety of the data that has been downloaded during your most recent download, or enter the date range from which you wish to download the data. In the event that you haven't yet downloaded data from PayPal before, the second option will download just the information from the previous week.
4. To ensure full compatibility with the QuickBooks program, select "QuickBooks (.iff)" from the "File Type for Download" drop-down option. Select "Download History" from the menu.
5. Give your PayPal account a name that QuickBooks is going to employ, as well as titles for your Other Expenses and Other Income entries. QuickBooks will use these names accordingly. The following options can be utilized for tracking items like PayPal fees and cash back payments if you have a debit card that is issued by PayPal when you make purchases. After you have finished downloading the file, you should log out of your PayPal account and then click the "Download Log" button.
6. Open QuickBooks and select the profile that you wish to utilize to monitor your transactions processed through PayPal. Within the "Customer and Vendor Profile" part of the application, you will need to establish new entries for your PayPal transactions, expenses, and other income. This is similar to how you would do it with other sorts of accounts. On the PayPal

website, check to see that the names of the three listings are identical to those used on the website.

7. Open the File menu, hover over "Utilities" to display a new submenu, then hover over "Import" and select "IFF Files." Follow these steps to import files. In order to begin the process of importing, you must first choose the IFF file that you obtained from PayPal and then click the "OK" button.

8. Once the import is complete, the QuickBooks profile must be saved. As part of the import process, your PayPal data will be automatically categorized accordingly.

Connecting Card Payments
You can link an unlimited number of corporate and personal accounts.

Note: American Express Business accounts involve several distinct procedures.

1. Go to Accounting > Transactions > Bank transactions or go to Banking.

2. If this is your first time setting up a bank account, simply select Connect account. Choose Link account if you have already created an account.

Note: If you are migrating from QuickBooks Desktop, you will be required to reconnect your bank and credit card accounts for security purposes.

1. Enter the name of your credit card, bank, or credit union in the search area. Note: If you cannot locate your bank but still wish to submit your transactions, you can personally upload them.

2. Afterwards, select **Continue.** Then, enter your username and password to access your bank account.

3. Follow the steps on-screen. This may involve security checks required by your bank. The connection could take a few minutes.

4. Choose the accounts you wish to link, then choose the account type from the drop-down menu. Choose the account type that corresponds to your QuickBooks chart of accounts.

If you do not see the appropriate account type in the drop-down menu, simply;

1. Select the number of transactions to download from the past. Some banks allow you to download the 90 most recent transactions. Others may look back up to 24 months.

2. Choose **Connect.**

Manually Adjusting Inventory

1. To adjust inventory in QuickBooks Desktop, access the "Adjust Quantity/Value on Hand" box by selecting "Vendors > Inventory Activities > Adjust Quantity > Value on Hand" from the Menu Bar.
2. From the "Change Type" drop-down box, choose the type of inventory adjustment to perform. You can modify the "Quantity", "Total Value", or both the "Quantity" and "Total Value" fields.
3. The adjustment date must then be entered in the "Adjustment Date" box.
4. Choose the account that will be affected by the adjustment from the "Adjustment Account" drop-down option.
5. Insert an adjustment reference number in the "Reference No." area on the right.
6. If necessary, you can also assign a "Customer:Job" or "Class" to the transaction.
7. Enter the explanation for the inventory adjustment in the "Memo" area at the bottom of the form.
8. Then, on the first available row, choose the "Item" column.
9. Choose the first item to be modified from the drop-down menu that appears.
10. To create a "Quantity" adjustment, enter either the "New Quantity" or the "Quantity Difference" in the appropriate column.
11. If you submit a loss in the "Qty Difference" column, be careful to enter a negative amount!
12. To make an adjustment to "Total Amount," put the new total value in the "New Value" column.
13. After making inventory adjustments in QuickBooks Desktop, select "Save & Close" to complete the process.

Basic Sales

How to Create an Invoice or Sales Receipt

If you utilize QuickBooks Payments, this is how to handle consumer credit card payments.

1. Choose + **New**.
2. Select **Sales receipt**
3. Choose the customer from the dropdown menu Customer.

Note: If you have not yet created the customer in QuickBooks, click **Add a new customer.**

1. Enter the sales information, like the method of payment.
2. Enter the products and services you sold as line items.
3. Select **Save** and submit to email the receipt when you're finished.

How to Find Transactions

1. To locate transactions in QuickBooks Desktop, access the form window corresponding with the type of form you wish to locate.
2. Then, from the Menu Bar, click "Edit| Find [form type]...", where [form type] is the title of the form type for which you are searching.
3. Click the "Find" button on the "Main" tab of the Ribbon located at the top of the form.
4. In the resulting "Find [form type]" window, input the value or values by which you wish to locate the transaction.
5. Then, click the "Find" button to display the matching form or, if there are numerous matches, to open the result set in a "Find" window.
6. For multiple matches, double-click the desired item within the list of results to open it.

How to Apply Credit to Invoices

Apply this credit memo to the invoices that you intend to write off.

1. Select **+New** in the upper left corner.
2. From the list of options, simply select **Receive payment**
3. Fill out the form for payment:
4. Name of Customer
5. Date
6. Check the boxes to the left of the bills you intend to write off, and the payment box will populate with the amount ($) corresponding to the invoice's open balance.
7. In the credit memo section, the credit note must be ticked, and the amount ($$) in the payment box must match the amount in the open balance column.
8. Check that the number in bold in the upper right corner is $0.
9. Close and save

Recording Sale on Account

You do not need to record sales receipts or purchases for your expenses and revenues because you do not utilize QuickBooks to track your inventory. To keep track of your income and expenses, you may utilize diary entries. I'll guide you how.

1. Create an account for QuickBooks Online (QBO).
2. Click the + **New icon,** then the **Journal entry option** under Other.
3. Complete the required fields before saving the transaction.

A professional accountant might be consulted for precise accounting. They are the only ones who can provide you with strategic assistance about the management of journal entries and financial records.

Printing Sales Receipts

You can print customer receipts using QuickBooks by producing a sales receipt for cash, cheque, or credit card. You can print sales receipts from the Print Forms menu or after completing their creation. Upon the approval of a credit card transaction using a Merchant Service in conjunction with a receipt printer and POS system, you have the option to utilize the processed payment receipt window. Credit card transactions are automatically displayed in the window for processed payments.

1. Create Sales Receipts. Choose "Enter Sales Receipts" from the "Customers" option.
2. Leave the Customer. Unless you wish to track client payments, Job field blank. Choose a customer from a list of existing clients, or create a new customer and enter the relevant information.
3. Select an invoice template by clicking the "Templates" drop-down menu. Modify the form as necessary and then click "Print Preview."
4. Verify the Date, Invoice or Sale Number, Bill To or Sold To, and Terms fields in the upper portion of the sales form.
5. Click a line within the Detail section. Choose the item from the drop-down menu and input the quantity in the Qty column.
6. Select the Payment Method drop-down menu and choose a method for making a deposit. Choose from Cash, Check, or Credit Card.
7. To print your sales receipt, select "Print" and then "Print" again. To save the receipt, choose the "Save & Close" button on the form window.

Team: Employee and Payroll Management

How to Set Up Payroll in QuickBooks

If you already use QuickBooks Online and need to pay staff, consider adding QuickBooks Payroll to your membership package. It is accessible from the same system that you use to handle your company's books, allowing for the smooth transfer of payroll costs to the relevant general ledger accounts.

Setting up employee payroll in QuickBooks is simple; employees can not only view and download their pay stubs, but they can also enter their own information.

All that is required is to send them an email inviting them to log in and enter information about the activity they have completed or the workforce before they are set up in QuickBooks.

Below are the steps to set up Payrolls:

1. Log in to QuickBooks Online.
2. From the left menu bar, click Payroll, then Overview.

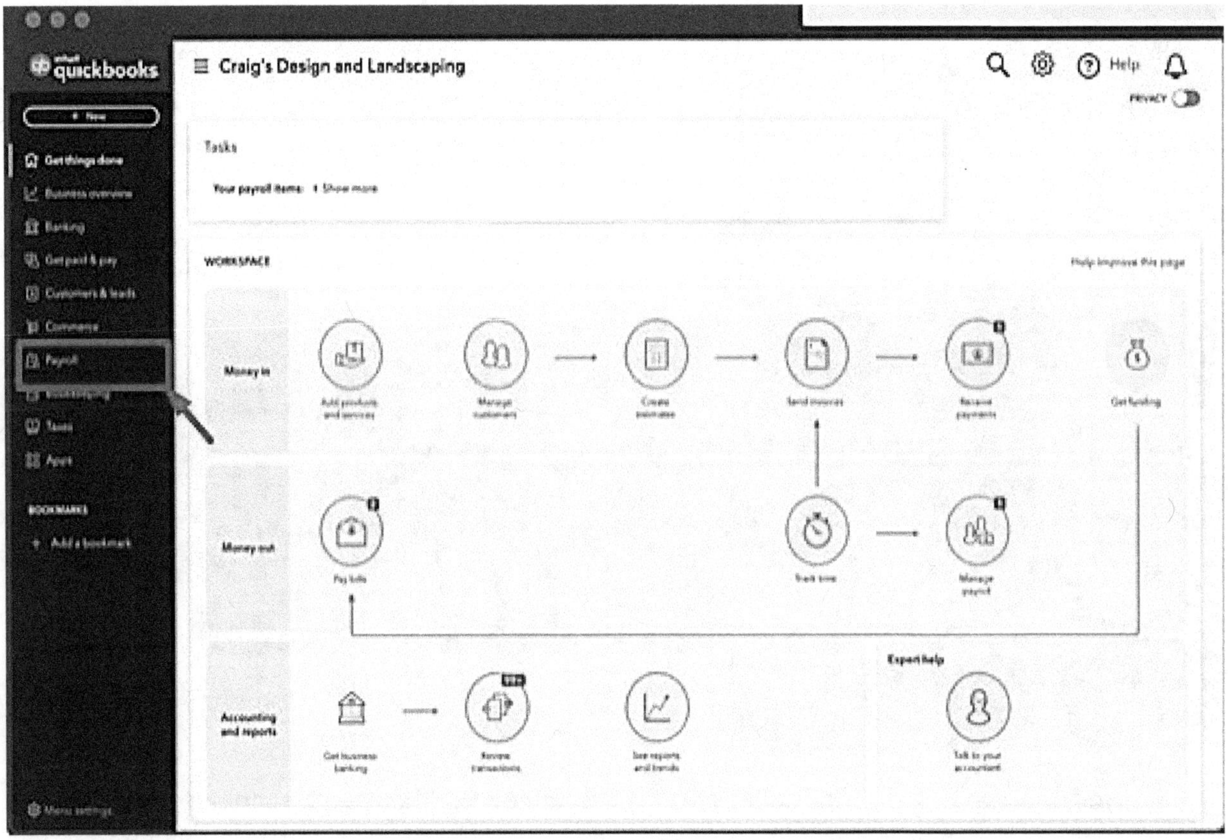

3. If this is your first time setting up payroll, the Get Started option will show; click on it.
4. Fill in the needed information by following the on-screen directions.

- The date of your next paycheck (or the date you want to begin paying your team in QuickBooks)
- The actual location where all or the majority of your workers work
- The name, email address, and phone number of the payroll contact. This is the primary person in charge of paying your team.

5. After you have completed the Business information section, you may begin adding your first employee.

How to Add Employees

Gathering basic information on your workers, like their name, pay info, direct deposit info, date of birth, and current contact information etc., is necessary before you begin.

1. Select Payroll from the menu on the left, then click Employees.
2. Click Add an employee.

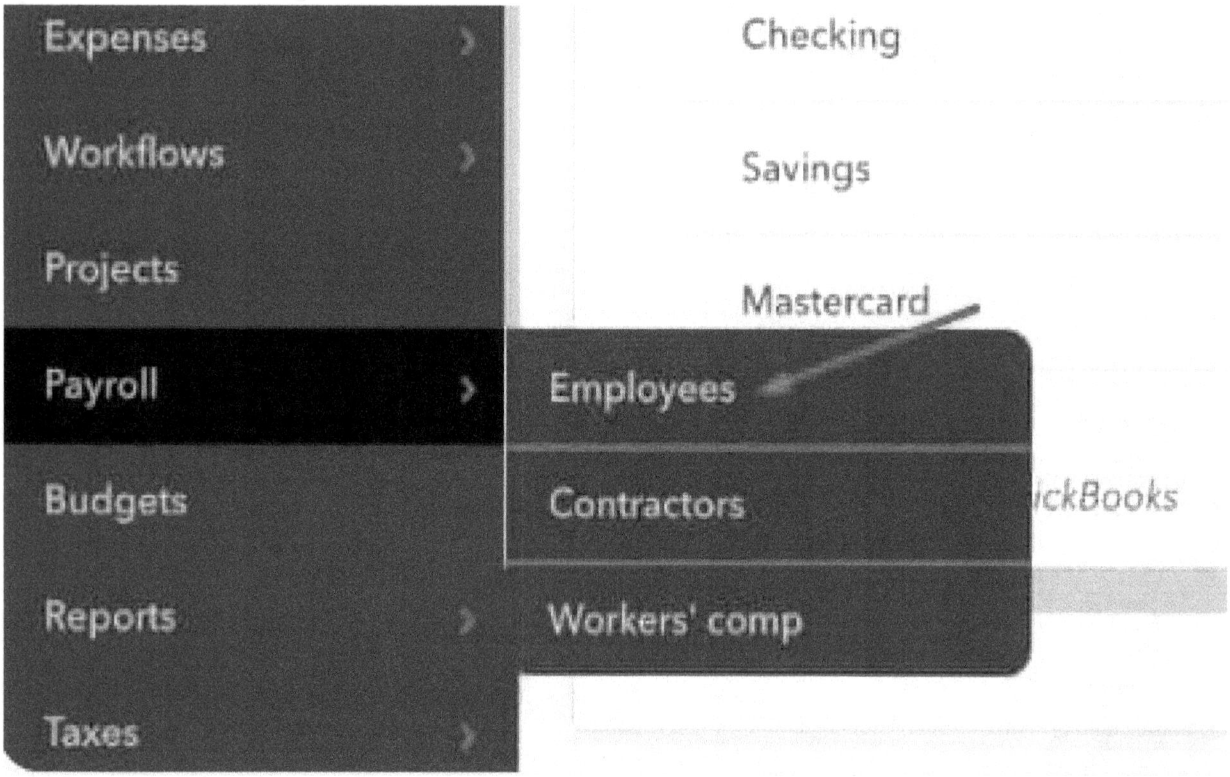

3. Add the name and email address of your employee. Make sure Employee self-setup is enabled if you want them to submit their own personal, tax, and banking information.

QuickBooks will send them an invitation to QuickBooks Workforce automatically. Your employee may provide their address, SSN, W-4, and banking information.

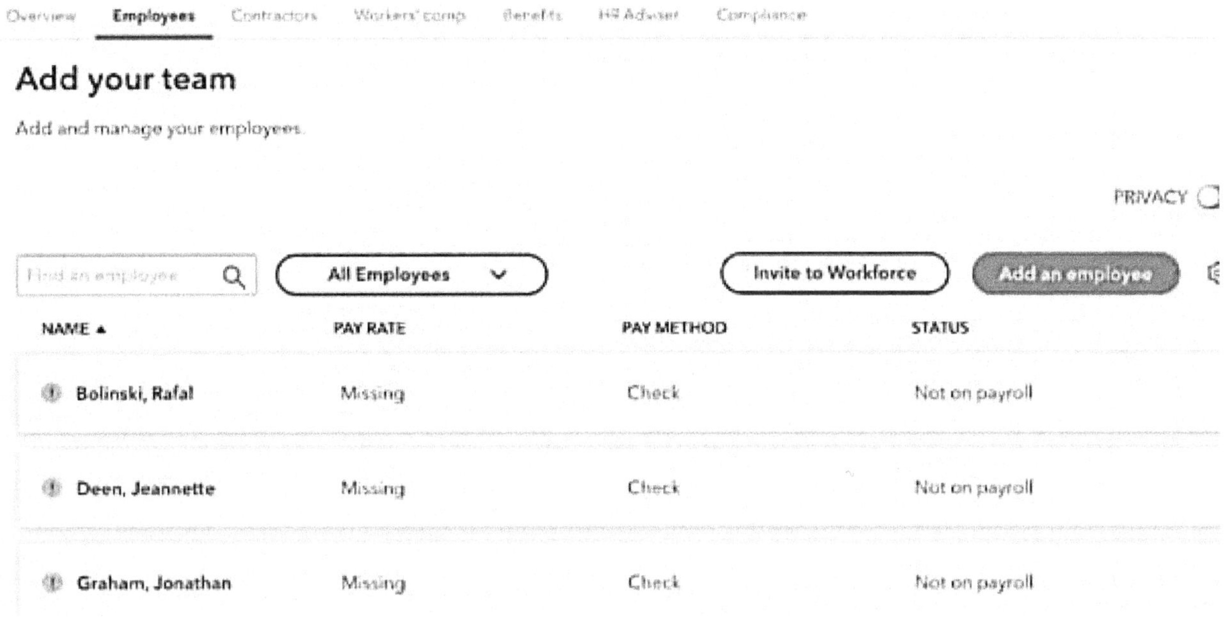

4. Once all of the information has been entered, click Add employee.
5. Select any box to enter the remaining personnel information.

- You will not be able to alter some data on the Personal details, Tax withholding, or Payment method cards if employee self-setup is enabled. If you wish to change those tabs, go to Personal Info and uncheck Employee self-setup.

6. When you're finished adding information to a tab, click Save.

How to Process a Pay Run

After you've finished configuring payroll in QuickBooks, you may begin processing your first pay run. Now comes the exciting part: paying your employees! A pay run only needs to be set once for the date part, after which all subsequent pay runs will be moved to the next pay date period.

1. Go to the main payroll screen and click *Run Pay Roll.*

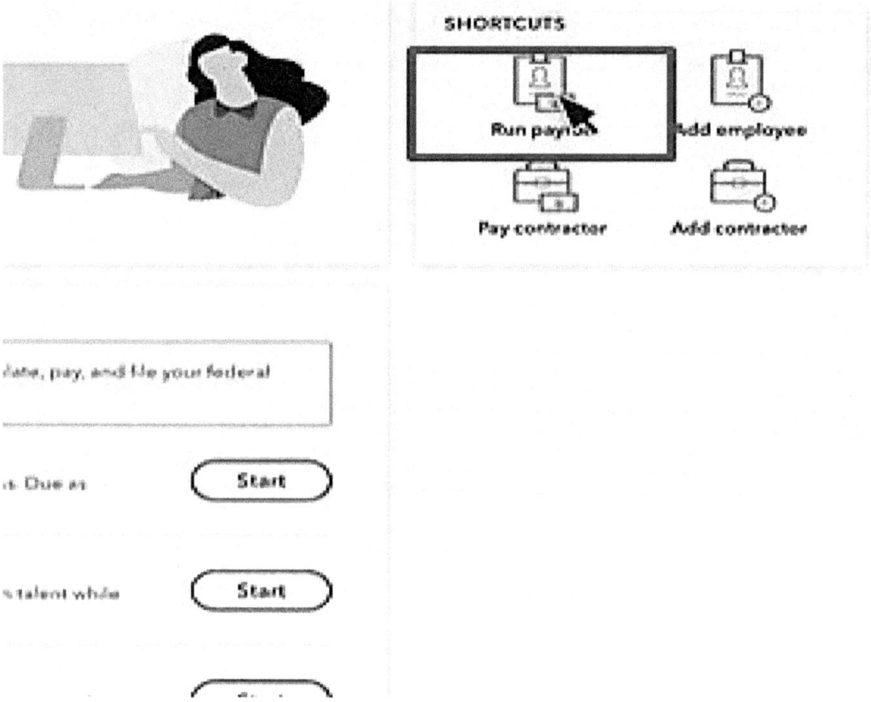

2. Once you open the pay run screen, select *Pay Schedule*. Input the date for the pay period ending and when the pay run is paid, then click *Create*.

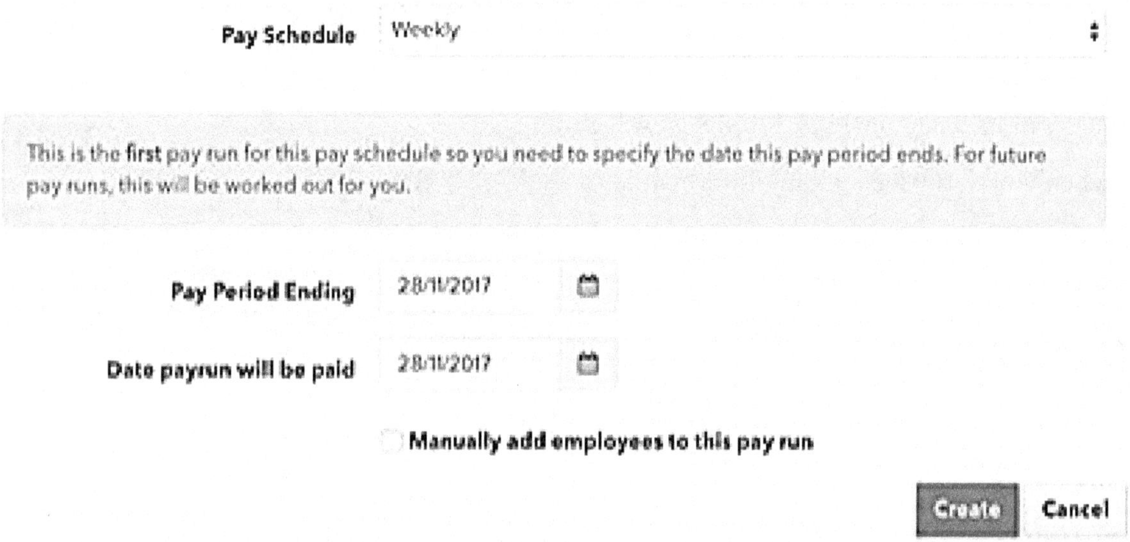

3. The next screen displays a summary of all employees in that run, including tax and their salaries or earnings. By clicking on the individual employee, you can view more information about them.

1 - 8 of 8 total employees.

	TOTAL HOURS	GROSS EARNINGS	PRE-TAX DEDUCTIONS	TAXABLE EARNINGS	POST-TAX DEDUCTIONS	WITHHELD AMOUNTS PAYG	SFSS	HELP	SUPER CONTRIBUTIONS SGC	EC	EXPENSES	EMPLOYER LIABILITIES	NET EARNINGS
> Arthur Authurson	38.00	$1,442.31	$0.00	$1,442.31	$0.00	$336.00	$0.00	$79.00	$137.02	$0.00	$0.00	$0.00	$1,027.31
> Felix Pickles	20.00	$599.50	$0.00	$599.50	$0.00	$59.00	$0.00	$0.00	$56.95	$0.00	$0.00	$0.00	$540.50
> Howard Finkle	28.00	$745.00	$0.00	$745.00	$0.00	$94.00	$0.00	$0.00	$70.78	$0.00	$0.00	$0.00	$651.00
> Jane Mills	28.00	$931.25	$0.00	$931.25	$0.00	$159.00	$0.00	$0.00	$88.47	$0.00	$0.00	$0.00	$772.25
> John Mills	37.00	$1,167.25	$0.00	$1,167.25	$0.00	$241.00	$0.00	$0.00	$110.89	$0.00	$0.00	$0.00	$926.25
> Mario Belic	38.00	$1,250.00	$0.00	$1,250.00	$0.00	$270.00	$0.00	$56.00	$118.75	$0.00	$0.00	$0.00	$924.00
> Ron Burgundy	38.00	$1,634.62	$0.00	$1,634.62	$0.00	$402.00	$0.00	$106.00	$155.29	$0.00	$0.00	$0.00	$1,126.62
> Sandy Stevens	38.00	$1,826.92	$0.00	$1,826.92	$0.00	$475.00	$0.00	$128.00	$173.56	$0.00	$0.00	$0.00	$1,223.92

4. The action button is important because it allows you to make additional selections to correct or amend the employee pay run.

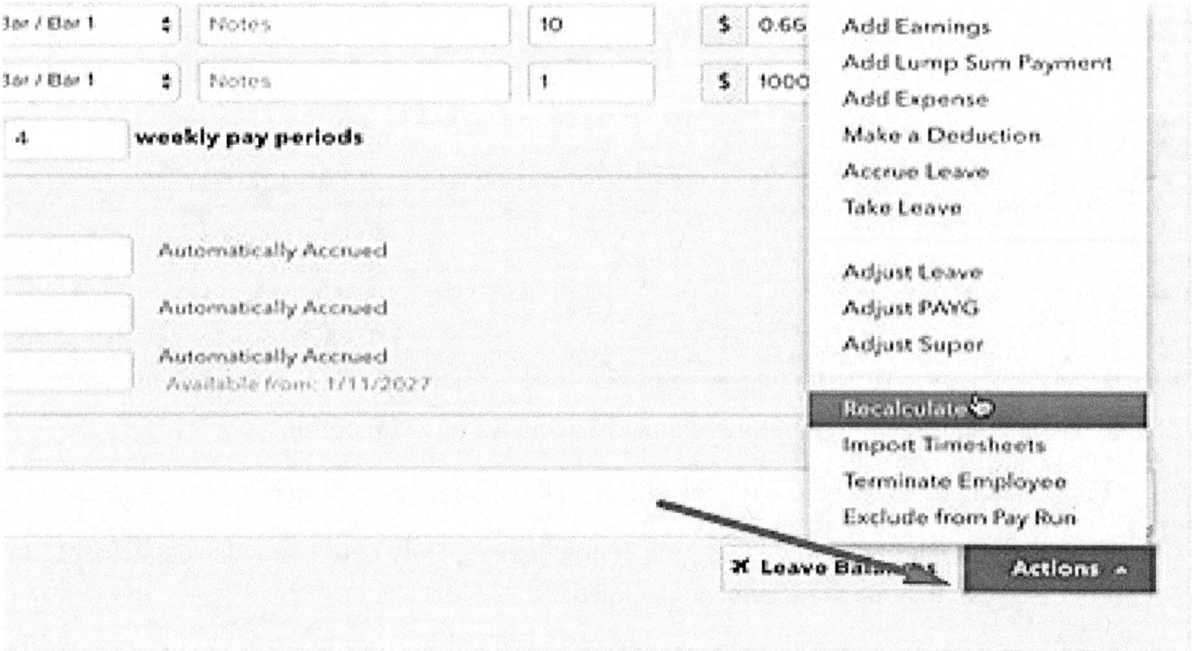

5. Check that you have chosen the right bank account, pay month, and pay date. You can also make changes as needed.
6. Change the employee's pay method as appropriate.
7. If relevant, enter the number of hours worked. TIP: To hide or reveal pay types, click the Settings button below the TOTAL PAY.
8. Select Payroll Preview.
9. After filling in the information needed, click *Save* and note any prompt alerts for an action.
10. To amend or preview a specific cheque, click the Edit icon next to the net pay, then click OK when finished.
11. To finish the pay run, click on *Finalize Pay Run* and verify that the date paid is correct, then click *Finalize*.

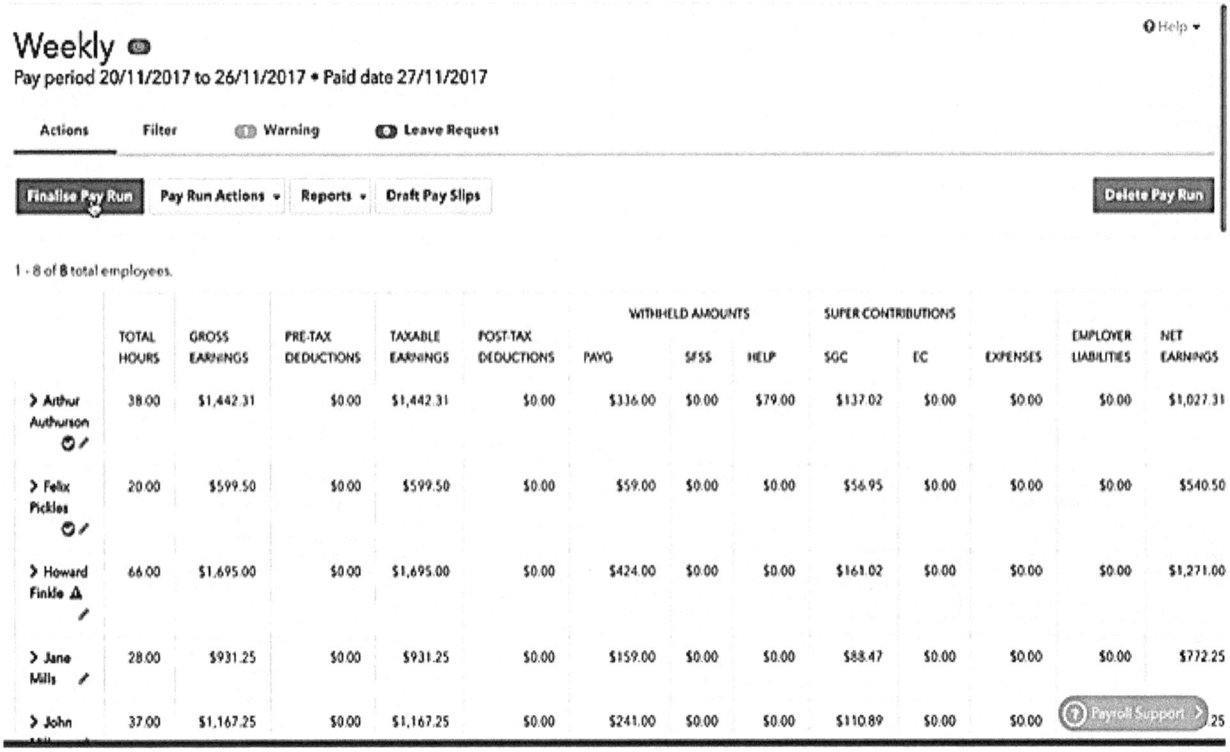

Help
Weekly
Pay period 20/11/2017 to 26/11/2017 • Paid date 27/11/2017
Actions
Filter
Warning
Leave Request
Finalise Pay Run
Pay Run Actions
Reports
Draft Pay Slips
Delete Pay Run
1 - 8 of 8 total employees.
TOTAL HOURS
GROSS EARNINGS
PRE-TAX DEDUCTIONS
TAXABLE EARNINGS
POST-TAX DEDUCTIONS
WITHHELD AMOUNTS
PAYG
SFSS
HELP
SUPER CONTRIBUTIONS
SGC
EC
EXPENSES
EMPLOYER LIABILITIES
NET EARNINGS
Arthur Authurson 38.00 $1,442.31 $0.00 $1,442.31 $0.00 $336.00 $0.00 $79.00 $137.02 $0.00 $0.00 $0.00 $1,027.31
Felix Pickles 20.00 $599.50 $0.00 $599.50 $0.00 $59.00 $0.00 $0.00 $56.95 $0.00 $0.00 $0.00 $540.50
Howard Finkle 66.00 $1,695.00 $0.00 $1,695.00 $0.00 $424.00 $0.00 $0.00 $161.02 $0.00 $0.00 $0.00 $1,271.00
Jane Mills 28.00 $931.25 $0.00 $931.25 $0.00 $159.00 $0.00 $0.00 $88.47 $0.00 $0.00 $0.00 $772.25
John 37.00 $1,167.25 $0.00 $1,167.25 $0.00 $241.00 $0.00 $0.00 $110.89 $0.00 $0.00
Payroll Support

12. Pay slips can be sent to employees quickly using the pay slip option.
13. You're ready to go! Select Print pay cheques, then Finish payroll to print pay cheques.
14. After it has been finalized, the pay run is now locked. Only before any bank statements are processed can they be unlocked and changed.

15. Once the pay run is complete, download the files that will be uploaded to the bank, run any payroll reports, and send pay slips.

How to Create Timesheets, Leave, and Expenses for Employees

Creating Employee's Timesheets
Employees who are required to use timesheets will be able to view, create, and delete timesheets on their own from within the Work Zone app.

Employees must use timesheets in the employee details, Pay Run defaults page, Payroll Settings, and Employee Portal Settings if they want to access timesheets in Work Zone. To create a timesheet and enter leave:

1. Select the timesheet icon on the bottom of the screen.
2. Tap the timesheet area on the homepage.
3. Click on *Employees.*
4. Click on the *Manage Employees* tab.
5. Select *Create a Timesheet.*
6. Select the employee's name and choose the week.
7. Select the *Work Time*. Put the start time, end time, break taken, and their location.
8. Click *Save.*
9. Click *Manage Employees.*
10. Select *Create Request* and choose the employee.
11. Select *Leave Category* and enter the period the employee will be on leave on the first and last days of the leave. The system will calculate and estimate the number of required leave days.
12. Click on *Approve Immediately*.

Creating Expenses for Employees

1. Click on Manage Employees.
2. Click on Create Expense Request.
3. Select the employee and the description of the expense being paid for
4. Input the expense date, the category, and the location. You can add a note choosing the tax code and the amount of the expense.

5. You can add an attachment that can be in the form of a pdf.
6. You can click on approve immediately or leave it empty and click on Create.
7. Now your expense request will reflect on the next payroll.

How Employees Can Self-Service

If an employer grants access to the portal, the employee will be instructed to activate their account and log in.

The following steps are for the employee to activate their account:

1. To begin, open the email inbox associated with the email address that you provided to your employer.
2. Find and open the email with the subject line "Login Information for Your Company Payroll."
3. To create a password, click on the link in the email you received.
4. Return to your email inbox and locate the email with the subject line "User Account Created."
5. In this email, you will be provided with the username for your portal account. This is the username for which you have created a password.
6. Click the email link that directs to the employee dashboard, which will take you to the login page.
7. To access the self-service portal, log into the portal using the password and the username
8. You now have access to the self-service portal. It's recommended that you bookmark the login page for easy access to the portal in the future.

How to Reset Your Password

If you have forgotten your password for the ESS Portal, follow the steps below to reset it.

1. Go to the Employee Self-Service Portal and log in.
2. Select *Forgotten Password* on the login page.
3. Enter your email address and select *Recover Password.*
4. A reset prompt will be sent to the email address provided during the signup.
5. Open the email and choose the link to reset your password.
6. Create a new password and enter it a second time to confirm the password.
7. Select *Set Password.*

8. Select the link to log back into the portal.

9. Enter your email and new password to log in.

The Work Zone App for Employees

Work Zone integrates with QuickBooks payroll, allowing employees to access self-service on their Android or iOS device.

Setting the Work Zone App for Employees

1. Download Work Zone from the Google Play Store on Android or the App Store on iOS.

2. Enter the email address and password to log in to access your employee service portal.

3. Create a pin that you will use each time you open the app.

Getting Around the Work Zone

To access the menu, click the hamburger icon. You can do a variety of things from here, including:

1. Logging out of the app.

2. Viewing login settings in the gear button.

3. Viewing your own personal payroll details on employees list.

4. View the business access.

Contents on the Home Screen

- Any content which requires employee acknowledgment
- Leave balances
- The last pay slips
- Timesheet
- Expense summary
- Next shift time

Contents in the Profile Icon

- Employee details
- Bank account
- Payment summaries
- Super funds
- Leave
- Emergency contacts
- Other documents

If you log out of the app, you will be prompted to enter your email address, password, and PIN to re-enter it. If you exit the app and return later, you will only need to enter your PIN.

Enabling Work Zone

This feature is not enabled by default. You will enable it in the business portal so that employees can use it from their smartphones. You must navigate to *Payroll Settings* and then *Employee Portal Settings*.

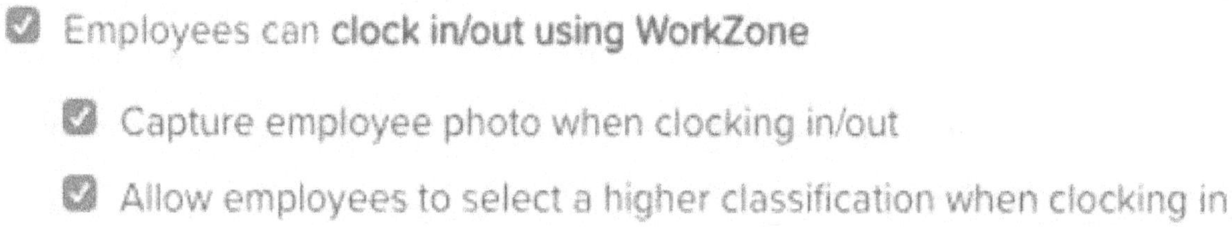

Employees can clock in/out using WorkZone
Capture employee photo when clocking in/out
Allow employees to select a higher classification when clocking in

The first step is to check the box next to "Employees can clock in/out using WorkZone."

The sub-settings in the picture below the first step are optional, but clearly affect the employee process when clocking in and out. After that send reminder emails to employees.

Generating Financial Reports

Profit & Loss/Income Statement

How to Navigate to Profit and Loss
To generate a new P&L report, select Reports from the menu on the left. Launch the Business overview group and tap on Profit and Loss.

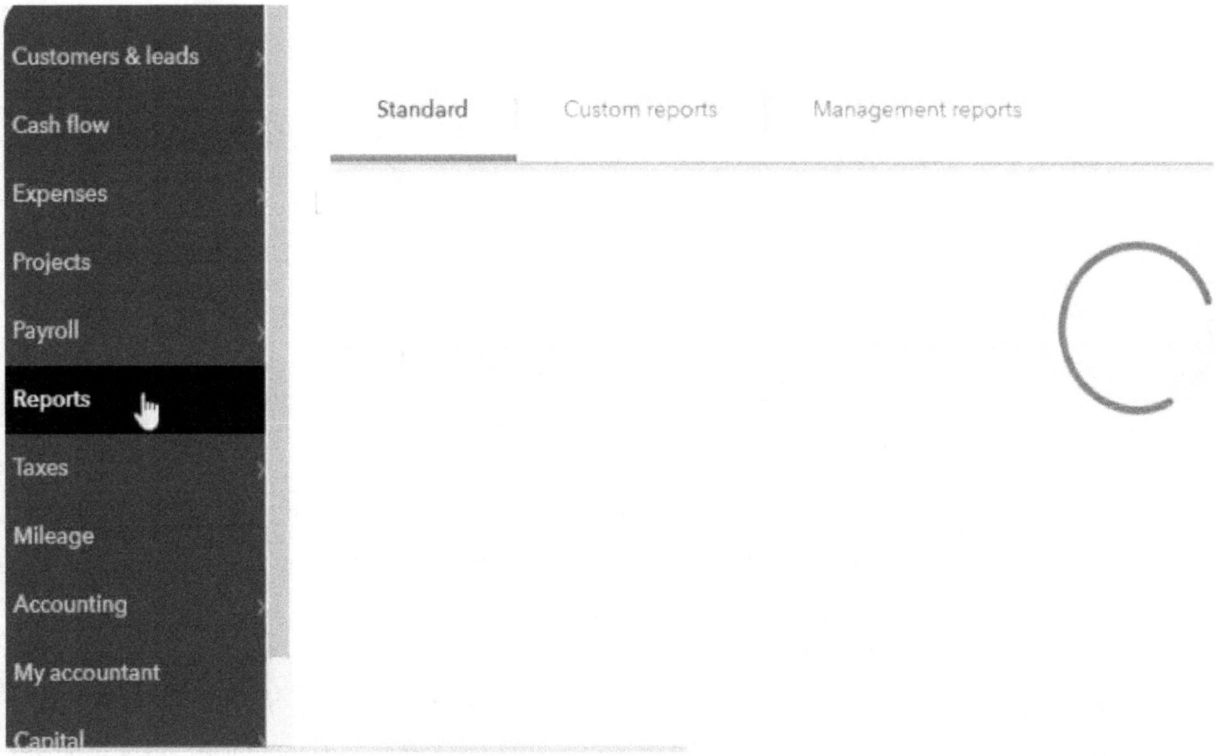

Profit and loss can be added to your favorite reports for quick access by clicking the star icon next to them. Then, it will be immediately accessible in the Favorites group, which will appear at the top when you select Reports.

How to setup Basic Options for the Profit and Loss Report

1. Scroll towards the top of the Profit and Loss Report page to access the menu bar containing the report's basic options.

Set up basic options for the QuickBooks Profit and Loss report

2. Choose from the following report choices.

- **Reporting period**: Tell us how long you want to track your income and expenses for. You can either select a predefined period from the drop-down menu or input the start and end dates for a custom period.
- **Display columns by**: By default, the Profit and Loss report from QuickBooks simply displays a single column for the period total. Click the drop-down menu to select which subtotal columns to display. You can show subtotals for many categories, including time periods, consumers, vendors, courses, and places.
- **Show only non-zero or active values**: This option allows you to specify which rows or columns to include in the report. By default, only rows and columns with activity during the period are displayed. You have the option of selecting rows or columns containing all data, only active data, or simply zeros.
- **Compare to a different period**: You can compare your profit and loss statement to a different period, like the previous year or year-to-date (YTD).
- **Accounting Method**: Select whether the Profit and Loss Report is to be prepared on a cash or accrual basis. Accounts payable (A/P) are expenses in accrual accounting, while accounts receivable (A/R) are revenue.
- **Run report**: Click this button to save your modifications.

- **Customize**: Click this button if you want to further customize your report.
- **Save Customization**: Select this option and give your report a name if you've made numerous changes that you'll need to reproduce regularly. You will be able to select this customized report from the Reports menu in the future.

Note that your modifications will not be reflected until you click "Run report".

Customizing profit and loss/income Report

To enhance the customization of the Profit and Loss report, click the Customize button in conjunction with the basic options chosen at the top of the page. The following sections are included in the Customize report window:

General

The first section of the customize report menu consists of general settings.

General report options in QuickBooks Online

In addition to defining the reporting period and accounting technique, you may also format the numbers. You can 1) enter quantities in thousands of dollars by selecting Divide by 1000, 2) suppress cents, or 3) omit zero sums. By using the Negative Numbers drop-down menu, you can select a format for showing negative numbers.

Rows/Columns

In the Rows/Columns section, you may select columns to include in your Profit and Loss report and adjust their order.

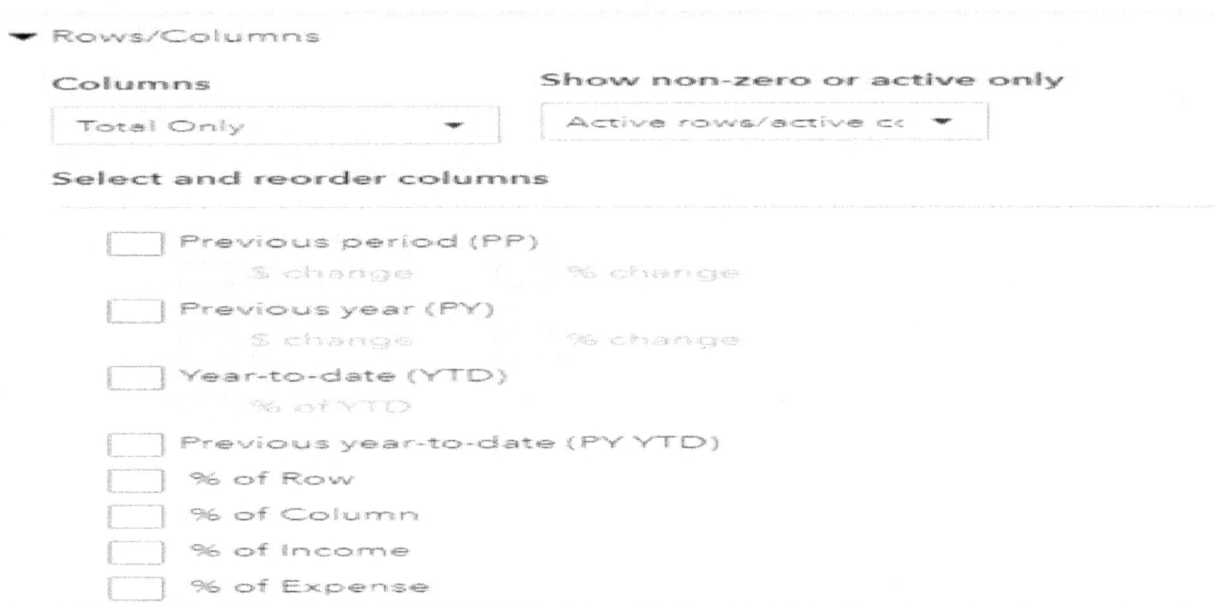

Row/columns report options in QuickBooks Online

Filter

These choices permit you to filter the report using the seven factors listed below.

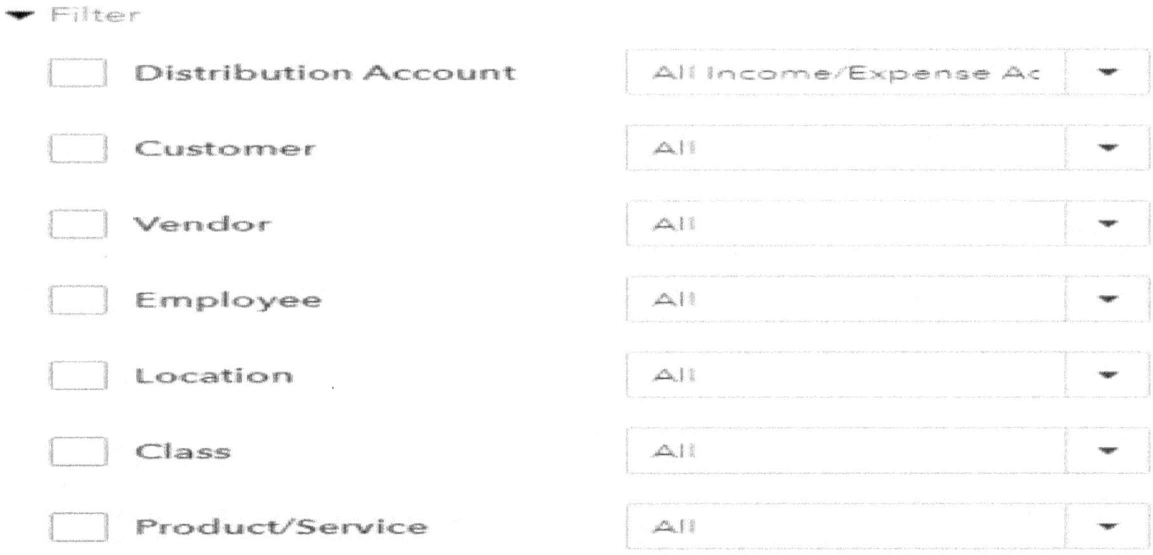

Filter reports by variables in QuickBooks Online

If you track income and expenses by class or location, you will likely wish to filter reports by these variables.

Header/Footer

In the final group of customization options, you can choose the information to display in the report's header and footer.

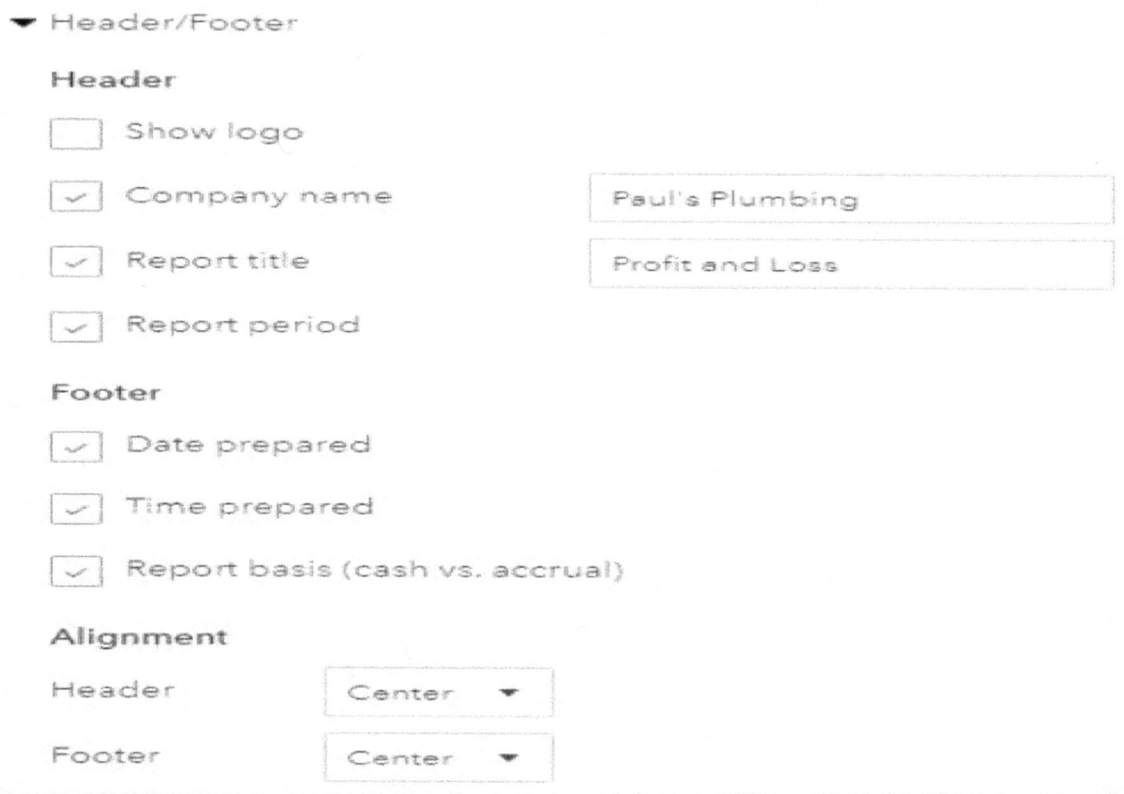

Header and footer report options in QuickBooks Online

By removing the checkmark next to a line's name, you can eliminate it from the report. In addition, you may modify the company and report names that show in the header by entering the desired content in the corresponding areas. If you upload a logo while setting up your company, you can choose the "Show logo" checkbox to display it in the P&L report's header.

When you are through designing your P&L report, click the "Run Report" button located at the bottom of the list of customization options.

Print, Email, and Export your Profit and Loss Report
Using the icons in the top right corner of the Profit and Loss report, you can print, email, or export the information as needed.

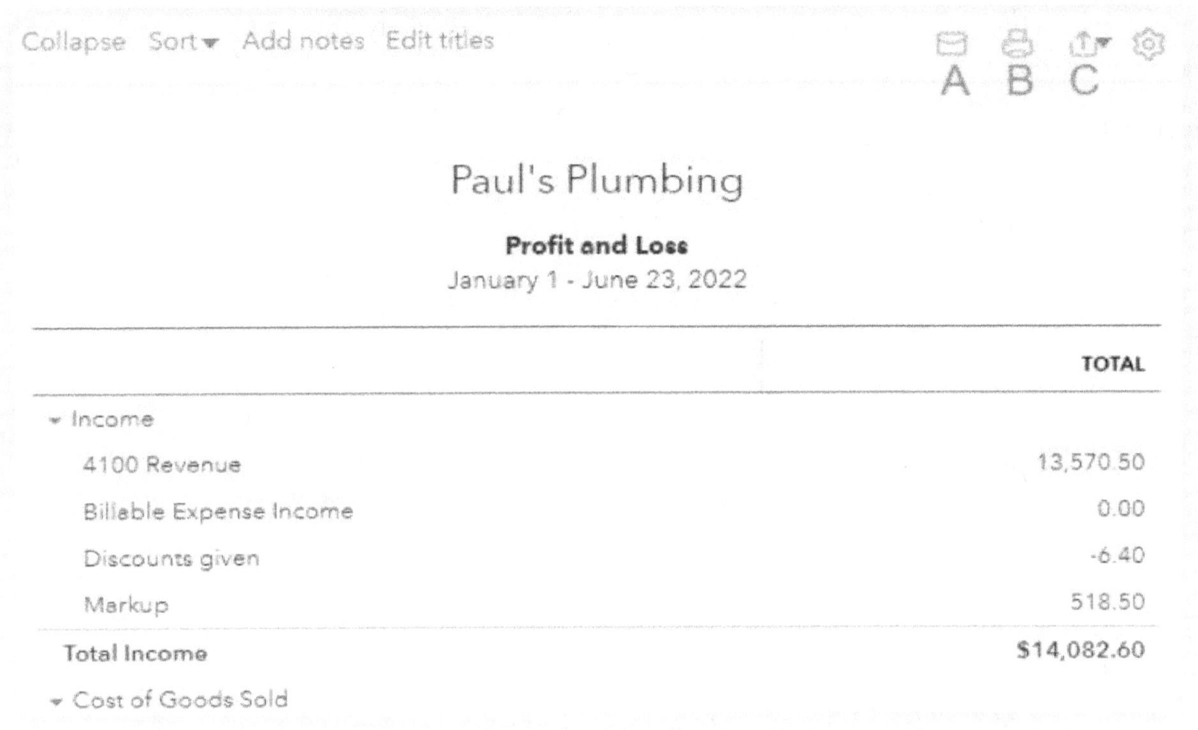

Collapse Sort Add notes Edit titles
A B C
Paul's Plumbing
Profit and Loss
January 1 - June 23, 2022
TOTAL
Income
4100 Revenue 13,570.50
Billable Expense Income 0.00
Discounts given -6.40
Markup 518.50
Total Income $14,082.60
Cost of Goods Sold

Email, print, or export your report in QuickBooks Online

1. Click the mail icon to send a PDF version of your report through email.
2. Choose the printer icon to print your report.
3. Click the arrow next to the export icon to export the report as a PDF or Excel file.

Reports and Graphs

How to Create a Graph

You can generate graphs for your sales, business and financial data, payables, and budgets. This is how.

1. From the Reports menu, choose the graph type you wish to create.
2. You may select from predetermined dates or enter your own.

Showing Your Reports as A Graph

Using QuickBooks Online to manage your business is a fantastic way to save time and effort on bookkeeping. The intuitive layout makes it simple to review your financial data, and it is essential that you make the most of the program's features.

The Dashboard is the principal location for reviewing report information in graph format. This is the homepage that appears when you log in to your account. Graphs will represent your bills, expenses, profit and loss, and sales data on the dashboard.

The other location where you can view information in graph format is the reporting center. The Business Snapshot report can be accessed by clicking the Reports option on the left navigation menu, then clicking the Business Snapshot report. This report will include graphs depicting the following data:

- My Revenue
- My Expenses
- The previous year's income comparison
- Previous Year's expense comparison

Other report details besides the Dashboard and the Business Snapshot report would need to be graphed outside of the software.

Creating a Custom Graph

Your Dashboard contains a graphical comparison of your income and expenses. However, there is no option to display monthly statistics for the preceding five fiscal years. This fiscal year and its predecessor are the only options available.

Additionally, you may choose to open the Business Snapshot report. This is how;

1. Select **Business Snapshot** under Business Overview on the Reports menu.
2. Scroll down to the **Previous Year Comparison of Income** and **Previous Year Comparison of Expenses sections.**
3. Click the period drop-down menu and pick Monthly for both.

In addition, you can generate a Profit and Loss Comparison report for the past five years. Then, export the report to Excel and design a graphic bar using the report's data.

Please follow these procedures to access your Profit and Loss account:

1. Head straight under the **Reports menu** to locate the Profit and loss account.
2. Change the date in the Report Period section to the correct Fiscal Year.
3. Select **Month** from the drop-down menu for Display columns by.

Additionally, you can click the down arrow next to **Compare another period** and select **Previous Period.** However, this just provides dates for the current and preceding time.

How to Hide Data in Your Graph

Occasionally, you may wish to hide the largest pie slice or bar in order to see the other parts of a graph more clearly.

1. Hold down the **Shift key** and then click the mouse button to hide a graph bar or slice.

2. You can reconstruct the graph if you wish to re-exhibit what you've hidden.

Note that concealing or hiding is distinct from filtering. When you apply a filter to report data, QuickBooks excludes specified quantities. When you conceal data in graphs, QuickBooks includes the concealed value when calculating the graph's values.

Safeguarding Your Data

In this day and age, information is one of the most imperative assets. If someone stole critical company information or customer banking details, it could leave a bad taste in the mouths of the patrons and business owners. This chapter is devoted to teaching you how to protect your data so that it's safe from malicious internet attacks.

Set Up User Permissions to Restrict Access

Limiting user access is the first step to restricting specific staff members from being able to view or open all reports. QuickBooks Online lets you set a “Standard User” that only gives the person access to A/P and A/R reports. This attribute allows the employee to create invoices and issue them to clients.

Follow the guide below to add Standard Users to your QuickBooks Dashboard:

1. Select the ‘Gear’ icon
2. Open your ‘Company’
3. Click “Manage Users”
4. Navigate to the ‘User’ tab and pick “Add User”
5. Select “Standard User”
6. Click ‘Next’
7. Select ‘Limited’
8. Checkmark ‘Customers’
9. Click ‘Next’
10. Adjust user parameters and choose ‘Next’
11. Fill in the new user credentials.
12. Once complete, click ‘Save’

Hints: Don’t utilize the same password and username if you have employees who also use QuickBooks. Ensure you have made a backup of your company file and save it on an external storage device (USB stick or CD) for safekeeping.

Backup and Restore Your Company

Once you have saved a backup of your organization, you'll permanently have access to your chart of accounts copy. You can also remove unwanted changes to critical data, settings, customers, and vendors.

Please Note: If you want to utilize pre-existing business information to begin a new one, create a copy instead of backing it up.

What Data Can and Cannot Be Backed Up?

You should know that while your chart of accounts can be backed up, there is some information you won't be able to save.

Data Capable of Being Back Up

- Transfers
- Time activities
- Refund receipts
- Purchase and purchase orders
- Journal entries
- Vendor credits
- Credit memos
- Bills and bill payments
- Deposits
- Payments
- Receipts
- Sales
- Estimates
- Invoices
- Vendors (except the Tax ID field)
- Terms
- Tax codes and tax rates
- Tax agencies
- Payment methods
- Items
- Employees (except their SSN)
- Departments
- Customers
- Currencies

- Classes
- Budgets
- Account
- Inventory shrinkage
- Adjustments backed up as journal entries
- Preferences
- Entitlements
- Company info
- Attachments
- Exchanges

Data That Can't Be Backed Up

- Audit log entries
- Custom form templates
- Custom reports
- Item-based billable expenses with markup
- Account-based billable expenses
- Reconciliation reports
- Bank feeds
- Links to transactions
- Bank rules
- Recurring transactions
- Belated credit and charges (however, affiliated invoices are recorded)
- Customer types of price rules
- QuickBooks Online payment information

What Data Cannot Be Restored?

The following items cannot be restored when reinstating a backup:

- Tax rates using expense accounts - This information is held in your liability accounts.
- Inventory: Not including inventory adjustment and inventory history.
- Budgets: Use a CSV file to export this data.

Switch on the Restore App and Online Back-Up

This feature is available to QuickBooks Online Advanced users only and automatically backs up your data. Once the task is complete, the program monitors any alterations made to your business's information. Now, whenever you require it, you can restore a backup.

1. Head to 'Settings'
2. Click "Back up Company"

Please Note: To proceed, you may be required to log in to your Intuit account.

Switch Off Automatic Backups

If you don't want your business information backed up regularly, here is how to switch off this feature:

1. Click on 'Settings'
2. Open "Back up Company"
3. Locate the organization you want to disable automatic backups for.
4. Select "Disable Backup" in the 'Action' dropdown menu.

Create a One-Time Backup Manually

If you want to save everything while you are busy with an essential project, you can do it with a manual backup. Follow the steps to configure everything:

Connect to Your Dropbox or Google Drive Account

1. Click on 'Settings'
2. Open "Back up Company"
3. Pick the "Local Backup" menu
4. Choose "Link a Service"
5. Decide where you want the backup saved; either 'DropBox' or "Google Drive."
6. The interface provides you with the steps to create a backup in QuickBooks.

Decide How Often You Need to Back up Your Data

1. Navigate to the "Local Backup" menu
2. Choose "New Local Backup Schedule"
3. Ensure the correct enterprise is selected
4. Adjust the time and date for the first time you want to backup.
5. Choose the recurrence of the backups.
6. Click "Create Local Backup Schedule" once everything is entered accurately

Restore Backup Data

You can utilize the backup to reinstate information from a particular time and date. In most cases, it may take up to 60 minutes to restore the data. However, your computer, the internet, and the amount of dossier you have affect the loading times.

Crucial Advice: While the Online Back-up and Restore app compiles your data, ensure you don't make any changes to your company. Once the process is complete, it'll be safe to return and make edits to your company.

1. Open 'Settings'
2. Click "Back up Company"
3. Open the 'Restore' menu
4. Choose "New Restore"
5. Use the 'Company' dropdown menu to find the organization you want to restore and overwrite your financial information to.
6. Click the 'Restore' dropdown menu
7. Choose a 'Date' that you want to reinstate the data.
8. Select "Create Restore" once everything is confirmed
9. Fill in your business's name.
10. Click 'Restore'

Keep Your System Safe

There are a multitude of ways to keep your system safe while using QuickBooks Online for your business's accounting. One of the best ways to safeguard your information is to keep the computer you're using QuickBooks Online on in excellent working order.

Ensuring the data and security of all programs on your PC is crucial to maintaining a secure system. Use a reputable antivirus or malware application to monitor and remove any malicious files.

Another great way to protect yourself while using QuickBooks Online is to utilize a Virtual Private Network (VPN) for an additional layer of protection.

Updates and Backups

Ensuring your QuickBooks is updated and backed up aids the protection of your data in the event of a malicious attack. I recommend setting up automatic updates, but if you prefer to perform them manually, that is possible too. Helping include crucial security protocols in its backend automatically updates your software.

Networks and Smartphones

If your network is not in good condition, it leaves the possibility of hackers stealing your business credentials. Typically, multiple computers are connected to a server, so make sure all PCs are updated and in the best shape possible. When a single workstation is infiltrated, it may affect all machines in the company's network.

Internal Fraud

There are cases where internal fraud occurs on QuickBooks Online, and this can be mitigated by ensuring particular users have limited access. In an ideal world, you'd want confidence your staff isn't stealing from you.

However, business owners quickly find out that there are unethical people in the world. Look out for three indications that may suggest internal fraud or theft is occurring.

Working Extended Shifts

If a staff member works on weekends, leaves the office late, or arrives early, it may indicate a problem. The holidays are also a perfect time for a worker to commit theft because no one is at the workplace to watch them. Keep a close eye on these individuals if you have any suspicions.

Buying Flashy Things

A big red flag would be an employee coming to work with a new luxury watch or a new automobile. If you are aware that these products are out of their wages, it may be something to look into. Staff members who go on elaborate holidays are also a signal that something may be up.

Exuberant Stress at the Office

If your finance staff is worried about a future audit, it may be that they're hiding something. Take a look at your books and determine if there are discrepancies that may seem normal.

Protecting Your Small Company Against Internal Staff Fraud

With the various scams and threats your staff members could encounter, it is crucial to know what to look out for. Below are seven steps you can use to safeguard your company and detect fraud before it happens.

Know Your Staff

Company owners trust their employees wholeheartedly but sometimes forget to take the time to learn about them. Background checks can help you determine who is worth hiring before starting the process.

Employees who access the payment accounts or money should be the primary parties you need to be cautious of. This tiny step may minimize internal fraud by those particular workers.

Substantiate Payments and Invoices

Considering who'll make payments or purchase decisions can help reduce the risk of fraud at your company. Once clear procedures are established for approving expenditures and invoices, assign the position to your most competent worker.

Check out your invoices before accepting details in case the person included fraudulent expenses.

Research Your Vendors

Monitor the behaviors and processes of your vendors. This can help you prevent losing money. Take time to research new companies you are working with or ask for references to see what others have experienced.

Type into Google "Business Name Scam" to find out what people are saying online. Social media is also a great way to read reviews and obtain insights into an organization's dealings.

Separating Accounting Duties

Individuals who manage your company's financials should each be assigned different tasks. It's bad business practice to employ one staff member for this job, as it gives them access and control of your company's capital.

Teach Your Workers to Notice and Stop Fraud

Identifying and stopping fraud should be taught to all employees in the workplace. Once your staff knows what to look for, they can report suspicious activity immediately.

Staff are the first people fraudsters speak to when reaching out to your company. Host an employee meeting and educate your front line of defense about potential fraud risks.

If you end up hiring more workers, ensure they receive the relevant education so they can be on top of things.

Utilizing a dark web scanner is another enterprising method to identify and prevent fraud cases. This application searches the dark web for your credentials on sites that share, sell, and buy stolen information.

They Offer Multiple Ways to Delineate Fraud

Vendors, clients, and staff can fill the whistleblower position to inform you of malicious acts in your company.

Hotlines are the most common method that most whistleblowers utilize to communicate apprehensive activity. Nonetheless, give these individuals many options for reporting dishonorable activities to improve their chances of discovering illegal undertakings.

These include, but are not limited to:

- Mailed forms or letters
- Web-based documents
- Email

Ensure your vendors, clients, and staff are aware that suspicious activity comes in all forms.

Remain Observant

Preventing identity theft requires that you be proactive in your approach. Knowing how to manage a data breach or scam event can be done by looking out for red flags. The worst nightmare of any business owner is a hacker who steals critical company information.

Look After Your Business

I understand that running a company is an unending process, and truthfully so. Operating your business takes time and energy, which means you may forget to take the necessary precautions to secure your data.

Without protecting your software and hardware, it could be a major cause for concern. If you don't have the time to perform such tasks, it may be a good option to hire a technician who can help maintain your systems.

Teaching your employees about intelligent email behavior can keep them in the loop regarding suspicious activity. Limit web browsing and application downloads on work computers to minimize the risk of installing malware or other phishing software.

Bonus – Tips and Tricks

QuickBooks is very popular and widely used by most small businesses. However, there are some features of this accounting program that are not being fully or efficiently utilized. Even your average CPA may not be aware of some of the strongest features that QuickBooks offers. If you want your business to make the most out of QuickBooks rather than simply relying on the basic features everybody knows about, you have to understand the shortcuts, tips, and tricks that you can use.

Here are some intermediate and advanced QuickBooks features that you should definitely learn how to use.

Memorizing Transactions

Every business has a significant number of transactions that are constantly recurring. Rather than trying to remember these transactions, use QuickBooks to automatically memorize these regular transactions. For example, if your business pays rent on a specific date every month, or you bill a customer for a monthly service, QuickBooks automatically memorizes them and helps you fill in the related information at programmed intervals. This feature enables you to save time, minimize errors, and improve accuracy. If you have complicated journal entries and templates that you have to remember, use this feature to make life easier.

To make use of this memorizing transaction tool, use the keyboard shortcut ***Ctrl + M***. Though the memorize transaction tool creates electronic payments, it does not send them automatically. You can send documents by going to ***File*** menu and clicking on ***Send Documents***.

QuickBooks Loan Manager

When it comes to recording loan repayment transactions, the majority of small business owners do not follow the correct process. Businesses fail to follow the loan repayment schedule by forgetting to separate the principal amounts and the loan interest accrued. QuickBooks makes loan repayment management easier by helping you set up every individual loan based on its related parameters. The QuickBooks Loan Manager tool makes sure the loan rate, term, balloon payments, compounding, and fees are filled in correctly every time. It then generates an accurate payment check every time a loan repayment is due. This not only reduces errors but also saves time.

To make use of this tool, click on ***Banking***, and then ***Loan Manager***.

Processing Multiple Reports

For a business to be managed effectively, it is important for the company personnel to have in their possession the relevant financial reports. In most cases, bookkeepers maintain the records well but then fail to generate and distribute these reports on a consistent basis. This is usually because preparing and printing all these reports takes too much time. To make this process easier,

QuickBooks contains a tool known as *Process Multiple Reports*. This tool works together with the *Memorize* function and helps you create and print a batch of multiple reports at the click of a button.

To make use of this tool, click on the ***Reports*** tab, then go to ***Process Multiple Reports***. One trick you can use is to add the name of the recipient in the title of the report when memorizing every report. This will make the report distribution process much easier.

Avoiding Prior-Period Changes

QuickBooks make it very easy for users to enter and edit transactions. Unfortunately, sometimes a user can unintentionally make a change in a prior period. To prevent such errors from occurring, you need to set up a special username and password for every person who uses the system, as well as set preferences for each user to stop them bypassing the closing date.

Once you have set up a closing date that is password protected, all you have to do is move the closing date forward each month as adjustments are made. To make use of this tip, click on the ***Company*** menu, and then ***Set Closing Date***.

Custom Data Fields

This feature can be considered as one of accounting software's most powerful features. Depending on the version of QuickBooks you are using, you have the option of between 20 to 50 generic custom data fields, each field being content-specific. Data fields are very handy when it comes to overcoming the many shortcomings that an accounting system has. If for instance, you are running a boat rental service in a marina, you can use custom data fields to keep track of a client, the details of the boat they rented, the slip number where they have parked, and whether they subscribe to your monthly cranking service.

More than that, QuickBooks provides you with the option of filtering reports using your custom data fields. For instance, your boat rental service could easily determine how many boats need cranking every month. This can be done by filtering the customer records to show only those who have a subscription for the cranking service.

To make use of this tool, click on the ***Customer Center*** tab, choose a specific ***Customer***, and go to ***Edit Customer***. Click on the ***Additional Information*** tab and select ***Define Fields***. Another tip about this QuickBooks feature is that you can include the information generated by Custom Data within an invoice, financial report, or any QuickBooks document.

Batch Invoicing

QuickBooks allows you to generate multiple invoices at a go. For instance, if you want to send invoices to your 1000 clients every month, you can easily create 1000 invoices in one process. QuickBooks' batch invoicing feature also enables you to find specific customers based on custom data fields, and then invoice that select group.

Using the example of the boat rental service, the accountant would be able to send invoices to all the customers who have signed up for the monthly cranking service –all in one step. To make use of this tool, go to ***Customers*** menu, and click on the ***Create Batch Invoices*** tab at the bottom of the screen.

Editing Templates

In QuickBooks, all types of documents are referred to as templates, whether it is an invoice, statement, purchase order, or sales order. QuickBooks makes it possible for you to change these templates by rearranging the structure of a document. If you need to include some extra information like additional columns, images, data fields, or text, you can do so easily.

For instance, you may decide to include your sales agent's name and telephone number in a company invoice. You may also decide to add extra columns to show information like rates and quantities. All this is possible by using the Editing Templates functionality. Any smart business owner will see the need to tweak their templates to effectively meet their business goals.

To make use of this tool, click on the ***Lists*** menu and go to ***Templates***. You will see several template options. Right-click on a template, select ***Edit Template,*** and then click on the ***Layout Designer*** tab. You can also choose to download extra templates and colorful themes from the Internet if you wish.

FAQ

1. What is QuickBooks Online, and how does it differ from other accounting software?

QuickBooks Online is a cloud-based accounting software developed by Intuit. It differs from traditional accounting software by offering users the flexibility to access their financial data anytime, anywhere through an internet connection. Unlike desktop-based solutions, QuickBooks Online's cloud architecture allows for real-time collaboration, automation, and ease of use, making it a preferred choice for small businesses.

2. How secure is QuickBooks Online, and what measures are in place to protect my financial data?

QuickBooks Online prioritizes the security of user data. The platform employs robust security measures like data encryption, multi-factor authentication, and routine system updates to safeguard sensitive financial information. Additionally, Intuit ensures compliance with industry standards and regulations, providing users with confidence that their data is secure and in adherence to legal requirements.

3. Can I use QuickBooks Online on different devices, and is there a mobile app available?

Yes, one of the key advantages of QuickBooks Online is its multi-device accessibility. Users can access their accounts through various devices, including desktops, laptops, tablets, and smartphones, as long as they have an internet connection. QuickBooks Online also offers a mobile app for both iOS and Android devices, allowing users to manage their finances on the go.

4. How user-friendly is QuickBooks Online for someone with limited accounting knowledge?

QuickBooks Online is designed with a user-friendly interface, making it accessible to individuals with limited accounting knowledge. The platform features an intuitive dashboard that provides a clear overview of key financial metrics. Guided workflows and easy-to-navigate menus simplify tasks like invoicing, expense tracking, and reconciliation, enabling users to manage their finances efficiently without a steep learning curve.

5. What automation features does QuickBooks Online offer to save time on routine tasks?

QuickBooks Online is equipped with various automation features to streamline routine tasks. Automatic bank feeds update transactions in real-time, reducing the need for manual data entry. The platform also supports recurring invoicing, automated bill payments, and categorization of expenses, saving users valuable time and minimizing the risk of errors.

6. Can multiple users collaborate on QuickBooks Online simultaneously?

Yes, QuickBooks Online supports real-time collaboration among multiple users. This feature is particularly beneficial for businesses with diverse teams, including business owners, accountants, and bookkeepers. Users can work concurrently on the same financial data, enhancing transparency and ensuring everyone is on the same page. The collaborative nature of QuickBooks Online fosters efficient communication and collaboration, facilitating a more integrated approach to financial management.

7. What reporting tools does QuickBooks Online provide, and how can they benefit my business?

QuickBooks Online offers a robust suite of reporting tools to provide users with valuable insights into their business performance. Users have the capability to generate standard reports, including profit & loss statements, balance sheets, and cash flow statements. Moreover, the platform facilitates the creation of customized reports, empowering users to analyze specific aspects of their business. These reports serve as essential tools for informed decision-making, compliance with tax regulations, and strategic planning.

8. Can QuickBooks Online help with tax preparation and compliance?

Yes, QuickBooks Online is equipped to assist users with tax preparation and compliance. The platform automates many aspects of financial record-keeping, making it easier to gather the necessary information for tax reporting. Additionally, QuickBooks Online generates reports that are essential for tax filing, like profit and loss statements and expense reports. Users can also integrate the platform with tax preparation software for a seamless tax filing process.

9. Is there customer support available for QuickBooks Online users?

QuickBooks Online does, in fact, offer customer assistance which is available to assist consumers with any inquiries or problems that they might experience. Users can access a knowledge base, tutorials, and community forums for self-help. For more personalized assistance, QuickBooks Online offers customer support through phone and chat options. The support team is trained to address a wide range of issues, from technical difficulties to general inquiries about using the platform effectively.

10. Can QuickBooks Online integrate with other business applications?

Yes, QuickBooks Online offers integration with a variety of third-party business applications. This integration allows users to connect QuickBooks Online with other tools they use for tasks like e-commerce, payroll, project management, and more. By integrating these applications, users can streamline their workflow, reduce manual data entry, and enhance the overall efficiency of their business processes.

11. How does QuickBooks Online handle inventory management?

Some of the capabilities that are included in QuickBooks Online are for basic inventory management. Users are able to monitor and handle their inventory, decide whether to place reorders, and receive notifications when their stock levels are getting low. While it may not have the advanced capabilities of dedicated inventory management software, QuickBooks Online provides small businesses with the tools they need to keep track of their products and make informed decisions about inventory levels.

12. What subscription plans are available for QuickBooks Online, and how much does it cost?

QuickBooks Online offers several subscription plans to cater to different business needs. The plans vary in terms of features and pricing. Common plans include Simple Start, Essentials, and Plus, each offering different levels of functionality and support for users. The pricing is typically based on a monthly subscription fee, and Intuit frequently offers promotions or discounts, especially for new users.

Conclusion

There are many accounting programs you will come across in the course of running and managing your business. The QuickBooks suite has been around longer than most of the programs in the market at the moment, hence the popularity as a result of its reputation. There are many businesses that have used QuickBooks as the backbone of their accounting processes for years. When you get into the world of accounting, QuickBooks is one of the accounting packages you might need to learn.

You have a better chance of learning and implementing QuickBooks when you have some background knowledge in accounting or finance. However, this is not always necessary. You will realize from this step-by-step guide that learning QuickBooks is not difficult. We have outlined the important steps and procedures with illustrations so that you can follow through on your own and learn how to manage your accounts.

There is so much to learn from using this QuickBooks tutorial that will help you understand the way your business operates. One thing you will realize is that the point at which you create accounts in QuickBooks matters a lot. At this point, you can create default settings for every customer and vendor account. These settings will cut across all accounts unless you specifically edit them for individual customers and vendors. Why is this important?

QuickBooks monitors and updates all transactions you perform. Therefore, it can keep up with your transactions better than you can. In accounting, no account transactions can be isolated. Every transaction must always affect at least one other account. Each time you make a transaction, QuickBooks updates all the relevant accounts that are affected by the value of the said transaction. This is why by the end of your accounting period, QuickBooks can populate the necessary financial statements reflecting the financial health status of your business.

When setting up accounts, there are two types of accounting that you can use. Many small and new businesses use cash accounting over accrual accounting. We looked at both of these methods in detail, explaining the content of each one of them and why it is relevant to your business. The cash accounting method is preferred by many businesses because it is simple and easy to understand. After all, you are in the business of making money, so you record money when you receive or pay for something.

The accrual mode of accounting is relatively complicated, which is one of the reasons why many small businesses avoid it. However, as your business grows, you will realize the need for switching to accrual accounting, especially if you are ever planning on getting financial support. The good thing about using QuickBooks is that you can prepare your financial accounts using any of the two methods whenever you need to. Since banks prefer accrual accounting, this will be a worthy consideration down the line.

There are different categories of users in QuickBooks, each of whose roles eventually culminate into the overall performance of the business. You can use QuickBooks to account for different types of users. To make this learning process easier, we created specific learning points to help you learn how to use QuickBooks for vendors, customers, your company, banking and so forth. The reason behind this is to create an organized learning process such that each time you come across any transactions, you already know which type of user you need to account for.

One area where many business owners struggle is managing the payroll system. Payrolls are an important part of your business, and as long as you have employees, you will need to sort this out at some point. The payroll system is elaborate and deals with important tasks like paying and filing taxes and paying employees on time. There are different rules that apply to each scenario. You must obtain specific tax forms for the purpose of filing federal and state taxes as required by law. All this information is aimed at helping you manage your payroll systems effectively.

At the end of your financial year, every business must prepare different financial statements that show the position of the business in light of all the trade that has taken place. For accounting purposes, there are many financial statements and reports that you can produce. However, we must focus on the important statements because these are the statements that at a glance, tell the story of your business.

We looked at how to prepare the balance sheet, cash flow statement, income statement, accounts receivables and accounts payables. When prepared accurately, anyone who has access to these statements can immediately tell whether your business is doing well or not.

By the end of this book, you will have learned how to get around QuickBooks even if you do not have prior accounting or finance knowledge. QuickBooks will play an important role in your career, especially if you plan to start a business and manage your accounts and finances on your own. Even as you do that, remember that there is no harm in asking for help whenever you need it.

Wishing you all the best as you learn to manage your business, and grow it to scale greater heights.

www.ingramcontent.com/pod-product-compliance
Lightning Source LLC
LaVergne TN
LVHW081344050326
832903LV00024B/1311
* 9 7 9 8 8 7 8 3 4 9 5 6 7 *